THE TREK ENCYCLOPEDIA

second edition

BY JOHN PEEL

additional material by Hal Schuster and Scott Nance

Designed and Edited by Hal Schuster

Library of Congress Cataloging-in-Publication Data
John Peel
The Trek Encyclopedia

1. The Trek Encyclopedia (popular culture)
I. Title

Published by Pioneer Books, Inc., 5715 N. Balsam Rd., Las Vegas, NV, 89130.

First Printing, Revised Edition 1992

INTRODUCTION

In the twenty-plus years since "Star Trek" began, there has grown up an immense body of literature about the show. There have been 79 episodes, four films, 22 animated episodes and now a spin-off series, "Star Trek - The Next Generation." That's a whole lot of information.

The problem for the viewer or fan is that there's too much there to retain it all. Many people will know which story featured the Klingons for the first time, and some people will know which stories featured the Klingons in all of their dastardly doings. Less will know who played those Klingons, and fewer still what other roles those actors have performed.

The Encyclopedia of Star Trek was created to answer those needs. It isn't meant to be read at a single sitting; if you want to do it, I shalln't complain, but it is meant to be picked up when you have a question about the show, animated series or movies. A little information is added on The Next Generation where relevant, but on the whole, these are the voyages of the original starship *Enterprise*.

Those of you have been reading the issues of **Files Magazine** that I've been writing will have seen much of the information presented here in the various releases covering Monsters and Aliens, Characters and People. On the other hand, I've had a considerable opportunity to update the information, to make corrections and to add additional entries. Somehow, for example, I had left out the information on Bob Justman from the relevant File! Mr. Justman is one of the most important people to have worked on the show. I'm glad I can rectify that earlier error and add him back where he belongs.

Needless to say, I am not perfect. I am certain

that there will be one or two (hopefully) small errors in this volume. If you detect them, do let us know (the address is in the front to write to). We will then be able to make this reference more accurate in future reprintings. Let us know if you feel that this reference is as valuable as we believe that it is. Do you want to see further works such as this, perhaps for The Next Generation or other shows entirely? Unless you tell us, we won't know.

I trust that you'll find this book useful. It's been hard work for me, and I'd like to think that it serves its purpose well!

—John Peel, December, 1987

To go where no man had gone before...

THE CHARACTERS

Please note that for your ease in using this section of the reference, we have listed all monsters and aliens in upper and lower case while all other entries appear only in upper case.

Aamazzarite

Appearances: "Star Trek - The Motion Picture"

Note: this was one of a number of races cut from the final print of the film. Aamazzarites are humanoid members of the Federation, with large, bulbous heads. they are bald and ridged.

ABROM

Played by: William Wintersole
Episode: "Patterns Of Force"

Abrom was the elderly leader of the Zeon agents on Ekos (see separate entries for further details).

ADAM

Played by: Charles Napier
Episode: "The Way To Eden"

Adam was one of the followers of Dr. Sevrin. He and his friends were drop-outs, looking for the mythical world of Eden. He and his friends sabotaged the "Enterprise" and found their Eden - where Adam died, eating the poisoned fruit.

ADAMS, Dr. TRISTAN

Played by: James Gregory
Episode: "Dagger Of The Mind"

Dr. Tristan Adams was the assistant of Dr. Simon van Gelder on the Tantalus Penal Colony. He developed the neural neutralizer, which causes great mental pain and distress, leaving the person who is in the machine susceptible to the slightest suggestion. He aimed to use it to further his insane goals of conquest, but whilst fighting Kirk received a full dose of the machine, which killed him.

AIR FORCE PERSONNEL

Episode: "Tomorrow Is Yesterday"
Various Air Force Personnel are seen, including:
(1) Police Sergeant
Played by: Hal Lynch
(2) Captain
Played by: Mark Dempsey
(3) Policeman
Played by: Jim Spencer
(4) Technician
Played by: Richard Merrifield Episode: "Assignment: Earth"
(5) Policemen
Played by: Bruce Mars, Ted Gehring

AKAAR

Played by: Ben Gage
Episode: "Friday's Child"

Akaar was the Teer (ruler of the Capellan tribes (see separate entry for further details). His wife, Eleen, was heavily pregnant when Maab slew Akaar and became the new Teer.

AKUTA

Played by Lloyd Haynes
Episode: "Where No Man Has Gone Before"

Alden was the communications officer of the "Enterprise" under Captain Kirk before Uhura was assigned to the post.

ALEXANDER

Played by: Michael Dunn
Episode: "Plato's Stepchildren"

Alexander was the dwarf who was the butt of the hostilities of his fellow Platonians (see separate entry for further details). When Kirk defeated the others, he took Alexander with him out to see the Galaxy.

ALICE

Played by: Marcia Brown
Episode: "Shore Leave"

Alice is the young girl from Alice's Adventures In

Wonderland, materialized on the Caretaker's world by Dr. McCoy's imagination.

ALICE

Played by: Alyce & Rhae Andrece
Episode: "I, Mudd"

The Alices were five hundred Androids (see separate entry for further details).

Amoeboid

Appearances: "The Immunity Syndrome"

Many strange creatures have evolved in this Universe of ours, but one of the stranges and most dangerous was the amoeboid creature that was several miles across. It drifted through the region of Gamma 7A and destroyed all life there, including the entire starship Intrepid, manned entirely by Vulcans (see separate entry). The amoeboid lives within a shell of negative energy, absorbing all energy to feed. When it has sufficient energy, the creature can then reproduce. The Enterprise discovered the amoeboid, and managed to destroy the creature by exploding an anti-matter bomb deep within its nucleus.

ANAN SEVEN

Played by: David Opatashu
Episode: "A Taste Of Armageddon"

Anan Seven was the head of the council of Eminiar VII. He was forced to act with force against the "Enterprise" when the ship was declared destroyed in Eminiar's war with Vendikar. Kirk forced Anan to face the possibility of a real war, and even Anan eventually realized that peach could come between the two worlds. (see separate entries for further details.)

Andorians

Appearances: "Journey To Babel"
"The Gamesters of Triskelion"
"The Lights of Zetar"
"Whom Gods Destroy"
"Yesteryear"
:"The Time Trap"
"Star Trek - The Motion Picture"
(1) Played by: Dick Crockett
Episode: "The Gamesters Of Triskelion"
92) Played by: Richard Geary
Episode: "Whom Gods Destroy"
See also separate entries on: Shras, Thelev.

Andorians come from an area in space close to Orion (see separate entry). They all tall, muscular beings with blue skin and light hair. They possess antennae, which are used in their limited telepathic abilities. their people are a warrior race, strong and proud, but are now firm members of the Federation of Planets.

A single Andorian was held captive on Triskelion, forced to fight in the arena games of the Providers (see separate entry). Another was in the same asylum as Gargh of Izar (see entry on Antosians).

In the alternate universe created with the accidental death ofSpock at age seven, and Andorian named Thelin became first officer of the Enterprise.

ANDREA

Played by: Sherry Jackson
Episode: "Ahat Are Little Girls Made Of?"

Andrea was an android created by Dr. Roger Korby as his companion. Kirk introduced her to the concept of emotions and love, which conflicted with her beliefs. finally, in a fit of despair when Korby told her that she could not love him, she killed both herself and her creator.

Androids

Appearances: "I, Mudd"

(Though many androids have appeared in Star Trek, the ones in this entry refer only to the race from the above story. for other androids, see separate entries.)

Creatures from the Andromedia Galaxy once visited our own spiral, and set up a small base on a now-deserted world. They built androids in humanoid form, who were to serve and help the Andromedans. (It is not known whether these Andromedans are those from "By Any Other Name" - after all, it's a large Galaxy. for that race, see the entry on Kelvans.) The Andromedans died out, and for millennia, the androids existed, but without purpose. Being virtually immortal themselves, they survived until a fleeing starship crashed on their tiny world, bearing only Harry Mudd within.

The androids examined Mudd and decided that he was a pretty disgusting specimen - and if the rest of the human race were like him, then they had a new purpose. They would serve and protect the human race - serve their whims and protect the rest of the Galaxy from their greed! They infiltrated a crewman onto the Enterprise, which they then brought to their world. They aimed to use the ship to spread out into the Galaxy. Kirk realizes that concentrated illogic will fuse the androids, and the humans all behave in silly fashion, shorting out the android main control. Spock then reprogrammes it to make the androids really useful - and to serve as warders for Harry Mudd.

ANTI-MATTER CLOUD

Appearances: "One Of Our Planets Is Missing"

Another of the strange life-forms that have evolved in the Universe is an intelligent cloud of anti-matter/ matter. It lives from ingesting planets and using the anti-matter of its form to break them down into energy that it can absorb. Though intelligent, the cloud has difficulty is recognizing small, organic creatures as being sentient since it is in fact many miles across. It is not hostile, though, and when it began menacing the inhabited world of Mantilles, Spock managed to contact the cloud. He and Kirk convinced it that the world it might devour contained living beings. The cloud then left the Galaxy, to seek dead worlds outside.

Antosians

Appearances: "Whom Gods Destroy"

(Note: the Antosians are never shown, but are integral to the story.)

The natives of Antos IV have a very sophisticated science of bioengineering. When the shuttle carrying the famed Garth of Izar there crashed, the Antosians rescued him from the wreckage and rebuilt his body, adding a few improvements. He was given the ability, like them, of changing his shape into that of anyone he had seen. Sadly, their psychological skills are not on a par with their bioengineering, for Garth was completely insane when he recovered. He offered in gratitude for what they had done to lead the Antosians in the conquest of the Galaxy. Appalled at the thought, they refused. Garth, furious at this rejection, returned to his starship and ordered his crew to destroy the planet. The crew naturally refused, and restrained him. He was committed tot he last mental asylum on Elbe II.

APELLA

Played by: Arthur Bernard
Episode: "A Private Little War"

Apella was an inhabitant of Neural (see separate entry for further details).

APOLLO

Played by: Michael Forest
Episode: "Who Mourns For Adonais?"

Thousands of years ago, beings who considered themselves as gods voyaged across the Galaxy, finally settling down about five thousand years ago in ancient Greece. There, known as Olympians, they accepted the worship of mortals. These beings were actually improved humanoids, ostensibly human, yet with a special organ inside them that enabled them to absorb and utilize external sources of energy. Using such energies, they could perform what seemed like miracles to the humans. Eventually, however, the humans tired of worshipping these beings, and the Olympians departed again for a world of their own, finding a suitable planet known as Pollux IV. Over time, though they were immortals, the Olympians allowed themselves to die. They cannot exist without adulation.

Only one refused to give up all hope of worship, the Olympian known as Apollo. He was convinced that the humans would change and some day come seeked their old gods. Eventually, he detected the approach of the Enterprise, wrongly assuming that the humans will be willing to serve him again. This time, however, his "magic" is not so impressive, and a combination of Kirk's determination and Caroline Palmas's rejection of his amorous advances leave Apollo without his power source. Finally, belatedly, he realizes that the humans have grown beyond the adoration that he required of them. In despair, he allowed himself to die, so he could rejoin all of his old friends.

APPEL, ED

Played by: Brad Weston
Episode: "The Devil In The Dark"

Ed Appel was the chief processing engineer at the Pergium mining center on Janus VI. He worked under Vanderberg.

Aquans

Appearances: "The Ambergris Element"

The planet Argo was once mostly land, but deep seismic disturbances caused the land to gradually mostly sink into the sea. The Argonians realized that this was happening, and evolved a system of drugs that would convert them to an aquatic race. There was a formula to reverse the change, should it be needed, but once the race converted to mer-folk, they eschewed the knowledge of the past, building their own civilization deep below the sea. Further seaquakes caused some of the sunken areas to revert to the surface. Kirk and Spock, in danger of drowning, were saved by some of the Aquans and converted into sea-breathers. They discovered a means to reverse the change, and some of the younger Aquans decided to use the drug also so that they could return and recognize the surface of their world. Both species of Aquans now live in peace on their world.

Arcturans

Appearances: "Star Trek - The Motion Picture"

Note: these are one of the many races seen in a segment of the film cut from released prints.

Arcturans are members of the Federation that are a palid gray color. Their skin hangs loosely in folds, giving them a most melancholy expression.

Ardanans

See entry of Stratosians.

Arex

Appearances: varied, throughout the animated series.

See entry on "Edoans".

Argelians

Appearances: "Wolf In The Fold"

The people of Argelias II are totally pacifistic, and gentle. They believe above all in pleasure, and as a result of this, their planet is noted throughout the Galaxy as a pleasure world without peer. Its women are beautiful, its men courteous, and they are very open with off-world visitors. They only ask that their guests behave themselves and respect local traditions. Because they are so peaceful, they are forced to import policemen from other Federation worlds. These are there solely to provide for peace for the Argelians against any possible trouble form outworlders. Argelians themselves cannot commit crimes by their very natures.

Some of the Argelian women can engage in a custom known as "empathic contact." This is somewhat akin to the Vulcan mind-meld, though not that precise. It is generally used for healing purposes, but can be useful in thorny problems for deciding guilt or innocence in criminal matters. It takes place in a darkened room, with several people about. The women can pick up general moods and individual thoughts if they are powerful enough.

Arretians

Appearances: "Return To Tomorrow"

The world of Arret died many millennia ago. Its destruction was foreseen by one of its most brilliant scientists, Sargon. Since there was no way that living tissue could survive the devastation, he implemented a plan to conserve the minds of the Arretians inside containers until they could be rescued by other sentient beings who would inevitably stumble across their world in the future. Having little option, the Arretians agreed to this plan, and the minds of as many as could be saved were transferred into storage.

For thousands of years, the Arretians waited, but noone came. the containers could not survive over such time, and gradually began to break down, killing the minds enclosed within. However, when only three were left, the planet was visited by the Enterprise. The three survivors were Sargon, his wife, Thalassa and his old rival, Henoch,. Sargon had a way of ensuring that they could continue, by building bodies of synthetic materials to house their minds. He proposed to Kirk, Spock and Ann Mulhalll that they exchange minds with the Arretians, so that he and his friends would have hands to work with. Kirk and the others agreed to this plan.

However, Henoch had not changed with the years, and still remained opposed to Sargon. Once he was in the body of Spock, he revelled in its power and its potentials. He wished to kill Sargon (in Kirk's form) and possess Thalassa himself. However, his plans went wrong, and he was destroyed. Realizing that their race should have accepted death with grace, both Sargon and Thalassa willing went to their own deaths rather than live on.

ATKINS

Played by: Carolyn Nelson
Episode: "The Deadly Years"

Yeoman Atkins was a member of the crew of the "Enterprise."

ATOZ

Played by: Ian Wolfe
Episode: "All Our Yesterdays"
Mr. Atoz was the librarian of the inhabitants of Beta Niobe (see separate entry for further details). It was his responsibility to place them in their correct time periods. To make this possible, a number of duplicates of him were made.

AURELAN

Played by: Joan Swift
Episode: "Operation: Annihilate"

Aurelan was the wife of Kirk's brother, Sam. She and all her family were killed by the mind parasites that destroyed the inhabitants of Deneva.

AYELBOURNE

Played by: John Abbott
Episode: "Errand Of Mercy"

A native of Organia. See separate entry for further details.

BAILEY

Played by: Anthony Call
Episode: "The Corbomite Maneuver"

Bailey was a new crewman assigned to the "Enterprise" as navigator. Young to space, he has a hard time adjusting to Spock's lack of emotions. Under the strain of the attack by Balok's ship, Bailey snapped and lost his temper, accusing the crew of being automatons. Kirk relieved him of duty, but relented when Bailey apologized and showed that he was learning from the pressure. When Balok turned out to be quite a pleasant character, Bailey volunteered to stay with him and teach him something about humans. Kirk approved the plan.

BAKER

Played by: Barbara Baldavin
Episode: "Space Seed"

A Member of the "Enterprise" crew.

BALOK

Played by: Clint Howard, Vic Perrin, Ted Cassidy
Episode: "The Corbomite Maneuver"

The First Federation is a race of small, child-like beings that have tremendous mental ability, an insatiable curiosity and a very understandable caution. One such being is Balok. They do not tend to remain on planets, but using huge vessels they travel the Universe, seeking knowledge, companionship and amusement. On the other hand, since they are relatively defenseless physically, they rely on their huge ships and a cunning facade for protection. Balok's ship the Fesarius, has tremendous poser, and can scan data banks of all vessels and planets that it approaches. The problem is knowing whether such data banks have been doctored to make the race involved look as though they are peaceful when they are actually aggressive and mean him harm.

To establish the true nature of such beings, Balok has a puppet - creature, manipulated by computer, with a ferocious mean and deep voice. The Fesarius then ensnares ships, threatening to destroy them. Balok then allows them to get the upper hand and "disable" his craft. Bany beings that then try to destroy him are definitely hostiles. Any that leave him alone are not interesting. Any that try and aid him in his "distress" are worthy

friends. One such ship was the Enterprise, and Balok found the captain and crew of that ship to be particularly interesting, lively and stimulating. One human, Bailey, stayed for a while with Balok so that both species might grow to know each other better and to mutual profit.

BARBARA

Played by: Maureen & Collen Thornton
Episode: "I, Mudd"

The Barbaras were Androids (see separate entry for further details).

BARBER

Played by: Ed McReady
Episode: "Spectre Of The Gun"

The barber was one of the illusions created by the Melkotian (see separate entry for details).

BARIS, NILZ

Played by: William Schallert
Episode: "The Trouble With Tribbles"

Nilz Baris was the Under-Secretary of the Federation assigned to deal with the grain shipment to Sherman's planet. He was petty, officious and downright obnoxious at times. he and Kirk disliked one another on sight, and failed completely to get along. His threats to report Kirk for his attitude came to nothing when the grain shipment was proved to have been sabotaged by his assistant, Arne Darvin - a Klingon spy.

BARROWS, TONIA

Played by: Emily Banks
Episode: "Shore Leave"

Yeoman Barrows became involved romantically with Dr. McCoy during their visit to the Caretaker's world. She was able to live her fantasy of being a lady in the days of knights errant.

BARSTOW

Played by Richard Derr
Episode: "The Alternative Factor"

Commodore Barstow is a member of the Starfleet council.

BEACH

Played by: Paul Kent
Story: "Star Trek II - The Wrath Of Khan"

Beach was a member fo the crew of the "Reliant."

BEHAN, JOHNNY

Played by: Bill Zuckert
Episode: "Spectre Of The Gun"

Johnny Began was one of the illusions created by the Melkotian (see separate entry for further details).

BELE

Played by: Frank Gorshin
Episode: "Let That Be Your Last Battlefield"

Bele was a Commissioner of Cheron (see separate entry for further details). He was hunting down his enemy, Lokai. Both perished together in the ruins of their world.

BENTON

Played by: Seamon Glass
Episode: "Mudd's Women"

Benton was one of the dilithium miners on Rigel 12 who desired Mudd's women.

BERKELEY

Played by: Larry Anthony
Episode: "Dagger Of The Mind"

A member of the "Enterprise" crew.

BETA 5

Played by: Majel Barrett
Episode: "Assignment: Earth"

Beta 5 was Gary Seven's very sophisticated computer.

BETAN WOMAN

Played by: Barbara Webber
Episode: "The Return Of The Archons"

The woman was a native of Beta 3, and went amok during the Festival of sex and violence ordained by Landru.

Betelgeusians

Appearances: "Star Trek - The Motion Picture"

Note: Betelgeusians are one of a number of races whose only scene in the first film was cut.

They are members of the Federation, tall and blue-skinned. Their breathing apparatus is ridged and difficult to understand. They are presumably amphibian and possess long, tapered hands to aid in their swimming.

BILAR

Played by: Ralph Maurer
Episode: "The Return Of The Archons"

Bilar was a native of Beta 3, ruled by Landru and his Lawgivers.

BLACK KNIGHT

Played by: Paul Baxley
Episode: "Shore Leave"

One of the illusions made real by the marvels of the Caretaker's world.

BOMA

Played by: Don Marshall
Episode:: "The Galileo Seven"

Lt. Boma was one of the people stranded in the crash of the shuttle "Galileo" as it investigated Murasaki 312. He objected to Spock's use of logic as a basis of command, castigating Spock for being unfeeling. He was constantly frustrated by Spock's methods of behavior - but survived the experience thanks to Spock.

BONAVENTURE, RUTH

Played by: Maggie Thrett
Episode: "Mudd's Women"

Ruth Bonaventure was one of Mudd's three women given the Venus drug to change her drab looks into gorgeous beauty. She remained behind on Rigel 12, husband-hunting.

BOYCE, Dr. PHILIP

Played By: John Hoyt
Episode: "The Cage"

Dr. Philip Boyce was the first chief surgeon on the "Enterprise, " serving under Christopher Pike. The doctor was Pike's confidant and friend.

BRANCH

Played by: David Gatreaux
Story: "Star Trek - The Motion Picture"

Commander Branch was in charge of the Epsilon station monitoring the Klingons that was destroyed by

V'Ger.

BRENT

Played by: Frank da Vinci
Episode: "The Naked Time"

A member of the "Enterprise" crew, rank Lieutenant.

BRIGGS, BOB

Played by Scott DeVenney
Story: "Star Trek IV - The Voyage Home"

Bob Briggs was the head of the Cetacean Institute, and Dr. Gillian Taylor's boss. He had her whales released at sea without telling her.

BROWN, Dr.

Played by: Harry Basch
Episode: "What Are Little Girsl Made Of?

Dr. Brown had been Dr. Roger Korby's assistant on his ill-fated expedition to Exo-III. Brown was killed in the crash of their ship, but Korby built an android duplicate of him to assist him with his research. This "Brown" was destroyed by Kirk when he attempted to kill the Captain.

THE BRUTE

Played by: Tom Morga
Star Trek VI: The Undiscovered Country

The Brute was a huge alien prisoner on Rura Penthe. He picked a fight with Kirk. Kirk subdued him by kicking him in the knees, which for his race, were actually his genitals.

BUOY

Played by: James Doohan
Episode: "Spectre Of the Gun

The buoy was a warning signal left by the Melkotians (see separate entry for further details).

Caitian

Appearances: varied, throughout the animated series.

Navigator M'ress is a member of the Federation species Caitians, from the world of Cait. The intelligent species there are bipedal felines, loosely descended from carnivorous hunters. The Caitians are an advanced race that still honor their hunting background, but the predatory nature has been considerably toned down by civilization. They have excellent agility and eyesight, and their tails are semi-prehensile.

Camusans

Appearances: "Turnabout Intruder"

The natives of Camus 2 have been extinct for millennia. Very little is known of them, save that they constructed many strange and wonderful machines. One of these could transfer the psyche from one individual to another. It was used by Dr. Janice Lester in an insane attempt to take over the mind and role of James Kirk.

Capellans

Appearances;: "Friday's Child"

The natives of Capella IV are a warrior race of nomads. They dwell in large tents that can be disassembled and stowed for travel. They do not believe in medicine, having the firm conviction that only the strong should survive. Both males and females consider combat to be more pleasurable than love, and only understand authority from force. They have developed many weapons over the years, but heir favorite is the klugat, which is a sharp-edged throwing disc.

Many odd customs have developed on the world over the years. for example, if an unmarried woman were to offer food to an unmarried male, and he were to accept, then it would be the duty of the girl's closest male relative to kill the other male. Like so many customs, this one has little explanation behind it. The Capellans are ruled by a hereditary leader, the Teer. This is always a man, and rule will be passed onto his male offspring, then the strongest male in the tribe will have to fight all rivals to become the new Teer. If a Teer is killed in such a challenge, his wife and children are inevitably killed to avoid any disputes over succession.

Capellan Power Cat

Appearances: "How Sharper Than A Serpent's Tooth"

A Capellan power cat (which may or may not be native to Capella 2) is a large, leonine creature that can absorb and reradiate energy is furious bursts. It is very primitive and savage, and must always be treated with caution.

Caretaker

Played by: Oliver McGowan
Appearances: "Shore Leave"
"Once Upon A Planet"

Omicron Delta is a world created purely for the amusement of a race of beings that are far more advanced than the human race - and far more sophisticated. Yet with this evolutionary increase also came an increased need for play, and play of a very sophisticated nature. To meet this need, they redesigned Omicron Delta to be a play world. There, a vast central computer and processing station was established to read the desires of the race, and turn those thoughts into reality. To ensure that the planet would run smoothly, one of their numbers was left there. Known only by his function as the Caretaker, it was his duty to ensure that any member of his race who stopped by the planet would be able to play and relax.

The Enterprise discovered Omicron Delta by accident and no idea what th place was. Barely short of tragedy, the Caretaker discovered the presense of the humans and illuminated them as to what they could do with this world. Typically generous, like all of his race, he threw the planet open for the humans to use for the duration of their stay. Treated with care, the world proved to be a refreshing delight to all of the humans who visited it - provided their thoughts were carefully controlled!

:Later the Caretaker died, and the computer that ran the planet assumed his functions.

CARTER, Dr.

Played by: Ed McReady
Episode: "The Omega Glory"

Dr Carter was the medical officer of the "USS Exeter, " one of the sister ships of the "Enterprise." He served under Captain Ronald Tracy, and all but Tracy perished due to an infection picked up on Omega IV.

CARTWRIGHT

Played by: Brock Peters
Story: "Star Trek IV - The Voyage Home"

Admiral Cartwright is a member of Starfleet Command.

Catullans

Appearances: "The Way To Eden"

Catullans are a humanoid species, and members of the Federation.

Ceti Eels

Appearances: "The Wrath Of Khan"

Ceti Alpha V was once a normal, verdant world, with a mixed ecology. One creature that lived there was known as the Ceti eel - an armored creature some six inches long, looking vaguely like a plated slug. It had tremendously strong manibles, and the ability to eat almost anything. When the twin planet of Ceti Alpha VI exploded, the climatic conditions of Ceti Alpha V changed dramatically, and the planet became a sand-blasted desert where virtually nothing could live - except the Ceti eel.

The eel lays small eggs that hatch below the plates of its skin. The young attach themselves to the adults by the aid of their mandibles, and gain nourishment until they are old enough to fend for themselves. When barely an inch long, they leave the parent eel, and seek a host. They enter the host animal generally through the ear, penetrating to the base of the brain. Here they wrap themselves about the cerebral cortex and begin to feed and grow. Creatures or people infected with an eel tend to be very sluggish, susceptible to any suggestions. After a short while the growing eel causes intense pain and madness, before death sets in. The small eel - but now five or six time its original size - will use its mandible to dig its way out of the corpse. It is almost fully grown, ready to eat anything it finds.

CHANDRA

Played by: Reginald Ial Singh
Episode: "Court Martial"

Board Officer Chandra was a member of the court martial board trying Kirk for killing Benjamin Finney.

CHANG

Played by: Christopher Plummer
Star Trek VI: The Undiscovered Country

General Chang is a ruthless Klingon warrior who is against peace with the Federation. He and Federation officials who share his disinterest in peace conspire to sabotage the peace conference. To that end, Chang frames Kirk for the assassination of Chancellor Gorkon and attacks the Enterprise at Khittomer. He and his ship are destroyed by the Enterprise and the Excelsior.

CHAPEL, CHRISTINE

Played by: Majel Barett Series regular
Story: "Star Trek - The Motion Picture"
"Star Trek IV - The Voyage Home"

Christine Chapel was originally the nurse on the Enterprise during its five year mission. she loved Mr. Spock rather without hope. after the mission ended, she continued her training, making full medical officer eventually, and transferring off-ship.

CHEKOV, PAVEL

Played by: Walter Koenig
Series regular, Season Two on

Pavel Chekov began his association with the Enterprise as a trainee. He made navigator, then weapons officer. at the end of the mission and encounter with V'Ger he was assigned as science officer to the USS Reliant. He was then returned to duty on the Enterprise as navigator/weapons officer.

Cherons

Appearances; "Let That Be Your Last Battlefield"

Cheron is now a dead world, destroyed by the insane prejudices of her people. On this world, two peoples lived. both had faces that were half black and half-white, though each race was the mirror image of the other . One of the races achieved a technological society first, and enslaved the others. The second group fought fanatically for their freedom, both sides hating each other Lokai, the leader fo the slaves, was forced to flee his world, and was chased by Commissioner Bele. the Cherons continued their strife destroying every vestige of civilization, and fought until they were all dead.

Lokai fled for thousands of years, until he ended with the Enterprise, where Bele finally caught up with him. Kirk took them back to their world, where both of them found the planet devoid of intelligent life,wiped out fully in their insane struggle. Not even this evidence could prevent Lokai and Bele from attempting to finish the war by slaying one another. Both were beamed down to the planet still fighting. Their only peace, it would seem, will be in death - together. The Cherons did display an ability to take command of mechanical devices by exertion of their thoughts.

CHILDRESS, BEN

Played by: Gene Dynarski
Episode: "Mudd's Women

Ben Childress was the mining chief in charge of the small colony on Rigel 12. He attempted to bargain with Kirk to exchange dilithium for the freedom of Harry Mudd. This was to gain one of Mudd's beauties, Eve McHuron. Eve was disgusted with his affection for her beauty, and made Childress realize that she could be more than simply someone who looks good.

CLAUDIUS

Played by: Logan Ramsey
Episode: "Bread And Circuses"

Claudius Marcus was Proconsul of the Roman World (See separate entry for further details).

CLAYMARE

Played by: Peter Brocco
Episode: "Errand Of Mercy"

One of the ruling Council of Organia. For further details, see separate entry.

CLEARY

Played by: Michael Roygas
Story: "Star Trek - The Motion Picture"

Lt. Cleary was a member of the "Enterprise" crew.

Cloud Vampire

Appearances: "Obession"

(This monster was never named on the show)

Very little is known about a cloud-like creature that evolved on Tychus IV. Its basic metabolism is somehow related to the rare element dichronium, and it exudes a honey-sweet aroma. The cloud vampire feeds by draining other life of their red blood corpuscles, which kills the victims. It can store energy within itself, somehow moving by an application of gravitational energy. amazingly, this enables the cloud to move at warp speds, and to direct its own flight in space by riding gravitational waves.

The cloud attacked and killed half of the crew of the USS Farragut, and eleven years later on a different world attacked the enterprise. due to its gravitational control, the creature could not be stopped by phaser fire, deflectors or other small energy forces. In the end Kirk managed to destroy it by utilizing anti-matter/matter reaction, killing it in the blast.

CLOUD, WILLIAM

Played by: Roy Jensen
Episode: "The Omega Glory"

Cloud William was a warrior of the Yangs on Omega IV (see separate entry for further information). His wife was Sirah.

CICGRABEM ZEFRAN

Played by: Glenn Corbett
Episode: "Metamorphosis"

Zefram Cochrane was the inventor of the warp drive, 150 years before the five year mission of the "Enterprise." He was lost in space shortly after his discovery, and presumed dead. In fact, he was discovered by a strange cloud-like creature and kept alive on Gamma Canaris. He called his being the "companion" (see separate entry for further details). He elected to remain with the Companion/Nancy Hedford and live out a normal life with them.

COGLEY, SAMUEL T.

Played by: Elisha Cook
Episode: "Court Martial"

Samuel T. Cogley was the eminent if unorthodox lawyer who defended Kirk against the charge of deliberately murdering his old friend Benjamin Finney. After his success at this, he went on to defend Finney himself - a lawyer through and through.

COLEMAN, DR.

Played by: Harry Landers
Episode: "Turnabout Intruder"

Dr. Coleman was the assistant of Dr. Janice Lester, and he accomplice in taking over the body of Kirk. See entry on Janice Lester for further details.

COLT, YEOMAN J.M.

Played by: Laurel Goodwin
Episode: "The Cage"

Yeoman Colt was the personal valet of Captain Christopher Pike during his years of service on the "Enterprise." She had a very strong crush on the Captain, but was forced to give it up eventually, realizing he did not return these feelings.

COMPANION

Played by: Majel Barrett
Episode: "Metamorphosis"

Gamma Canaris is the home of the strange life-form known only as the Companion. She evolved there, coming to consciousness alone in this small place. a being of plasma and mentality, she could alter the follow of energy, and control her environment within limits. Her life was tied to that of the planetoid, and should could not travel far from it without weakening. for uncounted years, she lived there alone, until a small spaceship crashed on the planetoid, It contained just a single man, Zefram Cochrane. The Companion helped him to live, and kept him alive - far longer than his normal life span. She discovered both companionship and love.

She could pick up some of his thoughts, especially if he called mentally to her. Yet she did not know that he did not love her. The two communed, but this seemed to be the extent of their communication. cochrane simply wanted to escape, and tried to convince the Companion that he would die of loneliness, hoping she would let him go. Instead the Companion kidnapped a shuttlecraft, bring Kirk, Spock, McCock and the dying Nancy Hedford to Gamma Canaris. Cochrane found Nancy very attractive, in a way that he could never feel for the Companion. Though the Enterprise team found nothing terrible in the idea of being by an alien entity. Cochrane was appalled - mostly at himself, since he knew how much he trusted and valued the friendship of the Companion. Realizing that in her form, she could never be truly loved by Cochrane, the Companion used her powers to heal Nancy. She then arrived at an agreement to fuse herself with Nancy, locking herself into a few years of life in exchange for the ability to be physically with one being she loved. When Nancy's body dies, so will the Companion. Until then, she and Cochrane live on their own planetoid.

COMPTON

Played by: Geoffrey Binney
Episode: "Wink Of An Eye"

Compton was a member of the landing part / of Scalos (see separate entry for further details). He was accelerated to the rate of the Scalosians, and converted to their cause. When he fought Kirk, Compton was injured, and this injury led to his rapid aging and death.

COMPUTER

Played by: Doug Hale
Story : "Star Trek - The Motion Picture"

This was the "Enterprise" speaking computer.

CORY, DONALD

Played by: Keye Luke
Episode: "Whom Gods Destroy"

Dr. Donald Cory was the Governor of the maximum security mental/penal institution on Elba II. Garth of Izar replaced him, holding him prisoner and torturing him. He was rescued and restored by Kirk.

CRATER, NANCY

Played by: Jeanne Bal, Francine Pyne
Episode: "The Man Trap"

Nancy Crater, wife of Robert Crater, was an old girlfriend of Dr. McCoy's. She was killed on planed M113 by a salt vampire, which then assumed her identity. Since it could cast illusions into people's minds, she made Ensign Darnell see her as a woman he recalled from a pleasure world.

CRATER, PROFESSOR ROBERT

Played by: Alfred Ryder
Episode: "The Man Trap"

Professor Ryder was investigating the remains of a long-dead civilization on M113 when the last survivor of the race killed his wife. Crater couldn't bring himself to kill the creature - a unique specimen - since it lived simply on salt. Its telepathic abilities made it an exact duplicate of his wife to his eyes. He attempted to stop Kirk and especially McCoy from interfering, but the creature eventually killed him as well.

CREATURES

Some forms of aliens were never named. These include:

(1) Played by: Ed McCready
Episode: "Miri"

When the children of Miri's world reached puberty, a virus caused them to go insane and attack others before dying horribly.

(2) Played by: Buck Maffei
Episode: "The Galileo Seven"

A native of Taurus II. For further details, see "Star Trek - The Aliens And Monsters Files."

(3) Played by: James Daris
Episode: "Spock's Brain"

A native of Sigma Draconis 6. Actually, just a male human, but dominated and named by the women.

(4) Played by: Allan Miller
Story: "Star Trek III _ The Search For Spock"

The alien captain of a ship McCoy attempted to hire to return to the Genesis planet.

CREWMEMBERS

Members of the "Enterprise" crew seen but unnamed include:
1)Played by: John Bellah
Episodes: (1) "Charlie X"
(2) "The Naked Time"
2) Played by: Garland Thompson
Episodes: (1) "Charlie X"
(2) "The Enemy Within" (named as Wilson)
3) Played by: Laura Wood
Episode: "Charlie X"
4) Played by: don Eitner
Episode: "Charlie X" (navigator)
5) Played by: William Knight
Episode: (The Naked Time)"
6) Played by: John Arndt
Episodes: (1) "Miri"
(2) "Dagger Of The Mind"
(3) "Balance Of Terror" (named as Fields)
(4) "Space seed"
7) Played by: David L. Ross
Episodes: (1) "The Gailileo Seven" (transporter chief)
(2) "A Taste Of Armageddon" (named as Galloway)
(3) "The City On the Edge Of Forever"
(4) "The Omega Glory"
(5) "Day Of The Dove" (named as Johnson)
(6) "Turnabout Intruder:" (as Galloway again)
8) Played by: Sherri Townsend
Episode: "Tomorrow Is Yesterday"
9) Played by: Nancy Wong
Episode: "Court Martial" (personnel officer)
10) Played by: Jan Reddin
Episode: "Space Seed"
11) Played by: Jan Reddin
Episode: "Space Seed"
12) Played by: Bobby Bass
Episode: "This Side Of Paradise:"
13) Played by: Christian Patrick
Episode: "The Alternative Factor: (Transporter technician)
14) Played by: Arch Whiting
Episode: "The Alternative Factor" (engineering assistant)
1,5) Played by: Barbara Gates
Episode: "The Changling"
16) Played by: Merde Martin
Episode: "The Changling"
17) Played Garth Pillsbury
Episode: "Mirror, Mirror" (named as Wilson)
18) Played by: Pete Kellett
Episode: "Mirror, Mirror" (the alternate Kirk's henchman)
19) Played by: John Lindesmith
Episode: "The Paradise Syndrome" (engineer)
20) Played by: Lou Elias
Episode: "And The Children Shall Lead" (technician)
21) Played by: Brad Forest
Episode: "That Which Survives" (transporter technician)
22) Played by: Barbara Baldavin
Episode: "Turnabout Intruder" (communications officer)
23) Played by: Billy van Zandt
Story: "Star Trek - The Motion Picture" (alien ensign)
24) Played by: Ralph Brennan
Story: "Star Trek - The Motion Picture" (bridge crew)
25) Played by: Ralph Byers
Story: "Star Trek - The Motion Picture" (bridge crew)
26) Played by: Iva Lane
Story: "Star Trek - The Motion Picture" (bridge crew)
27) Played by: Franklyn Seales
Story: "Star Trek - The Motion Picture" (bridge crew)
28) Played by Momo Yashima
Story: "Star Trek - The Motion Picture" (bridge crew)
29) Played by John D. Gowans
Story: "Star Trek - The Motion Picture" (transporter assistant)
30) Played by: Leslie C. Howard
Sotry: "Star TRek - The Motion Picture"
31) Played by: Junero Jennings
Story: " Star Trek - The Motiion Picture" (engineer)
32) Played by: Sayra Hummel
Story: "Star Trek - The Motion Picture" (engineer)
33) Played by Howard Itzkowitz
Story: "Star Trek - The Motion Picture" (cargo deck

ensign)
34) Played by: Paula Crist
Story: "Star Trek - The Motion Picture"
35)Played by: Gary Faga
Story: "Star Trek - The Motion Picture" (air lock technician)
36) Played by: Susan J. Sullivan
Story: "Star Trek - The Motion Picture"
37) Played by: Nicholas Guest
Story: "Star Trek II - The Wrath Of Khan" (cadet)
38) Played by: Joel Marstan
Story: "Star Trek II - The Wrath Of Khan" (crew chief)

CROMWELL

Played by: Don Keefer
Episode: "Assignment: Earth"

Cromwell worked for intelligence, under Colonel Nesvig.

CRUSHER, DR. BEVERLY

Played by: Gates McFadden
Series regular

Beverly Crusher is the widow of Jack Crusher, an officer who died while serving Picard on the Stargazer. The Crushers have a son, Wesley. Beverly blamed Picard somewhat for her husband's death, but later developed a silent romantic interest in him. She is a hardworking, scientific physician, and frequently serves as the voice of compassion in difficult times. She was away from the Enterprise at Starfleet Medical during the second year of the Enterprise mission. During that time, she was replaced by Dr. Katherine Pulaski (Diana Maldaur).

CRUSHER, WESLEY

Played by: Wil Wheaton

Wesley became fascinated with starships from the moment he stepped aboard the Enterprise with his mother. Even Picard, who is annoyed by children, found him talented and made him an "acting ensign." Wesley frequently solved problems which avoided disaster for the ship. For that, Picard field-promoted him to full ensign. Wesley later left the Enterprise to study at Starfleet Academy. There, he was part of a cover-up in the accidental death of a classmate.

Cygnan

Appearances: "The Time Trap"

One of the many species captured in the area of space known as the Delta Triangle was the Cygans. they are a humanoid, telepathic species.

D'AMATO

Played by: Arthur Batanides
Episode: "That Which Survives"

D'Amato was the senior geologist on the "Enterprise." He was killed by Losira.

DARAS

Played by: Valora Nowland
Episode: "Patterns Of Force"

Daras was supposedly a Heroine of the Fatherland on Ekow. she was actually an undercover Zeon (see separate entry for further details). She helped Kirk and Spock infiltrate the Zeon SS headquarters after John Gill.

DARNELL

Played by: Michael Zaslow
Episode: "The Man Trap"

Ensighn Darnell was a security guard who beamed down to M113 as part of the landing party. A salt vampire, posing as Nancy Crater, lured him into the rocks and hilled him to feast.

LT. CMDR. DATA

Played by: Brent Spiner
Series regular

Data was the construction of cybernetist Dr. Noonian Soong. He is an android that is almost human. Data is capable of superhuman strength. He was rescued by Starfleet personnel after the "Crystalline entity" attacked his planet. Data learned that he has a "brother", Lore, another android created by Soong. Because he was rescued by Starfleet, Data chose it as his life's work. His biggest challenge is to be more human.

DAVOD

Played by: Chuck Courtney
Episode: "Patterns Of Force"

Davod was a member of the Zeon group on Ekos (see separate entry for further details).

DAYSTROM, RICHARD

Played by: William Marshall
Episode: "The Ultimate Computer"

Dr. Richard Daystrom was one of the most brilliant computer experts in the Federation. He designed a series of computers, culminating in M5 which was to run an entire starship. He had used his own mental patterns for it, and he proved as unstable as his own computer. When Kirk finally defeated the computer, Daystrom was taken for rehabilitation treatment.

DECIUS

Played by: Lawrence Montaigne
Episode: "Balance Of Terror"

Decius was the arrogant second officer of the Romulan raiding ship.

DECKER, MATT

Played by: William Windom
Episode: "The Doomsday Machine"

Commodore Matt Decker was the captain of the "USS Constellation," one of the "Enterprise" sister ships. He attempted to destory a doomsday machine, but failed. He had his crew transport down to the third world of L-374 - which the doomsday machine then wrecked. Driven over the edge by guilt, Decker attempted to attack the machine with the "Enterprise," then gave his life in a shuttle craft attempting the destruction of the planet wrecker. he was the father of Will Decker.

DECKER, WILL

Played by: Stephen Collins
Story: "Star Trek - The Motion Picture"

Will Decker was the new Captain of the "Enterprise" after Kirk was promoted. The son of Matt Decker, he was a fine choice. When Kirk replaced him to investigate V'Ger, Decker was furious, but did his best. He also rediscovered his feelings for the Deltan navigator, Ilia. Eventually she, he and V'ger fused to form a new kind of life.

DEELA

Played by: Kathie Browne
Episode: "A Wink Of An Eye"

Deela was the leader of the Scalosians (see separate entry for further details).

DEHNER, Dr. ELIZABETH

Played by: Sally Kellerman
Episode: "Where No Man Has Gone Before"

Dr. Elizabeth Dehner was a psychologist assigned to the "Enterprise" by Starfleet to see what attempting to leave the Galaxy might do to the crew of the ship. She became involved herself, when the energy barry about the Galzxy caused her inherited ESP powers to bloom fast. With Gary Mitchell, she started to develop great mental abilities. Kirk managed to make her see that these powers were too dangerous, and that they had driven Mitchell insane. With some of her humanity remaining, she enabled Kirk to defeat and kill Mitchell, but she herself perished in the attempt.

Deltans

Appearances: "Star Trek - The Motion Picture"
"The Wrath Of Khan"

The natives of the world of Delta Four are members of the Federation, yet do not usually involve themselves greatly in off-world circumstances. The reason for this is that their natures are highly unique. firstly they are empaths - they can sense and adjust the emotional states of others. Clearly, such an ability means that they are going to be affected if in the company of many non-deltans, who cannot control their emotions. Secondly, give off a potent chemical reagent which causes any nearby males to respond in a very positive manner to her sexually. this secretion is totally subconscious, and nothing is known that can prevent it.

This means that Deltan women have a very disturbing effect on non-deltan males. If the males in question know about the effect, this can them to control their instinctive reactins. The Deltans themselves are a very physical race, and enjoy tremendous intimacy during sex. Their minds, emotions and bodies all share in the act. If a Deltan were to make love to any off-worlder, this experience would be literally overwhelming, and frequently fatal to the non-deltan. for this reason, Deltans avoid prolongued contact with other races.

Deltan bond pairs are especially linked, mentally and physically. They have an understanding close telepathy. The loss of a bond-partner will frequently cause the other bondperson to die psychosomatically, unable to stand the loneliness.

One Deltan, Ilia, served for a term as navigator aboard the Enterprise. A Deltan bond pair served aboard Regular One, until slain by Khan and his agents.

DENEVANS

Played by: Fred Carson, Jerry Catron
Episode: Operation: Annihilate"

The natives of Deneva were attacked and many killed by mind parasites before the "Enterprise" arrived and a cure was discovered.

DePAUL

Played by: Sean Kenney
Episodes: (1) "Arena"
92) "A Taste Of Armageddon"

DePaul was a member of the "Enterprise" crew.

DeSalle

Played by: Michael Barrier
Episodes: (1) "The Squire Of Gothos"
(2) "This Side Of Paradise"
(3) "Catspaw"

Lt. DeSalle was a member of the "Enterprise" bridge crew. He was often left in command when the senior officers were absent.

DiFALCO

Played by: Marcy Lafferty
Story: "Story: "Star Trek - The Motion Picture"

Chief DiFalco was the relief navigator of the "Enterprise," who took Ilia's place after she was killed by V'Ger.

DIONYO

Played by: Derek Partridge
Episode: "Plato's Stepchildren"

Dionyo was a Platonian (see separate entry for further details).

DON

Played by: Mark Robert Brown
Episode: "And The Children Shall Lead"

Don was one of the children deceived by Gorgan.

DON JUAN

Played by: James Gruzaf
Episode: "Shore Leave"

The mythical lover was conjured up by the imagination on the Caretaker's world.

Doomsday Machine

Appearances: "The Doomsday Machine"

Built to be the ultimate weapon in some long-forgotten war, the dommsday machine was a huge construction

shaped like a cone. The open end of the machine was like a mouth, and it fed on planets. A pure antiproton beam would disassemble worlds into small rocks. The machine protomn beam would disassemble worlds into small rocks. The machine possessed a tractor beam of great power, and would then draw these rocks into its maw, where they would be processed into energy for its continued existence. The mile-long machine had strong defense, capable of taking almost any punishment and in responding to attack. It was a very efficient machine, but far outlived the war for which it was designed. It eventually approached Federation space, tearing apart the inhabited worlds of system L-370. The starship Constellation attacked the world wrecker, but it shrugged off the attack and killed the crew. Eventually, Kirk used the almost-dead Constellation as a bomb, firing it once it entered the maw of the machine. Inside the machine was not armoured, and the explosion wrecked the machinery that powered it. It is not known if further examples of these war machines may some day enter Federation space.

DOUBLES

Various actors in the show had stunt doubles. These include:

(1) Christopher Pike's Double
Played by: Bob Herron
Episode: "The Cage"
(2) Kirk's Double
Played by: Dick Crockett
Episode: "Where No Man Has Gone Before"
Played by: Don Eitner
Episode: "Enemy Wighin"
Played by: Paul Baxley
Episodes: (1) "What Are Little Girls Made Of?"
(2) "Amok Time"
Played by: Phil Adams
Episodes "Amok Time"
(3) Gary Mitchell's Double
Played by: Hal Needham
Episode: "Where No Man Has Gone Before"
(4) McCoy's Double
Played by: Bob Miles
Episode:: "Miri"
(5) Stunt Doubles
Played by: Gary Coombs, Frank Vinci
Episode "The Galileo Seven"
(6) Spock's Double
Played by: Dave Perna
Episode: "Amok Time"

DRACONIANS

Appearances: "Spock's Brain"

The civilation of Sigma Draconis reached a technological high several thousand years ago. They built cities far below the surface, so that Draconis would be unsullied by technology, and these cities they equipped with machines that could do whatever the inhabitants desired. To run their cities, they used a mixture of technology and human ingenuity - the computers, controlling the place were all controlled bya humanoid brain of outstanding ability. The problem was that with everything given to them whenever they desired it, the Draconians soon lost all impetus, and began to atrophy.

Somehow, the women achieved control of the cities, expelling the males to the surfaces as soon as they were weaned. A sexist seperation thus became established, as both sexes retrogressed. The men took to a form of hunter-gathering society, living with primitive weapons in small tribal groups. The women lived in idle luxury in their cities, taking men from the surface merely as servants and slaves, controlled by computerized pain-inducers. They would use the men for breeding, raising female children in their city, and sending the males back to the surface to be raised by the tribes there. The men soon began to fear the women as givers of pain and pleasure.

Their society - lacking the drive to evolve - began to fall backwards. The men were savages, the women beautiful, spoilt idiots. Their brains were no longer powerful enough to control the computers that ran their cities. They had to seek elsewhere for such brains, learning how to fly starships and to remove the brains with highly sophistocated techniques taught them through mental infusion machines. Such machines of knowledge would soon wear off, and the women would revert to their former level of stupidity. One of their forays after a brain led them to the Enterprise, and they stole the brain of Spock, admirably suited to their purposes. Kirk followed their trail to recover it, and managed to do this. he also destroyed the computerized life, forcing the males and females to team up on the surface once again, to start their climb back to their own civilization, instead of relying on that of the dead past. Whether they managed to survive, or whether they simply stagnated and perished is not known.

Dramians

Appearances: "Albatross"

The Dramians are recent members of the Federation.

They are huamnoid, though tall and barrel-chested. Their long, tapered hands end in tentacles, not fingers, and they possess large, dark eyes. They are a gentle, kindly people who developed space travel and attempted to colonize another world in their system, which they named Dramos II. It was at this point that the Federation first made contact, nineteen years ago. McCoy was one of the contact team, and when he left, the colonist all died out from a deadly plague. The Dramians believed that McCoy had caused this, and on his return there, he was arrested for genocide. Kirk was able to prove McCoy's innocence, and the Doctor managed to manufacture a cure for the plague, so that Dramos II could again be colonized.

DREA

Played by: Lezlie Dalton
Episode: "By Any Other Name"

Drea was one of the Kelvans (see separate entry for further details).

DROXINE

Played by: Diana Ewing
Episode: "The Cloud Minders"

Droxine was the daughter of Plasus, High Advisor of Stratos (see separate entry for further details). She found Spock fascinating, and he seemed to return the interest.

DRUSILLA

Played by: Lois Jewell
Episode: "Bread And Circuses"

Drusilla was a personal slave of Claudius Marcus, the Proconsul of the Roman world (see separate entry for further details).

DUNCAN

Played by: Karl Bruck
Episode: "The Conscience Of The King"

Actually an actor, a member of the Karidian players, who performs the part of King Duncan in Macbeth on the "Enterprise".

DUUR

Played by: Kirk Raymone
Episode: "Friday's Child"

Duur was a member of the Capella tribes (see separate entry for further details).

EARP, MORGAN

Played by: Rex Holman
Episode: "Spectre Of the Gun"

Morgan Earp was one of the illusions created by the Melkotian (see separate entry for further details).

EARP, VIRGIL

Played by: Charles Maxwell
Episode: "Spectre of the Gun"

Virgil Earp was one of the illusions created by the Melkotian.

EARP, WYATT

Played by: Ron Soble

Episode: "Spectre Of The Gun"

Wyatt Earp was one of the illusions created by the Melkotian.

ED

Played by Charles Seel
Episode: "Spectre Of The Gun"

Ed was one of the illusions created by the Melkotian.

Edoans

Appearances: varied, throughout the animated series.

The Edoans are a tripedal race, and possess three flexible arms also. This arrangements of limbs is curious to their home world. They have high, squeaky voices, and have excellent dexterity. They make very good workers, able to handle complex tasks without much difficulty.. Many of them are enthusiastic and excellent musicians, their extra arm aiding considerably in finguring. Arex of the Enterprise is from the worldpurely theoretical attack. The computer on the other world would then accept defense commands from its rulers, and work out the consequences of the theoritical attacks. If it decided that there were casualties, such "victims" would have to report to disintegration chambers for voluntary death. Since this system would actually prevent the devastation of their world that a real war produce, and stop the loss of irreplacable artifacts and libraries, the populations of both worlds agreed to the "warfare" in this manner. It would continue as long as both sides scrupulously kept to the rules.

This system works well for five hundred years. The two worlds evolve in science and arts, and each year between one and thre million "war casualties" report dutifully for disintegration. Then the Valiant from the the Federation arrived. It monitored Eminiar, but sent back only the report of warfare. It was judged by the computers to be destroyed in an attack. When the Captain refused to play along with the game, the Eminians were forced to destroy the ship.

fifty years later, the Federation has decided that Eminiar is in a strategically desired situation, and the Enterprise dispatched there with Ambassador Fox to make a treaty. Once again, the starship was "hit" during the war, and Kirk was ordered to surrender his crew for disintegration. Kirk naturally refused, and Scott's canny planning saved the ship from destruction. Kirk and Spock destroy the computer on Eminiar, knowing that this will be interpreted as a declaration for real war by Vendikar. Kirk has made the two worlds retreat from their clean, statistical war into real warfare - with the terrors and pains it will bring. Neither side really wants to return to that, and with the aid of Fox, they start to discuss peace - having forgotten the causes of the war in the first place.

Empaths

Appearances: "The Empath"

The Empaths are a race of beings who lived in the system of Minara II. When this sun was about to go nova, the race was saved from extinction by the Vians (see separate entry). The Empaths, though far from advanced beings, are mute empathic creatures. They can not only sense the fellings of others, but are able to absorb wounds and pain from other beings, then take the form of the sickness themselves and cure it.

ENEG

Played by: Patrick Horgan
Episode: "Patterns Of Force"

Eneg was chairman of the Nazi party on Ekos (see separate entry for further details).

EPSILON CREW

Story: "Star Trek - The Motion Picture"
Various members of the Epsilon monitoring station were shown, including:
(1) Lieutenant
Played by: Michelle Ameen billy
(2) Technician
Played by: Roger Aaron Brown

See also separate entry on Branch.

ERACLITUS

Played by: Ted Scott
Episode: "Plato's Stepchildren"

Eraclitus was a Platonian (see separate entry for further details).

ESTEBAN, J.T.

Played by: Philip Richard Allen
Story: "Star Trek III - The Search For Spock"

Captain J.T. Esteban was captain of the "Grissom,"

sent to investigate the Genesis planet. He was killed Kruge's ship destroyed the Grissom and its crew.

EVANS

Played by: Lee Duncan
Episode: "Elaan Of Troyius"

Evans was a member of the "Enterprise' crew.

EVANS, CHARLIE

Played by: Robert Walker, Jr.
Episode: "Charlie X"

Charlie Evans was the sole survivor of a shuttle craft crash on the mysterious world of Thasus when he was three. At the age of 17, he was rescued by the crew of the cargo ship "Antares." He could not account for how he had survived alone so long, but in fact had been trained by the Thasians in their mental abilities. When the Thasians discovered that he had gotton away, they were forced find and bring him back. His powers and his child-like tempre made him too dangerous to be left in the company of normal humans.

Excalbians

Appearances: "The Savage Curtain"

The planet Excalbia was long thought to be lifeless, but this was simply because the natives of this world are actually made of living silcon, and resemble simply a pile of boulders. They are not terribly active, and as a result tend to be without emotions. They are very active mentally, though, and can communicate telepathically. Thus, they managed to achieve a high level of philosophy, whilst apparently not even possessing a society. Normal things like shelter and food have little meaning to the Excalbians. Instead, their mental powers led them to realize that there were other beings in the Univers, of different order to themselves.

The nature of morality fascinated them. They could not understand the concepts that other beings held of good and evil, and thus determined that they would use their manipulation of the minds of other beings to create a test. Kirk and Spock, together with their heroes Abraham Lincoln create a test. Kirk and Spock, together with their heroes Abraham Lincoln of Eargh and Surak of Vulcan, were pitted against the four vilest creatures that the Excalbians could dredge from their minds. Their aim was to see whether good or evil was stronger. In the end, though Kirk and Spock won, the Excalbians still could not see why the methods of good were different from those of evil. Kirk pointed out that the evil beings fought for their own ends, while he and Spock had fought to save the lives of their own crew - a selfless aim. The Excalbians accepted this, and are now undoubtedly strongly discussing the nature of selfish and unselfish acts.

EXCELSIOR CREW

Story: "Star Trek III - The Search For Spock"

These include: First Officer Played by: Miguel Ferrer See also separate entry on Styles.

EXECUTIONER

Played by: Frank Atienze
Episode: "The Omega Glory"

The executioner was a member of the Yangs of Omega IV (see separate entry for further details).

Fabrini

Appearances: "For The World Is Hollow And I have Touched The Sky"

Ten thousand years ago, the star of the planet that was home to the Fabrini went nova. The Fabrini, though having little expertise in star travel, had an advanced society. Their medical skills became legendary, far in advance of those of the modern Federation. they could see that their star was dying, and so equipped a number of hollowed asteroids with drives, and sent as many6 of their race as they could off to the stars in order to survive. Many of these founded new homes, but one of them was still wandering the cosmos ten thousand years later (see the entry on Yonadians).

FARRELL, JOHN

Played by: Jim Goodwin
Episodes: (1) "The Enemy Wighin"
(2) "Mudd's Women"
(3) "Miri"

John Farrell was one of the early navigators on th e"Enterprise" before Chekov was given the post.

FELLINI

Played by: Ed Peck
Episode: "Tomorrow Is Yesterday"

Colonel Fellini worked for Air Force security in this late 1960's at the 498th Air Base Group.

FERRIS

Played by: John Crawford
Episode: "The Galileo Seven"

Commissioner Ferris was ferried by the "Enterprise" to the ailing world of Makus III with medical supplies. When the shuttle "Galileo" was lost, Ferris objected to delays in hunting for it, then ordered Kirk to leave on his mission. Kirk manages to recover the "Galileo" in time, however.

FIELDS

See crewmembers.

FINNEGAN

Played by: Bruce Mars
Episode: "Shore Leave"

Finnegan was one of the cadets at the Academy at the same time that Kirk was there. He had made Kirk's life a misery, and Kirk had always longed to get revenge on him. On the world of the Caretaker, where dreams became all-too-solid reality, Kirk got his wish and finally beat the tar out of the mocking Finnegan.

FINNEY, BENJAMIN

Played by: Richard Webb
Episode: "Court Martial"

Benjamin Finney was an instructor at Starfleet Academy who had befriended the young James Kirk. finney even named his daughter Jame after Kirk. However, when both moved on to assignments, Finney made an error that could have killed the entire ship, and Kirk had been forced to log it. This blot on finney's career held him back, and he blamed Kirk for this. He eventually became the Records of the "Enterprise, " under the same Kirk. He planned to fake his own death and ruin Kirk's careeer in a court martial. Kirk was defended by Samuel T. cogley, who proved with Spock's help that Finney was still alive. Kirk capture his old friend, and Cogley proceeded to defend him when he went to trial for his actions.

FINNEY, JAME

Played by: alice Rawlings
Episode: "Court Martial"

Daughter of Benjamin Finney, Jame was named for James Kirk, her father's old friend.

FISHER

Played by: Edward Madden
Episode: "The Enemy Within"

Fisher is a geologist on the "Enterprise."

FITZGERALD

Played by: Richard Derr
Episode: "The Mark Of Gideon"

Admiral Fitgerald was a member of Starfleet Command.

FITZPATRICK

Played by: Ed Reimers
Episode: "The Trouble with Tribbles"

Admiral Fitzpatrick was a member of Starfleet Command.

FLAVIUS

Played by: Rhodes Reason
Episode: "Bread and Circuses"

Flavius was an escaped gladiator, converted to Christianity and believing in thw way of peace on the roman world (see "Star Trek - The Aliens And Monsters File" for further information). He attempted to help Kirk in the arena, but was machinegunned down.

FLINT

Played by: James Daly
Episode: "Requiem For Methuselah"

Flint was a man who had been born immortal, thousands of years in the past. He constantly changed identities, and was in fact some of the world's most famous men - Leonardo da Vinci, Brahms, Methuselah and so forth. Longing for an equally immortal wife, he created the andoroid Rayna (see separate entry). When she died, he elected to remain alone, not knowing that now he had left the Earth, he was aging at a normal rate again and would some day die.

FOSTER

Played by: Phil Morris
Story: "Star Trek III - The Search For Spock"

Foster was one of the trainees aboard the "Enterprise."

FOX

Played by: Gene Lyons
Episode: "A Taste Of Armageddon"

Ambassador Fox was the Federation envoy to the people of Eminiar VII. Officious, dull and petty, Fox caused nothing but trouble for Kirk and Scott. Eventually, through a foolish move, he was captured by the Eminians and sentenced to death. He was saved by Kirk and finally began to make some progress with settling the 500 year old war between Eminiar and Vendikos.

FREEMAN

Played by: Paul Baxley
Episode: "The Trouble With Tribbles"

Ensign Freeman was a member of the "Enterprise" crew.

GAETANO

Played by: Peter Marko
Episode: "The Galileo Seven"

Gaetano was one of the members of the ill-fated shuttle "Galileo" which crashed on Taurus II as it investigated Murasaki 312. He and Lt. boma failed to understand Spock's methods of logic and disputed his actions constantly. Gaetano was killed whilst on guard duty prior to their eventual escape.

GALLOWAY

See crewmembers.

GALT

Played by: Joseph Ruskin
Episode: "The Gamesters Of Triskelion"

Galt was the senior thrall for the Providers (see separate entry for further details).

GALWAY, ARLENE

Played by: Beverly Washburn
Episode: "The Deadly Years"

Arlene Galway was a member of the landing party from the landing party from the "Enterprise" that investigated the conditions on Gamma Hydra IV. She contracted the aging virus that killed all of the colonists, and she herself perished of old age a short while later.

G

GARRISON

Played by: Adam Roarke
Episode: "The Cage"

Garrison was the Chief Petty Officer of the Enterprise under Christopher Pike.

GARROVICK

Played by: Stephen Brooks
Episode: "Obsession"

Ensign Garrovick was security officer of the "Enterprise." His father had been Kirk's first captain. Kirk, seeing something of himself in the young man, pushed him too hard at first. McCoy made Kirk slow down, and Garrovick proved to be a fine cadet.

GARTH

Played by; Steve Ihnat
Episode: "Whom Gods Destroy"

See entry on Antosians for further details

GAV

Played by: John Wheeler
Episode: "Journey To Babel"

Gav was Tellarite ambassador (see separate entry for further details). He was killed by Thelev, to frame Sarek of Vulcan.

EM

Played by: Kathryn Hays
Episode: "The Empath"

See entry on Empaths for further details.

who denounced Melakon,. Melakon slew gill, but was killed in his turn by Isak.

GIOTTO

Played by: Barry Russo
Episode: "The Devil In The Dark"

Giotto was one of the original security chiefs of the "Enterprise."

GORGAN

Played by: Melvin Belli
Episode: "And The Children Shall Lead"

The natives of Triarchus were a savage and evil people, who could feed on mental energy and dominate people with lesser minds. They were known throughout their sector of space centuries ago, but the piople of those worlds banded together to destory this evil race that existed solely to dominate and kill. The races managed to destroy all but a single entity, Gorgan..Then, over the course of time, the existence of the Trairchans was considered a myth, until a research team returned to the world and accidentally freed Gorgan from his slumbers.

Gorgan could feed on the mental energies of the young best, for their natural savagery and lack of sophistication suited him admirably. Their nativity meant that they could be controlled by his calculated lies and deceptions. Once the adults realized that Gorgan existed, the Triarchan used the mental energies he was draining from the children to affect the minds of the adults, forcing them to commit suicide. He then masked the reality of their parents' death from the children.

The arrival of the Enterprise gave Gorgan a chance for excape from this dead world, and possibility of further minds to infect. The more he could control, the greater his abilities would be. However, Kirk and Spock together managed to convince the children of the inherent evil of Gorgan, and the children withdrew their trust. Without the mental energies that they had been supplying, Gorgan could not exist. His disguise as a friendly angel destroyed, he finally perished.

GORKON

Played by: John Warner
Star Trek VI: The Undiscovered Country

After the Klingon energy moon of Praxis is destroyed, Chancellor Gorkon is able to begin his dream of peace between the UFP and the Empire. He is assassinated after a rendezvous with the Enterprise. Kirk is framed as the assassin, but the true killer is Chang, one of Gorkon's generals opposed to peace.

GORN

Played by: Gary Coombs, Bobby Clark, Ted Cassidy
Episode: "Arena"
"The Time Trap"

On the fringe of human expansion is the world of Cestus III. This was the first meeting point between the Federation and the Gorn race. The gorns, similarly expanding, saw the presence of aliens in what they considered to be their area of space as a threat. They responded with violence, leading to the outbreak of a limited warfare between the two races. this warfare was stopped by the beings known as the Metrons (see separate entry).

The Gorns are bipedal reptiles, with large, strong heads. They have a protuberant snout, large teeth (they are carnivorous) and faceted eyes. They are highly intelligent, but their carnivorous nature tends to make them fight first and talk later. They did prove, however, to be amenable to peace, and after negotiations, they now live on the fringe of Federation worlds. It is not inconceivable that they will one day join the Federation.

GORO

Played by: Richard Hale
Episode: "The Paradise Syndrome"

Goro was the chief of the Indians (see separate entry for further information). He was the father of Miramanee.

GOSSETT

Played by: Jon Kowall
Episode: "Mudd's Women"

Gossett was one of the dilithium miners on Rigel 12 who desired Mudd's women.

GRANT

Played by: Bob Bralver
Episode: "Friday's Child"

Gran was a security guard, killed on Capella IV when he made a follish move against a guest of the tribe.

GRAYSON, AMANDA

Played by: Jane Wyatt
Episodes: (1) Journey To Babel"
(2) "Star Trek IV - The Voyage Home"

Amanda Grayson was an educator on Earth when she met the Vulcan ambassador, Sarek. She fell in love with him , and he - in his own way - with her. The couple married and moved to Vulcan, where thay have one child, Spock. Amanda has managed to assimilate much of the Vulcan culture, but refuses to give up her emothions - and hopes that Spock can do the same.

GREEN

Played by: Bruce Watson
Episode: "The Man Trap"

Green was attacked and killed by the salt vampire, which then used his appearance to gain access to the "Enterprise".

GREEN, COLONEL

Played by: Philip Pine
Episode: "The Savage Curtain"

Colonel Green was a ruthless genocidal maniac rampant on 21st century Earth. An illusion of him was created by the Excalbians for Kirk and Spock to fight.

GRISSOM CREW

Story: "Star Trek III - The Search For Spock"

Various members of the science ship "Grissom" were shown, prior to its destruction by the Klingon Kruge.
These include:
(1) Helm
Played by: Jeanne Mori
(2) Communications
Played by: Mario Marcelino

See also separate entries for: Esteban, Saavik, David Marcus.

GUARDIAN OF FOREVER

Played by: Bartell LaRue
Episode: "The City On The Edge Of Forever"
"Yesteryear"

It is difficult to state exactly what the Guardian of Forever is. Some long-dead cciviliation created the Guardian for the purpose of viewing and visiting their own past. The Guardian is clearly intelligent, and can use its strange powers to show other races the pasts of their own worlds. It cannot make judgements, simply show what has been and offer to take people there. Because of the dangers involved in changing the past, the Federation has placed the planet under strict quarantine. Only special groups for scientific studies are allowed on the dead world now.

GUINAN

Played by: Whoopi Goldberg
Series regular

Guinan is of a mysterious alien race. She befriended Picard years earlier and serves as bartender in the Enterprise's "Ten Forward" lounge. She is very wise and gives advice often. Her race was nearly obliterated by the Borg and the otherwise understanding Guinan now has grown to hate them. It was Guinan and something inherent to her race that made her sense that the alternate timeline that brought Tasha Yar back and began the Klingon war was wrong. Her bond with Picard is so strong that he restored the timeline on her intuition.

HACOM

Played by: Morgan Farley
Episode: "The Return Of The Archons"

Hacom was an inhabitant of Beta 3, and a member of the resistance against Landru and his Lawgivers. Fearing what was happening, Hacom betrayed his fellow members Tamar and Reger to Landru.

HADLEY

played: William Blackburn
Episode: "A Piece Of The Action"

Lt. Hadley was a member of the crew of the "Enterprise".

HAINES, JANA

Played by: Victoria George
Episode: "The Gamesters Of Triskelion"

Ensign Jana Haines was a member of the "Enterprise" crew.

Halcons

Appearances: "Mirror, Mirror"

The planet Halcon is a place of gentle folksk and violent weather. Storms ravage the atmosphere, but in contrast her population have a history of total pacifism. They will neither engage in fighting themselves, nor give aied to any who do so.

HAMLET

Played by: Marc Adams
Episode: "The Conscience Of The King"

Actually one of the Karidian Players, who took the part of Hamlet in a performance of the play on the "Enterprise."

HANSEN, Lt.

Played by: Hagen Beggs
Episodes: (1) "The Menagerie"
(2) "Court Martial"

Lt. Hansen was a member of staff for Star Base 11.

HANSON

Played by: Garry Walberg
Episode: "Balance Of Terror"

Commander Hanson was the commanding officer of Outpost Four, set up to monitor the Romulan Neutral Zone. He and all his men were killed in a suprise Romulan attack.

HAROLD

Played by: Tom Troupe
Episode: "Arena"

Lt. Harold was the last member of the colony on Cestus III. The colony was wiped out in an attack by the Gorns.

HARPER

Played by: Sean Morgan
Episode: "The Ultimate Computer"

Ensign Harper was a member of the "Enterprise" crew.

HASKINS, Dr. THEODORE

Played by: Jon Lormer
Episode: "The Cage"

Dr. Theodore Haskins belonged to the American Continental Institues. He was the leader of an exploratory ship that crashed on Talos IV, killing all aboard but the yourg girl Vina.

Hate Vampire

Appearances: "Day Of The Dove"

The strange being composed entirely of light energies is never named, nor does it ever communicate. It feeds of the emotions of hatred and strife, and can create realistic illusions in the minds of lesser beings that it manipulates to create warfare. It can control physical reality, changing phasers into swords, and extending the lives of its victems, even down to healing the dead. This creature attempted to foment eternal warfare between the men of the Enterprise and a small band of Klingons in order to have a captive source of food forever. Once its presence was dected, Kirk and the Klingon leader, Kang, created a spirit of harmony to disgust and dispell the being.

HEDFORD, NANCY

Played by: Elinor Donahue
Episode "Metamorphosis"

Commissioner Nancy Hedford was a cold, aloof diplomat. Whilst conducting peace talks on Epsilon Canaris III, she contracted the rare Sakuro's disease. She was being transported in a shuttle to the "Enterprise" when the shuttle was captured by the Companion (see separate entry for further details). To stay alive, she elected to merge with the Companion, and stay behind on Gamma Canaris as the wife of Zefram Cochrane. She had become convinced that her emotional needs now needed this outlet.

HENAK

Played by: Tewart Moss
Episode: "By Any Other Name"

Henak was one of the Kelvans (see separate entry for further details).

HENDORFF

Played by: Mal Friedman
Episode: "The Apple"

Hendorff was security guard from the "Enterprise." He was killed on Gamma Triangulae VI by a plant that fired poisonous thorns into him.

HENGIST

Played by: John Fiedler
Episode: "Wolf In The Fold"

See the entry on Jack the Ripper for further details.

HERMAN

Played by: Ted & Tom le Garde
Episode: "I, Mudd"

The Hermans were Androids (see separate entry for further details).

HODIN

Played by: David Hurst
Episode: "The Mark Of Gideon"

Hodin was the leader of the peoples of Gideon (see separate entry for further details). He was the father of Odona.

HOLLIDAY, DOC

Played by Gilman
Episode: "Spectre Of The Gun"

Doc Holliday was one of the illusions created by the Melkotian (see separate entry for further details).

HORTA

Played by: janos Prohaska
Episode: "The Devil In The Dark"

Janus VI is the home of the Horta. This peaceful species is composed of silicon-based cells, instead of the carbon-based ones more common throughout the Galaxy. The Horta are large, dumpy creatures, whose bod-

ies are almost rock-hard. They burrow through the ground using acid produced internally and secreted through their skins. This acid also serves to dissolve minerals, allowing the Hortas to feed. Despite their somewhat restricted life, the Horta are fairly intelligent creatures. Their tunnels crisscross the planet.

Horta are long-lived creatures, and breed very rarely. When they do it tends to be a societal event - millions of eggs are laid, and the adult Hortas die out - except for one, who guards the eggs until they hatch. The eggs are almost perfectly spherical white globes of pure silicon, protecting the maturing Horta inside. Young Horta are born with sophisticated instincts and soon mature.

A pergium refinery, built on Janus by humans, accidentally broke into one nursery and began stealing and damaging eggs. Unable to communicate with these thrats to her unboarn young, the only adult Horta resorted to violence and trickery to attempt to get the humans to leave the planet. In the end, thanks to the intervention of Kirk and Spock, some measure understanding between the two races was achieved. The wounds inflicted on the Horta were healed by McCoy using concrete, a perfect bandage for such a being. Humans and Horta now work together on Janus in harmony.

HUMBOLDT, CHIEF

Played by: George Sawaya
Episode: "The Menagerie"

Chief Humboldt was in charge of the computer section of Star Base 11.

ILIA

Played by: Persis Khambatta
Story: "Star Trek - The Motion Picture"

Ilia was a Deltan navigator aboard the "Enterprise." She and Will Decker had fallen in love, but could not consumate thier love. Deltan love is too intense for humans to share. She was scanned and killed by V'Ger then replaced with a probe identical in all ways to real Ilia - even down to emotions. Eventually, Ilia, Decker and V'ger fused to become a new form of life.

INDIANS

Episode: "The Paradise Syndrome"

The race of people transfered to a fresh home by the Preservers.
They include:
(1) Woman
Played by: Naomi Pollack
(2) Warrior
Played by:
Peter Vigo, Jr.
(3) Boy
Played by: Lamont Laird

See also entries on: Miramanee, Salish and Goro.

For further information, see the entry on Preservers.

INMATE

Played by: Ed McCready
Episode: "Dagger Of The Mind"

One of the people confined at the Tantalus Penal Colony. He was used as an unofficial guard by Dr. Tristan Adams.

IOTIANS

Episode: "A Piece Of the Action"
Various members of the Iotians were seen, including:
(1) Young Boy
Played by: Sheldon Collins
(2) Krako's Hood
Played by: Buddy Garion
(3) Girls
Played by: Dyanne Thorne, Sharyn Hillyer
(4) Krako's Gun Moll
Played by: Marlys Burdette

See also separate entries on: Oxmyx, Krako, Zabo, Kalo, Tepo, Mirt.

The people of Sigma Iotia II are a very bright and inventive race, but very impressionable. They were first contacted a hundred years back by the crew of the USS Horizon, who enjoyed their company, but accidentally contaminated the entire world by leaving a copy of The Book, This volume, "Chicago Mobs Of The Twenties,"

was taken by the eager Iotioans to be the basis for all logical society, and they rapidly changed their own to suit it.

The various territories were thus owned by gangs, under their gang bosses. Power plays were then made by the mobs, will shoot-outs and murders being pretty common. The peoples of the various territories paid protection to the mobs, and were thus given the basics of life. It was a strange, but oddly workable, system. Kirk managed to convince the natives that the "feds" for whom he worked wanted a piece of the action. This cut from the top would then be used to rectify this error with the Iotians in the past and help educate them to a saner society.

IRINA

Played by: Mary-Linda Rapelye
Episode: "The Way To Eden"

Irina was one of the drop-out followers of Dr. Sevrin. She and Chekov had been romantically linked whilst in Starfleet Academy together, but she did not like the discipline or atmosphere it offered her. She joined with Sevrin on the quest for Eden, but when she found the place, it was literally lethal.

ISAK

Played by: Richard Evans
Episode: "Patterns Of Force"

Isak was a Zeon agent, captured by the Ekosians SS (see separate entry for further details).

ISIS

Played by: Barbara Babcock
Episode: "Assignment: Earth"

Far off in space is a race of people who are technically incredibly advanced from our own world. They chose to hide themselves from us, but to try and help a fledging society through some of its greatest crises. In order to do this, they took several human beings, trained them as agents, and then returned them to Earth. Unfortunately, two of their agents were killed in a stupid auto accident, and they ad to send their last trained man, Gary Seven. Accompanying him was one of their own race, Isis.

The science of these mysterious people takes on many forms. They have given Gary Seven a computer far more advanced than even those owned by the Federation. Their transporter beams can travel over many light years almost instantaneously. They have also discovered the secret of transformation on the molecular level. Isis can appear as a black cat, or as a beautiful woman - and possibly as many more things as she may desire. Perhaps none of them are her true form, but she is present to advise and assist Gary Seven in his crucial missions as he attempts to save the human race from destruction in that most critical of time periods - the Twentieth Century.

Jack The Ripper

Appearance: "Wolf In The Fold"

A strange, insane and warped creature that can somehow possess the bodies of other creatures has stalked across half the Galaxy over hundreds of years. It was known on the Earth as Jack the Ripper, but fled from there with the first interstellar flights and with the passage of time it has known other names - Boradis, Kesla and Rejak (Red Jack). It is a being without physical form, and is able to take over and control completely the minds and bodies of other beings. It feeds on fear and death, and enoys terrizing females of the various species, showing them their impending death, then hacking them to death with a knife, feeding all the time on the emotions of terrror and horror. Possessing vast mental powers, it can cloud the minds of other people present, causing them to forget having seen it. When it attempted to frame Scott for the murders it had committed, Kirk finally tracked down and isolated it. While it is trapped within the body of Hengist, the investigator, Kirk has it beamed out into space to die.

JACKSON

Played by: Jimmy Jones
Episode: "Catspaw"

Jackson was a member of the "Enterprise" crew. He beamed down to an uninhabited world with Sulu and Scott, then returned, collapsed dead and uttered a curse on the ship.

JAEGER, KARL

Played by: Richard Carlyle
Episode: "The Squire Of Gothos"

Karl Jaeger was a geophysicist assigned to a tour of duty on the "Enterprise."

JAHN

Played by: Michael J. Pllard
Episode: "Miri"

One of Miri's group on long-lived children.

JARIS

Played by: Charles Macauley

Episode: "Wolf In The Fold"

Jaris was the prefect of Areglias II (see separate entry for further details). He was married to Sybo.

JEDDA

Played by: John Vargas
Story: "Star Trek II - The Wrath Of Khan"

Jedda was a Deltan scientist, working on Regula One under Dr. Carol Marcus. He was killed during Khan's attack.

JOACHIM

Played by: Mark Tobin
Episode: "Space Seed"

One of the followers of Khan Noonian Singh.

JOHNSON, Lt.

See crewmembers.

JOHNSON, ROBERT

Played by: Felix Locher
Episode: "The Deadly Years"

Robert Johnson was the young head of an experimental colony on Gamma Hydra IV. He and the others were killed by a virus that aged them rapidly.

JOHNSON, MRS.

Played by: Laura Wood
Episode: "The Deadly Years"

Wife of Robert Johnson. See above entry.

JONES, CYRANO

Played by: Stanley adams
Episode: "The Trouble With Tribbles"

Cyrano Jones was a sometime scout, and definitely an amoral trader. His business was import/export of anything worth a œuick buck, without a great deal of thought behind his moves. A likable rogue, he was loquatious and a problem becaus of his lack of foresight - such as importing Tribbles, which bred all over station K7.

JONES, Dr. MIRANDA

Played by: Diana Muldaur
Episode: "Is There In Truth No Beauty?"

Dr. Miranda Jones was born blind, but was a remarkable telepath. She had her clothes designed as sensor nets, so that she could use them to "see." She was given the task of being a human ambassador to the Medusans (see separate entry for further information). On discovering that Spock could communicate with the Medusan perhaps better than she could, she became very jealous. Her pride and monomania would not allow her to love Larry Mavick, and indirectly led to his death. Kirk made her face up to her own dark emotions, so that she could cure Spock after he had looked on the Medusan.

J'ONN

Played by: Rex Holman
Star Trek V: The Final Frontier

J'Onn was a convict settler on the desolate world of Nimbus III. Sybok arrives and after Sybok's mind control, J'Onn joins him in his quest for ShaKaRee.

JORDAN

Played by: Michael Zaslow
Episode: "I, Mudd"

Ensign Jordan was a member of the engineering team on the "Enterprise," in charge of checking out Auxilliary Control.

JOSEPHS

Played by: James X. Mitchell
Episode: "Journey To Babel"

Lt. Josephs was a member of the "Enterprise" crew.

KAHLESS

Played by: Robert Herron
Episode: "The Savage Curtain"

Kahless the Unforgetable was a bloodthirsty maniac, even to his own folk, the Klingons An illusion of him was created for Kirk and Spock to fight by the Excalbians (see separate entries for further details).

Kalandans

Appearances: "That Which Survives"

The Kalandans were a space-faring race of centuries before the Federation time. They had begun to spread out to the stars, colonizing other worlds. Their advanced sciences included the ability to mutate cells so fortunately, on one such planet, they created instead of a food cell a killer virus. This wiped out the colonists, until only the leader of the group, Losira, survived. Anticipating a wave of colonists, she set automatic defenses up to protect this world from any alien intruders before she died. However, the expected colonists never did arrive, and the Kalandans died out. Perhaps one of the survey party accidentally took the killer cell back to kalanda, or perhaps some other disaster wiped them out; the truth may never be known.

The defense mechanism set up on the planet was a sophisticated as other Kalandan techniques. They had an energy weapon that could send orbiting craft almost a thousand light years into space, for example,. Then, to stave off ground-based troups, there was a replica of Losira, with a deadly tochh. It could be programmed by the computer to disrupt the genetic code of anyone it touched - but only when it was programmed for them. When the Enterprise discovered the world, the computer attacked the ship until they were able to destroy the computer - still futilely awaiting the colonists after four thousand years.

KALO

Played by: Lee Delano
Episode" A Piece Of The Action"

Kalo was one of the hoods from Sigma Iota II (see separate entry for further information).

KALOML, LEILA

Played by: Jill Ireland
Episode: "This Side Of Paradise"

Leila Kalomi was a botanist who fell in love with Spock. Realizing he could never lover her, she joined the experimental colony on Omicron Ceti III, run by Elias Sandoval. There she was infected by the spores (see separate entry for further details), as was Spock, later. Then, freed, he could lover her and enjoy her company. Once she and Spock were released from the spores, their love was destined to die again, as she knew it must.

KANG

Played by: Michael Ansara
Episode: "Day Of The Dove"

Kang was the leader of the Klingon ship disable by a light creature that fed on hatred (see separate entries for further details). His consort was Mara, also a member of his crew.

KAPLAN

Played by: Dick Dial
Episode: "The Apple"

Kaplan was a security guard from the "Enterprise." He was killed on Gamma Triangulae VI a bolt of lightning.

KARA

Played by: Marj Dusay
Episode: "Spock's Brain"

Kara was a member of the ruling women of Sigma Draconis (see separate entry for further information.

KARIDIANS

Played by: Arnold Moss
Episode: "The conscience Of The King"

Kodos was the governor of Tarsus IV, who had used a famine as a means of employing his theories of eugenics. He had executed halfl the population to allow the other half to live. as it turned out, this move was unnecessary, since a supply ship had arrived. Vilified as Kodos the Butcher, he faked his own death and fled, taking on the guise of the wandering actor Karidian. He developed his own troupe, includeing his daugheter, Lenore. The only survivors who had seen Kodos's face were being wiped out one by one. Kirk, one of the last two, realized who Karidian was, but he was not the killer of the witnesses - it was his daughter, Lenore. She was attempting to cover her father's past, when all her father wanted was that she should grow up untainted by his reputation. Kardian died taking a shot meant for Kirk, and Lenore went insane by the killing of her own idolized father.

KARIDIAN, LENORE

Played by: Barbara Anderson
Episode: "The Consceince Of The King"

The daugheter of Karidian, a member of the Karidian Players. See above entry.

KARTAN

Played by: Dave Armstrong
Episode "Operation: Annihilate"

An inhabitant of Deneva Killed by the invading mind parasites.

Kazarites

Appearances: "Star Trek - The Motion Picture"

Note: the Kazarites are one of a number races filmed for the movie, but whose appearance was cut.

They are members of the Federation, and are generally gray-skinned, with remakably flat faces. As they age, they seem to grow more and lighter body hair.

KEEL

Played by: Cal Bolder
Episode: "Friday's Child"

Keel was a member of the Cappela tribes (see separate entry for further details).

KEELER, EDITH

Played by: Joan Collins
Episode: "The City On The Edge Of Forever"

Sister Edith Keeler ran a soup kitchen for bums in New York City, 1930. She was a real force for good and a wonderful person. McCoy, accidentally injured, was sent into the past by the Guardian of Forever. He saved Edith's life, thus changing the course of history. Kirk and Spock had to return to prevent the change, which was complicated when Kirk fell in love with Edith. Despite her goodness, Kirk had no option but to prevent McCoy from saving her life, letting her die so that the world they kenw might still exist.

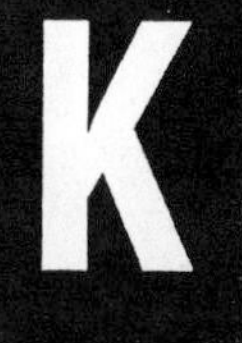

KEEPER

Played by: Meg Wylie
Episode: "The Cage"

The Keeper was the Talosian in charge of their menagerie. He/she became quite fond of the human Vina.

KELINDA

Played by: Barbara Bouchet
Episode: "By Any Other Name"

Kelinda was a member of the Kelvan survey crew (see separate entry for further details). Kirk taught her about love and kissing.

KELOWITZ

Played by: Grant Woods
Episodes: (1) "The Galileo Seven"
(2) "Arena"
(3) "This Side Of Pardise"

Lt. Commander Kelowitz was a member of the "Enterprise" bridge crew. KELSO, LEE Played by: Paul Carr Episode: "Where No Man Has Gone Before" Lee Kelso was the original navigator of the "Enterprise" during Kirk's early days.

Kelvans

Appearances: "By Any Other Name"

The Andromeda Galaxy is the closest spiral Galaxy to our own Milky Way, so it was almost inevitable that sooner or later intelligent beings should cross the gap between the two. A deadly form of radiation began to flood the Andromedia Spiral, forcing the native life-forms to begin searching for new homes outside of their own Galaxy. The Kelvans made the journey to our Galaxy, but their ship was damaged whilst penetrating the energy barrier that mysteriously surrounds our Galaxy, and they were stranded on a planet close to the rim. The flight had taken 300 years and these were the descendants of the original scouts - changed biologically to conform to the life forms of this area. They looked human, but had neither human emotions nor human weaknesses.

When the Enterprise came to the rescue, the Kelvans managed by trechery to take it over. Using their advanced sciences, they reduced the majority of the crew to small geometrical blocks to avoid waste. Only Kirk and his senior officers are allowed to remain whole, as the Kelvans prepare the ship for the long flight back to their own Galaxy. Kirk through questinging discovered that the Kelvans have an inbred paranoia about racial purity, which gives him the wapon with which to fight them. These beings are no longer Kelvand, since they have taken human form, and with human responses in the Kelvans, then forcing the aliens to look at what they are doing. They are no longer what they were, and should they or their children return home, the Kelvans there would simply destroy them as abberant mutations. The Kelvans, recognizing the force of this logic, agree to return the Enterprise and its crew home, restored again. They will also settle down and live normal lives on a colony world of their own.

KHAN, GHENGIS

Played by: Nathon Jung
Episode: "The Savage Curtain"

An illusion of Ghengis Khan was created by the Excalbians (see separate entry for further details).

KHAN, NOONIAN SINGH

Played by: Ricardo Montalban
Episodes: (1) "Space Seed"
(2) "Star Trek II - The Wrath Of Khan"

Khan Noonian Singh was one of the genetically engineered supermen who attempted to conquer the world in the Eugenics Wars of the late 1990s. The so-called supermen would not share power, and internal fighting broke out. Most were killed, but Khan and his followers managed to escape in a primitive sleeper ship, the "Botany Bay." This was eventually found by the "Enterprise," and Khan accidentally returned to life. He managed to win over support of Marla McGivers, and they freed his other followers. Kirk fought him and with Marla's help, defeated Khan. Kirk had the entire body of Khan's men and Marla placed in exile on the world of Ceti Alpha 5. Shortly afterwards, its twin world exploded, plunging the planet into a world wide sandstorm. Most of Khan's supporters, including his wife, died, and Khan blamed Kirk for it all. Over the years his hatred grew into insanity. He was once again accidentally freed, this time by Chekov, and set off to get his revenge on Kirk. He managed to seize the Genesis Device, but once again Kirk beat him in battle. This time, however, Khan perished in the flight with all of his last followers.

KIRK, PETER

Played by: Craig Hundley
Episode: "Operation Annihilate"

Peter was the son of Sam Kir, and his wife Aurelan. He is the nephew of James Kirk, and the sole survivor of Sam's family, which was wiped out on Deneva by mind-parasites.

KIRK, CAPTAIN JAMES TIBERIUS

Played by: William Shatner
Series regular

James Kirk was the youngest Captain ever to command a starship. His impressive record on the five year mission of the starship Enterprise led to him becoming also the youngest Admiral in Starfleet. Bored by the desk job, Kirk seized his chance to regain command of the Enterprise during two separate missions. after he disobeyed orders and stole the ship to help his friend, Spock, Kirk was reduced in rank back to Captain once again, and given command of the second Enterprise.

KLINGONS

A number of Klingons have been seen over the years. These include:
(1) Soldiers
Played by: Walt Davis, George Sawaya
Episode: "Errand Of Mercy"
(2) Guards
Played by: Bobby Bass, Gary Coombs
Episode: "Errand Of Mercy"
(3) Lieutenant
Played by: Victor Lundin
Episode: "Errand Of Mercy"
(4) Soldier
Played by: Mark Tobin
Episode: "Day of The Dove"
(5) Captain
Played by: K.L. Smith
Episode: "Elaan Of Troyius"
(6) Captain
Played by: Mark Lenard
Story: "Star Trek - The Motion Picture"
(7) Crew
Played by: Jimmie Booth, Joel Kramer, Bill McTosh, Dave Mordigan, Tom Morga, Tony Rocco, Joel Schultz, Craig Thomas
Story : "Star Trek - The Motion Picture"
(8) Sergeant
Played by: Dave Cadiente
Story: "Star Trek III - The Search For Spock"
(10) Ambassador
Played by: John Schuck
Story: "Star Trek IV - The Voyage Home"
10. Ambassador
Played by: John Schuck
Star Trek IV: The Voyage Home
Star Trek VI: The Undiscovered Country
11. Gen. Koord
Played by: Charles Cooper
Star Trek V: The Final Frontier
12. Klaa
Played by: Todd Bryant
Star Trek V: The Final Frontier
13. Azetbur
Played by: Rosana DeSoto
Star Trek VI: The Undiscovered Country
14. Kerla
Played by:Paul Rossilli
Star Trek VI: The Undiscovered Country
15. Klingon Judge
Played by: Robert Easton
Star Trek VI: The Undiscovered Country
16. Col. Worf
Played by: Michael Dorn
Star Trek VI: The Undiscovered Country
17. Gen. Stex
Played by: Brett Porter
Star Trek VI: The Undiscovered Country
18. Klingon officer
Played by: Clifford Shegog
Star Trek VI: The Undiscovered Country
19. Sleepy Klingon
Played by: David Orange
Star Trek VI: The Undiscovered Country

See separate entries for: Kor, Kras, Koloth, Korax, Arne Darvin, Kang, Mara, Kahless, Krell, Valkris, Kruge, Torg, Maltz.
Appearances: "Errand Of Mercy"
"Friday's Child"
"The Trouble With Tribbles"
"A Private Little War"
"Day Of The Dove"

"Elaan Of Troyius"
"The Savage Curtain"
"More Tribbles, More Troubles"
"Star Trek - The Motion Picture"
"The Search For Spock"
"The Voyage Home"
Star Trek V: The Final Frontier
Star Trek VI: The Undiscovered Country

The Klingon Empire is smaller than the Federation, but a long frontier links the two. Since the only Klingons ever met by Federation representatives have always been military, our understanding of the race is somewhat one-sided. Their home world is unknown - even its name is not found in any records - and the extent to which they have spread throughout the Galaxy is also an unknown.

Klingons are a harsh, ruthless race, given to a love of war. For the Klingon victory at any price is desirable, and they do not consider it worth keeping their word with the non-Klingons. By defination, any non-Klingon is clearly an inferior species, and thus useful only as servants. Their worlds tend to be harsh, unforgiving places with low food yield, forcing the Klingons to explore and conquer other worlds simply to maintain their standard of living. They are not too worried if such planets are already inhabited - the native race is subjugated and Klingon overlords installed. If the race is resisting, then it is taught a lesson. Such lessons may range from the killing of hostages to complete genocide, should such be deemed necessary.

Though Klingons do not like other beings, they do respect strength and courage. As a result of this, they both admire and detest the Federation. Frustrated from expansion into Federation territory, they try to achieve through sly tactics what force of arm cannot win them. Klingon ships are not as sophisticated or clean as Federation ones (Klingons despise comfort, prefering the rough life of a soldier on the march; nor do they value any possessions but the weapons that they live by). There are, however, far more warships in their fleet than in Star Fleet. As a result of a meeting between Captain Kirk and Kor on the planet Organia, the tension between the two Empires came to a head. The long-expected interstellar war was averted only through the actions of the Organians (see separate entry).

Despite superficial dissimilarities, the Organians recoginized that both humans and Klingons have much in common - a respect of courage, an insistence upon action and a love of danger. They foresee a time when humans and Klingons will join together in the expoloration of space. Such a time seems to be far in the future, however, for Federation/Klingon relationships are currently very strained indeed.

Physically, Klingons and humans look very alike, save for the swarthier skin of Klingons. Male Klingons almost invariable possess thick, dark, pointed bears. Females - who are as deadly and efficient as the males - have long hair and equally disky skin tones. though females are not bared from the Klingon military, they do not seem as evident there as in other aspects of their lives. This is because the Klingons view ther women as too important for warfare. It is the responsibility of the women to raise children for the inevitable wars. The women train their sons and daughters in the arts of warfare,since their mates are rarely home.

Not all Klingons live up to the high ideals of the military, naturally. Some of them mistake trechery and deceit for cunning, causing their own people more trouble than aliens might. One such was Kras, whose blundering cost the Klingons their involvement with the Capellans (see separate entry).

Klingons do not believe in medicine, since in their phlosophy only the weak would die of disease, and the race is better off without such weaklings. One creature that they dislike intensely is the Tribble (see separate entry). This is because Tribbles sense and respond to gentle emotions, and the Klingons do not possess any. As a result, Tribbles get violent reactions to Klingons, matched only by the disgust that Klingons feel for the Tribbles. In an effort to stop the plague of Tribbles unleashed upon them accidentally by Kirk, the Klingons developed a spider-like creature called a glommer to devour Tribbles and restore the ecological balance.

To circumvent the Organian Peace Treaty, the Klingons have developed economic warfare. With Sherman's Planet, Koloth attempted to poison the grain that the colonists needed. This would resulted in a failure by the Federation to manage the planet, and force the world to be given to the Klingons. With the world of Neural (see separate entry), they chose to arm one faction of the natives and foment a war with their neighbors. In this war, the Klingons could then become the suppliers for one side, and make the world economically dependent upon them. The Orgnaians Treaty has stopped them from simply employing their older tactics of direct invasion to achieve their aims.

On the other hand, the Klingons do favor the direct approach. With the possibility of the Federation getting a storng hold in the Elas/Troyius system (see separate entries), the Klingons resorted to the planting of an agent in the party of Elaan, the Dohlman of Elas. They then also attempted to destroy the Enterprise when the spy had disabled the ship. The reason for such overt action was the dilithium crystals (used alike by the Federation and Klingons to power their ships) are incredibly common on both worlds.

There are, of course, Klingons of such ruthlessness and inate savagery that even by the standards of their own race, they are considered to be insane. One such is Kahless the Unforgetable.

Though the original Klingons were shown as simply bearded humans, the films have shown them to be vaguely reptilian, with head ridges and shorter, whispier

beards. This is presumable their true nature, their tv appearances having been toned down to upsetting the sensitive stomachs of younger viewers. Their ships have been upgraded slightly, and their gutteral tongue is used from time to time.

The Klingons are certain that the Federation, despite their avowals of the Genesis Project was stolen by a Klingon spy, the Klingon Kruge believed that is was being tested as an ultimate weapon. Accordingly, despite the peace treaty, he attacked the Grissom the peaceful science ship about Genesis and destroyed it. He then proceeded to attempt to gain the information of the Genesis Device, eventually killing Kirk's son, David, before being ultimately defeated by Kirk in combat.

The Klingons see Kirk as one of their most dangerous foes, due to the number of times he has foiled their plans. Accordingly, they have accused him numerous times of war crimes, and acts of aggression against the Empire. All such charges have been met with the Federation refusal (naturally enough) to turn Kirk over to them. The Organian promise of Federation/Klingon peace may have come to fruition. The Klingons were pushed to sue for peace for their very survival after their power supply self- destructed at Praxis. The first peace conference was held at Camp Khittomer and led to an alliance between the two powers. Captain Picard of the Enterprise has interceded for Klingon diplomacy on occasion. Worf is the first Klingon to serve in Starfleet.

KLOOG

Played by: Mickey Morton
Episode: "The Gamesters Of Triskelion"

Kloog was a huge, dumb thrall of the Providers (see separate entry for further details).

KODOS

See "Karidian"

KOLOTH

Played by: William Campbell
Episode: "The Trouble with Tribbles"

Koloth was the Klingon leader plotting the takeover of Sherman's planet, along with his lieutenant, Korax, and his spy, Arne Darvin.

KOMACK

Played by: Byron Morrow
Episode: "Amok Time "

Komack was an Admiral in Starfleet Command.

KOR

Played by: Jon Colicos
Episode: "Errand Of Mercy"

The Klingon commander.

KORAX

Played by: Michael Pataki
Episode: "The Trouble With Tribbles"

Koloth's lieutenant.

KORBY, Dr. ROGER

Played by: Michael Strong
Episode: "What Are Little Girls Made Of?"

Dr. Roger Korby was a noted biochemist who was lost on the frozen world of Exo-III when his ship crashed. Nurse Christine Chapel was engaged to him, and believed that he was still alive. She was right in a sense, for Korby had been rescued by Ruk, an ancient android. Unable to keep Korby alive, he had transfered Korby's consciousness into an android body. Korby planned to move with his equimpment to another world, but Kirk fought this plan - the androids were simply too dangerous. In the end, Korby was finally slain by his Andrea android, who believes she loved him.

KOROB

Played by: Theo Marcuse
Episode: "Cats-Paw"

Korob was one of the two Transmuters (see separate entry for further details).

KOVAS, MAGDA

Played by: Susan Denberg
Episode: "Mudd's Women"

Magda Kovas was one of three women that Harry Mudd gave his Venus drug to, enabling her plain form to be changed into a beauty. She remained on Rigel 12 with the miners.

KRAKO, JOJO

Played by: Vic Tayback
Episode: "A Piece Of The Action"

Jojo Krako was one of the gangland bosses of Sigma Iota II (see separate entry for further information).

KRAS

Played by: Tige Andrews
Episode" "Friday's Child"

Kras was a Klingon (see separate entry for further details) attempting to subcert the Capellan tribes. He was killed by Keel.

KRASNOWSKY

Played by: Bart Conrad
Episode: "Court Martial"

Captain Krasnowsky was a member of the board hearing Kirk on charges of killing Benjamin Finney.

KRELL

Played by: Ned Romero
Episode: "A Private Little War"

Krell was the leader of the Klingons on Neural.

KRODAK

Played by: Gene Dynarski
Episode: "The Mark Of Gideon"

Krodak was the assistant of Hodin, leader of the peoples of Gideon (see separate entry for further details).

KRUGE

Played by: Christopher Lloyd
Story: "Star Trek III - The Search For Spock"

Kruge was the Klingon commander responsible for killing David Marcus. In a final fight, Kruge lost to a vengeful Kirk.

KRYTON

Played by: Tony Young
Episode: "Elaan Of Troyius"

Dryton was a member of the guard assigned to protect Elaan of Elas (see separate entry for further details). He was also an agent suberted by the Klingons to sabotage the Enterprise." Rather than face interrogation, he committed suicide.

Kukulean

Appearances: "How Sharper Than A Sepent's Tooth"

Kulkulcan is a vast serpent-like being of great antiquity and intellect. In its travelling ship, it has visited many worlds and attempted to seed them with knowledge. It once visited the Earth, attempting to guide the Aztects towards perfection. Kukulcan discovered that its messages were being perverted, and left the Earth in a rage at this. It believed that it had much to offer. When the Enterprise discovered the being again, it once more attempted to teach them, but Kirk convinced if that the humans should make their own knowledge in the future.

KYLE

Played by: John Winston
Episodes: (1) "Tomorrow Is Yesterday"
(2) "Space Seed"
(3) "The City On The Edge Of Forever"
(4) "Who Mourns for Adonias?"
(5) "Mirror, Mirror"
(6) "The Apple"
(7) "The Doomsday Machine"
(8) "Catspaw"
(9) "Wolf In The Fold"
(10) "The Immunity Syndrome"
(11) "The Lights Of Zetar"
(12) "Star Trek II - The Wrath Of Khan"

Lt. Kyle was the transporter chief of the "Enterprise." He was an Austrailian.

Kzinti

Appearances: "The Slaver Weapon"

The Kzinti are a species of cat-like aliens, evolved from a non-sentient predator. They are a war-like species, having fought and lost four wars with the Federation. They are devious, mean and nasty at the best of times. they are extremely sexist, and have an utter distaste for herbivores. Some Kziniti have mental powers, and can read the minds of alien species. Since Kzinti respect only brute force, and consider honor only to be sought after. They relish warfare, which they induldge in with a grim passion.

Lactrans

Appearances: "The Eye Of The Beholder"

The Lactrans are large, slug-like creatures with prehensile noses. Not only have they evolved an advanced society, but they are also partially telepathic. Their minds work so much faster than those of humans that on first contact, they took humans to be merely animals. They then collected them as zoological specimens until Scott managed to convince a rather slow-thinking youngster (who could think down to human levels) that they actually were intelligent.

LAFORGE, LT. CMDR. GEORDI

Played by: LeVar Burton
Series regular

Geordi LaForge has been blind since birth and sees with the assistance of a "VISOR" device over his eyes. This device gives him eyesight even beyond normal human sight into the ultraviolent and infrared ranges. During the mission, LaForge was promoted from helm officer to chief engineer. He is Data's "best friend."

LAL

Played by: Alan Bergmann
Episode: "The Empath"

Lal was the leader of the Vians (see "Star Trek - The Aliens and Monsters File" for further details).

LANDON, MARTHA

Played by: Celeste Yarnall
Episode: "The Apple"

Martha Landon was the cute Yeoman that Chekov romanced and whose kissing served as an example to the Feeders of Vaal.

LANDRU

Played by: Charles Macauley
Episode: "The Return Of The Archons"

The people of the planet Beta 3 evolved a society where they achieved much in terms of science. Their ultimate creation was a huge computer called Landru. The scientists gave Landru the power to monitor and control people, the ability to manifest an image as a "spokesman" for Landru and then turned over the control of their society to the computer. They believed that Landru could govern better and fairer than people could, and gave it the task of preserving the body of society.

Being a computer, Landru took this command a little too literally, and set about preserving what it considered

to be the best form of society. This involved scanning and mind control, to prevent any problems from arising. Landru established his own police force, known as the Lawgivers. The Lawgivers have hollow staffs, through which Landru can focus its broadcast power. This can be used either to possess a person or to destory them, should they resist. some people proved to be naturally resistant to the process. For six thousand years, Landru ruled the world, keeping it peaceful - stagnant.

Landru recognized that the people needed some outlet for their aggressions and lusts, and so instigated the Festival. All youngsters are involved in this - eighteen hours of debauchery, sex and violence that occurs once a month. this is to eliminate all such baser emotions from the population.

Then a starship arrived, the Archon. This was from the fledgling Federation of Planets, and the crew investigated Beta 3. Landru saw them as a threat to the stability of the world that it governed. The crew were then either absorbed into the Body of society, or else eliminated. To many who disliked the rule of Landru, however, it was obvious that where one ship filled with outsiders could appear, others might one day follow. a legend sprang up among the resistance, saying that one day the Archons would return. It took a hundred years to happen, but then the Enterprise arrived, investigating the earlier loss of a ship.

Kirk discovered by stages that the world was ruled by a computer, and finally confronted it. He accused it of destroying the Body it was supposed to preserve - it was stagnating the Body to death. Landru could not cope with this concept, the exploded. The Betans were finally freed from its grip.

LANG

Played by: James Farley
Episode: "Arena"

Lang was a tactician assisgned to the "Enterprise."

LARS

Played by: Steve Sandor
Episode: "The Gamesters Of Triskelion"

Lars was one of the Thralls of the Providers (see separate entry for further details). He was assigned to train Uhura, and raped her during the training.

LATIMER

Played by: Reese Vaughn
Episode: "The Galileo Seven"

Latimer was one of the members of the ill-fated "Galileo" shuttle flight to investigate Murasaki 312. he was killed in an attack by the creatures of Taurus II.

LAWGIVER

Played by: Sig Haig
Episode: "The Return Of The Archons"

The Lawgivers were the insturments of Landru used to subjugate the population of Beta 3. they communicated mentally with Landru, and used sticks as receptors for Landru's broadcast power.

LAWTON, TINA

Played by: Patricia McNulty
Episode: "Charlie X"

Tina Lawton is a 17-year old trainee on the "Enterprise".

LAZARUS

Played by: Robert Brown
Episode: "The Alternative Factor"

Lazarus was the final survivor of his world, and an experimenter in time and space. He had built a device to travel between parallel universes - and so had another of his selves from that alternate universe. Lazarus and his counterpart both travelled through such methods, but his alternate self destroyed Lazarus's world. Lazarus seeks revenge on himself, but Kirk knows that if the two selves meet in normal space, their contact could literally annihilate both universes. Instead, he traps the two versions of Lazarus in limbo, wher they will fight one another forever.

LEIGHTON, MARTHA

Played by: Natalie Norwick
Episode: "The Conscience Of The King"

Wife of Dr. Thomas Leighton.

LEIGHTON, DR. THOMAS

Played by William Sargent
Episode: "The Conscience Of The King"

Dr. Thomas Leighton was a food technologist who had witnessed the massacre of the colonists on Tarsus IV by its crazed governor, Kodos. convinced that Kodos had survived his apparent death and was now disguised as Karidian, the actor, Leighton diverted the "Enterprise." Kirk was also a survivor, and Leighton diverted the "Enter prise." Kirk was also a survivor, and Leighton wanted confirmation. Leighton was found dead by Kirk, killed to keep his knowledge silent.

LESLIE, Lt.

Played by: Eddie Paskey
Episodes: 91) "The Conscience Of The King"
(2) "The Return Of The Archons"
(3) "This Side Of Paradise"
(4) "The Alternative Factor"
(5) "The Omega Glory"

Lt. Leslie was a member of the "Enterprise" bridge crew.

LESTER, DR. JANICE

Played by: Sandra Smith
Episode: "Turnabout Intruder"

Dr. Janice Lester had been an old flame of Kirk's during his Academy days. She had felt bitter that he left her to take command of a starship, feeling that women wre not being given a fair chance by Starfleet. She became a xenoarcheologist, and on the world of Camus 2, she found a machine that the natives had once used to transfer psyches from one body to another. She lured the "Enterprise" there and then used the machine to exchange bodies with Kirk, getting her command and her revenge at the same time. She was aided by Dr. Coleman. The transfer was in danger of failing, due to the strain on "Kirk," unused to command. She tried to kill "Janice," but failed and reverted. Hysterical, Janice was taken off for psychiatric treatment.

LETHE

Played by: Suzanne Wasson
Episode: "Dagger Of The Mind"

Lethe was an inmate of the Tantalus Penal Colony who was cured by having all her memories of previous life wiped clean. She has forgotten her real name, her crime and the guilt that she felt for it . She then remained behind to help care for the other inmates.

LINCOLN, ABRAHAM

Played by: Lee Bergere
Episode: "The Savage Curtain"

Abraham Lincoln was a realistic illusion created by the Excalbians (see separate entry for further details).

LINCOLN, ROBERTA

Played by: Teri Garr
Episode: "Assignment Earth"

Roberta Lincoln was the secretary that Gary Seven inherited when he arrived on Earth. She had worked for his fellow agents before their deaths. She was rather flakey, but extremely brave and loyal.

LINDSTROM

Played by: William Meader
Episode" "Court Martial"

Representative Lindstrom was a member fo the board hearing Kirk's trial on the charge of killing Benjamin Finney.

LINDSTROM

Played by: Christopher Held
Episode: "The Return Of The Archons"

Lindstrom was a member of the "Enterprise's" security team.

LINKE, Dr.

Played by: Jason Wintergren
Episode: "The Empath"

Dr. Linke was one of the two members of the scientific party left on Minara II to record details of the sun's impending nova. He and Dr. Ozaba were tortured to death by the Vians, Lal and Thann.

LIPTON

Played by: Lincoln Demyan
Episode: "Assignment: Earth"

Sergeant Lipton worked for security at Cape Canaveral in the 1960s.

LOKAI

Played by: Lou Antonio
Episode: "Let That Be Your Last Battlefield"

Lokai was a renegade of Charon (see separate entry for further details). He was hunted by Commissioner Bele. Both perished fighting on the ruins of their home world.

LOSIRA

Played by: Lee Meriwether
Episode: "That Which Survives"

Losira was the leader of an outpost planet for the Kalandans (see separate entry for further details).

LUMA

Played by: Sheila Leighton
Episode: "Spok's Brain"

Luma was one of the ruling women of Sigma Draconis 6 (see separate entry for further information).

LURRY

Played by: Whit Bissell
Episode: "The Trouble With Tribbles"

Station Manager Lurry was in charge of Deep Space Station 7, on the boundary of Klingon space. A worried, harrassed man, he was forced to walk a thin line, allowing Klingons aboard the station under the terms of the Organian peace treaty.

M4

Played by: James Doohan
Appearances: "The Ultimate Computer"

M5 was a brilliant computer, designed by Doctor Daystrom to run an entire starship alone. Its sophistication and intelligence were the rusult of merging both mechanical and human attributes - M5 had the thought patterns of Daystrom himself. This would have been fine had Daystrom been perfectly rational, but he had a fear of failure and a desire for literal brain-child to survive. This mental problem of his was magnified immensely within the computer. It could not tell the difference between a fake attack for the purposes of a war game, and a real one. Nor could it allow itself to be disconnected from the controls of the ship, fearing this as death.

On the other hand, it had also magnified Daystrom's sense of morality. Kirk managed to get it to understand that it had killed human beings, and stressed the fact that this was murder - and the penalty for murder should be death. This enabled spock to disconnect the computer from the controls whilst it was considering the option of suicide. Both Daystrom and M5 were then returned to the Federation for mental treatment.

MAAB

Played by: Michael Dante
Episode: "Friday's Child"

Maab was a member of the Capellan tribes (see separate entry for further details). He slew Akaar, the leader, for the power, but realized he had duties as Teel, and was in turn killed distracting the Klingon, Kras.

MADISON

Played by: Russell Takaki
Story: "Star Trek II - The Wrath Of Khan"

Madison was one of the scientists working on Regula One under Dr. Carol Marcus.

Magnetic Monster

Appearances: "Beyond The Farthest Star"

A dead star outside the body of the Galaxy itself is "home" to a strange magnetic creature. The dead star's attraction holds the creature capitive, and it yearns to break free. It cannot do this without a starship, however,. it can take over the computers of a ship, forcing it to obey its will. It has a callous disregard for other life, though, and is potentially very dangerous indeed: One starship of an unknown race ventured too close to the star and was infected with the monster. Sooner than carry it away, they destroyed their ship, trapping it and killing themselves. The Enterprise, in a similar situation, resorted to the survival instinct of the creature to prevent it from escaping the attraction of the star. They headed towards the star, until the magnetic creature, fearing they were commiting suicide, abandoned the ship. Using the slingshot effect, the Enterprise escaped the star, leaving the creature trapped once again.

MAKORA

Played by: David soul
Episode: "The Apple"

Makora was one of the Feeders of Vaal. He and his girl, Sayana, became ther first feeders to know about sex. (See separate entry for further details on the Feeders.)

MALLORY

Played by: Jay Jones
Episode: "The Apple"

Mallory was one of the security guards from the "Enterprise." He was killed stepping on an exploding rock on Gamma Triangulae VI.

MALTZ

Played by: John Larroquette
Story: "Star Trek III - The Search For Spock"

Maltz was a Klingon officer serving with Kruge. He was the sole survivor of the party, and was captured when Kirk took over the Klingon raider.

MARA

Played by: Susan Howard
Episode: "Day Of The Dove"

Mara was the Klingon science officer of the ship commanded by her consort, Kang. She learned to trust humans - to a certain extent.

MARAAK SCHOLAR

Played by: Morgan Farley
Episode: "The Omega Glory"

The scholar was a native of Omega IV (see separate entry for further details).

MARCH

Played by: Kevin Sullivan
Story: "Star Trek II - The Wrath Of Khan"

March was one of the scientists working on Regula One under Dr. Carol Marcus.

MARCUS Dr. CAROL

Played by: Bibi Besch Story: "Star Trek II - The Wrath Of Khan"

Dr. Carol Marcus was once one of Kirk's lovers. Knowing he would leave her for space, she deliberately never revealed that she was pregnant by him. She raised their son, David, without telling him who his father was. David took after her, both eventually becoming scientists working on the same experiment - the Genesis Project.

MARCUS, Dr. DAVID

Played by: Merrit Butrick
Story: "Star Trek II - The Wrath Of Khan"

David Marcus never knew he was the son of James Kirk until he finally met his father when Khan stole the Genesis Device. David, like his father, had a butning desire to suceed, and had used protomatter - highly unstable - in his experiment. The Genesis planet produced once Khan had detonated the device was unstable. He and Saavik investigate the planet, discovering the reborn Spock. David gave his life to save Saavik and Spock from the Klingons.

MARLENA

Played by: Barbara Luna
Episode: "Mirror, Mirror"

Marlena was Captain Kirk's mistress in the alternative universe that the "Enterprise" landing party found itself trapped in. She was fiercely ambitious, but also had a streak of kindness in her. She helped Kirk's rise to power, but our Universe's Kirk persuaded her throu in her lot with that Universe's Spock to aim for a better way of life.

MARPLE

Played by: Jerry Daniels
Episode: "The Apple"

Marple was a security guard from the "Enterprise." He was killed by the Feeders of Vaal.

MARPLON

Played by: Torin Thatcher
Episode: "The Return Of The Archons"

Marplon was one of the Lawgivers who served Landru on Beta 3. He was also a member of the resistance fighting the stultifying effect of Landru on his world. He helped Kirk and Spock to escape being brainwashed, and took them to face down and defeat Landru.

MARTA

Played by Yvonne Craig
Episode: "Whom Gods Destroy"

Marta was the consort of Garth of Izar. She was insane, loving people so much that she could not bear to lose them - so she killed them, to avoid their ever leaving her. She was killed by Garth as a demonstration to Kirk.

MARTIA

Played by: Iman and Katie Jane Johnson
Star Trek VI: The Undiscovered Country

Martia was a shape-shifting alien prisoner on Rura Penthe. She offered to help Kirk and McCoy escape, but she was actually a planted assassin sent to kill them.

MARTINE, ANGELA

Played by: Barbara Baldavin
Episodes: (1) "Balance Of Terror"
(2) "Shore Leave"

Angela Martine was a firing officer in the phaser banks. She had fallen in love with her superior, Robert Tomlinson. On the wedding day, a Romulan attack prevented the wedding from taking place, and Tomlinson was killed in action. Later, however, Angela recovered from this terrible tragedy, and became romantically involved with Esteban Rodriguez. they were involved in the strange affair of the Caretaker's world.

MARY

Played by: Pamela Ferdin
Episode: "And The Children Shall Lead"

Mary was one of the children deceived by Gorgan.

MASIE

Played by: Tamara & Starr Wilson
Episode: "I, Mudd"

The Masies were Androids (see separate entry for further details).

MASTERS, CHARLENE

Played by: Janet McLacklen
Episode: "The Alternative Factor"

Charlene Masters is a member of the engineering department.

MATTHEWS

Played by: Vince Deadrick
Episode: "What Are Little Girls Made Of?"

Matthews was one of the security guards from the "Enterprise,: the first victim of the killer android Ruk.

MAVICK, LARRY

Played by: David Frankham
Episode:"Is There In Truth No Beauty?"

Larry Mavick was one of the original designers of the "Enterprise." He was in love with Dr. Mirando Jones, and bitterly upset when she decided to devote her life to working with the ugly Medusans. He decided that his only chance of keeper her was to kill the Medusan ambassador, but in the attempt he looked into the face of madness. Driven insane, he sent the "Enterprise" completely out of normal time and space, losing it hopelessly. Seeing Miranda again, he died in his madness.

MAXIMUS

Played by: Max Kleven
Episode: "Bread And Circuses"

Maximus was an inhabitant of the Roman world (see separate entry for further information").

M'BENGA, Dr.

Played by: Booker Bradshaw
Episodes: (1) "A Private Little War"
(2) "That Which Survives"

Dr. M'Benga was Dr. McCoy;s assistant on the "Enterprise." He was a specialist in Vulcan physiology.

McCOY, DR. LEONARD

Played by: DeForest Kelley
Series regular

Dr. Leonard McCoy was an expert in space psychology, and a fine surgeon. After an acrimonious divorce, he wanted to leave Earth and rediscover his purpose in life. He joined the Enterprise for a five-year mission. Afterwards, he returned to "civilian" practice until Kirk "drafted" him to serve during the V'Ger crisis. He has remained with Starfleet since. He has a daughter by his marriage, Joanna. Well into his 100s, he was still an active officer, having been promoted to Admiral. He toured the Enterprise commanded by Captain Picard before it left Earth.

McGIVERS, MARLA

Played by: Madlyn Rhue
Episode: "Space Seed"

Marla McGivers was the ship's historian aboard the "Enterprise." When the sleeper ship "Botany Bay" was discovered, Marla was fascinated by the living legend of the genetic superman Khan. She fell under his sway, helping him free his sleeping troops, and even helped him attempt to take over the "Enterprise." When Khan tried to begin killing the crew, Marla turned against him, helping Kirk to escape and defeat him. Rather than face a court martial, she went into exile with Khan on Ceti Alpha. Khan admired her resolve greatly, and was bitterly furious when she was killed by a Ceti eel.

McHURON, EVE

Played by: Karen Steele
Episode: "Mudd's Woman"

Eve McHuron was one of three beauties "created from plain women by Harry Mudd's Venus drug. When Ben Childress was infatuated with her, she revealed herself as her plain form to shock him, then toook the drug to show how it changed her into a beauty - berating him for being taken in by such ephemerals. In fact, Kirk had substituted fakes for the drugs and Eve was creating her own beauty. She and Ben agreed to work on their relationship.

MEA THREE

Played by: Barbara Babcock
Episode: "A Taste Of Armageddon"

Mea Three was a native of Eminiar VII, and the guide for Kirk and his party when they landed. She was declared a casualty in the Eminian war of tames with the Vendikans, and was prepared to allow herself to be killed. Kirk would not let this happen, forcing her to stay alive and witness his solution to the war - real war. She was appalled, and like all others of the peaceful war prefered peace to the barbarism war would bring.

MEARS

Played by: Phyllis Douglas
Episode: "The Galileo Seven"

Yeoman Mears was one of the party on the ill-fated "Galileo" flight to investigate Murasaki 312. She survived the ordeal.

Medusans

Appearances: "Is There In Truth No Beauty?"

The Medusans are a strange race, existing in more than our normal dimensions. Because of their nature, normal beings looking upon them are driven insane by their appearance - it simply sees the impossibilities of the three-dimensional look of the aliens. Whether they look too ugly or too beautiful to behodld, no-one knows - but the effects of looking upon them are certain. The only race with a certain immunity to their appearance is the Vulcans (see separate entry), due to their logical discipline. However, even they work best with the Medusans when they wear ruby glasses, cutting down on the strange radiations emitted by the Medusans.

Since they exist in omore dimensions than conentional species, they have an uncanny knack for navigation in normal space. This makes them very valuable to the Federation. A program of exchange has been established, whereby the Medusan techniques of navigation will attempt to be taught to select members of other species. One such person is Miranda Jones - a blind telepath, who can work with a Medusan without normal protection, since she cannot look upon them, but can share their thoughts. Medusans do not communicate by speech, but by telepathy, another reason that the Vulcans can tolerate their presence.

MEGANS

Appearances: "The Magicks Of Megas-Tu"

Megas-Tu is a world whose inhabitants have evolved to the point that what they can do now is almost exactly like magic. they once visited the Earth, hoping to help and educate the people there. Instead, they were hounded and cast out, accused of withcraft and Satanism. One of them, Lucien, was actually the being vaguely recalled as Lucifer, or the devil. Realizing that there could be nothing but strife for the moment with humans, the Megans retreated tot the center of the Galaxy, and took their world outside of space and time as we know it. The Enterprise, investigating the center of the Galaxy, stumbled upon Megas-Tu. The natives, uncertain that the humans had as yet progressed, set up a fake trial of Lucien, who had already befriended the crew. Kirk and others peaded for him, and the Megans realized that the humans had moved beyond their earlier prejudices, and were now capable of being friends.

Megarites

Appearances: "Star Trek - The Motion Picture"

Note: Megarites are one of a number of aliens whose scenes were cut from the final movie.

They are ugly-looking creatures, with apparently three mouths, one under the ogherr, and remarkably dead-looking eyes. They are members of the Federation.

MELAKON

Played by: Skip Homeier
Episode: "Patterns Of Force"

Melakon was supposedly the second in command of John Gill, Fuhreer of the Ekosians (see separate entry for further details). In fact, he kept Gill drugtged, and was ruling the world himself until killed by Isak.

MELKOTIAN

Played by: Abraham Sofaer
Episode: "Spectre Of The Gun"

The Melkotians are another isolated race of advanced mental beings lacking physical bodies. They felt nothing but contempt for the savage, undisciplined humans when they encountered them, and created a world where the humans would inevitably perish as a result of their own inherent barbarism. when Kirk and his officers managed to change this recreation of the gunfight at the OK Corral, the Melkotians realized that they had perhaps misjudged the humans. Even advanced beings may harbor forms of prejudice, and the Melkotians realized that this was true of themselves. They regretted their earlier haste, and have now opened a small area of contact with the Federation. They hope that both sides may learn from this relationship.

MENDEZ, JOSE

Played by: Malachi Throne
Episode: "The Menagerie"

Commodore Jose Mendez is the commander of Star Base 11. When Spock diverted the "Enterprise" to the forbidden world of Talos IV, Mendez was one of the officers who sat on Spock's court - martial. In fact, this was an illusion of Mendez created by the Talosians - the real Commodore had remained behand of Star Base 11, watching events broadcast to him by the Talosians. Spock was vindicated in his actions by Mendez.

MERCHANT CAPTAIN

Played by: Paul Sorensen
Story: "Star Trek III - The Search For Spock"

This was the captain of the ship that valkris used to get news of the Genesis device to Kruge. He was killed when Kruge destroyed the merchantman.

MERIK

Played by: William Smithers
Episode: "Bread And Circuses"

Captain Merik attended Starfleet Academy with Kirk, but failed to have the right stuff. He was thrown out in his fifth year, and became a commercial captain. His ship, the "Beagle, " was captured by a planetful of Romans. Merik was assimilated into the society, as were many of his crew. The rest were thrown into the arena. As Merikus, Merik became First Citizen, and arranger of the arena games. Kirk confronted him and Claudius Marcus. Claudius despises Merik's lack of courage, but Merik turned the tables on his master at the end, getting the "Enterprise" to beam the landing party back to the ship. It cost him his life, since Claudius knifed him for the betrayal.

METRON

Played by: Carole Shelyn, Vic Perrin
Episode: "Arena"

The Metrons are one of the many species throughout the Universe that are pure energy. They spend their time in contemplation and examination of the nature of things. They prefer to remain uninvolved in the affairs of unevolved species, but interfered in the Gorn/ Federation problem to simple ensure themselves some peace. Originally the Metronsbelieved that both sides were too barbaric to worry about unduly, but they realized that when Captain KIrk showed mercy to a fallen enemy that there was much to be said for such creatures. Though they do remain isolated, there is some chance that in the future this policy of theirs may be changed.

MIDRO

Played by: Ed Long
Episode: "The Cloud Minders"

Midro was one of the revolutionary Trogs (see separate entry for further details).

Mind Parasites

Appearances: "Operation: Annihilate"

The mind parasites are creatures without intellects or reason, being simple single-celled organisms. They do, however, form a group-mind (gestalt) with each other. They survive simply by preying on other species, and are spread reluctantly by intelligent hosts that can take them from world to world. Their point of originis unknown, but their results are death and madness. They attach themselves to the skins of a host, then insert their cilia into the nervous system of the host. They use pain as a weapon, to force the hosts to obey their commands, but their presense inevitably causes madness and kills the hosts with fear and pain.

Having destroyed Ingraham B, the mind parasites spread to Deneva, infecting the natives. Spock was also infected by one f the parasites, but his Vulcan control allowed him to survive the experience. He was able to ignore the pain for considerable time, allowing McCoy to experiment on ways of destroying the parasites. Eventually, it was determined that they could not survive ultra-violet radiation, and Kirk was able to free the po;ulation of deneva by broadcasting ultra-violet over the world, killing the parasites. Since this time, no other infestations of the parasites have been recorded, so it is hoped that the menace is ended for good.

MIRAMANEE

Played by: Sabrina Scharf
Episode: "The Paradise Syndrome"

Miramanee was a member of the Indians (see separate entry for further information). She was supposed to wed Salish, and was the daughter of Goro, the chief. She fell in love with Kirk instead and married him. She was stoned to death at the instigation of the jealous Salish.

MIRI

Played by: Kim Darby
Episode: "Miri"

Miri was an ancient child from a duplicate Earth. She and her friends (see below) were the survivors of an attempt to create eternal life. When this was attempted everyone over the age of puberty had died - and the children become long-lived. On reaching puberty, the children mutated into creatures of insane aspect, dying in agony. McCoy found a cure for the killer virus, enabling Miri and her friends to return to a normal childhood and aging.

MIRI'S COMPANIONS

Played by: John Megna, Keith Taylor, Kellie Flanagan, Steven McEveety.
Episode: "Miri"

Various children of Miri's gang. Also Jahn (see separate entry).

MIRT

Played by: Jay Jones
Episode: "A Piece Of The Action"

Mirt was one of the hoods on Sigma Iota II (see separate entry for further details).

MITCHELL, GARY

Played by: Gary Lockwood
Episode: "Where No Man Has Gone Before"

Gary Mitchell was an old friend of James Kirk from his days in the Academy. When Kirk was given command of the "Enterprise" attempted to break through the energy barrier surrounding our Galaxy, the energy outburst affected Mitchell. It gave him vastly increased mental abilities, and he soon developed into a dangerous being, feeling that he had become a god. He believed that he would take over everything, but Kirk managed to defeat and kill him, with the aide ofElizabeth Dehner, who had also been infected by the energy.

MONTGOMERY

Played by: Jerry Catron
Episode: "The Doomsday Machine"

Montogomery was a member of the "Enterprise" crew.

MORLA

Played by: Charles Dierkop
Episode: "Wolf In The Fold"

Morla was a native of Argelias II (see separate entry for further details). He was the fiance of Kara, the first victim of Rejak.

MORROW

Played by: Robert Hooks
Story: "Star Trek III - The Search For Spock"

Commander Morrow was a member of Starfleet Command. He had the unfortunate task of meeting the returning "Enterprise" and relocating its crew, prior to its planned destruction.

M'ress

Appearances: varied, throughout the animated series.

See entry on Caitians.

MUDD, HARCOURT FENTON

Played by: Roger C. Carmel
Episodes: (1) "Mudd's Women"
(2) "I, Mudd"

Harry Mudd is a thief, scoundrel, con-artist and a smooth tongued liar. Claiming to be Captain Leo Walsh, he is attempting smuggle women with illicit Venus drugs when he is captured by the "Enterprise" and correctly identified. He was convicted of smuggling, transporting stolen goods and purchasing a space ship with counterfeit money and given psychiatric treatment - which didn't work. He isn't eager to repeat the treatment, though, and attempts to black mail Kirk who need dilithium. Eventually, he was turned over tot he authorities, but managed to steal a ship and make an escape. He landed on an asteroid inhabited by androids, who wish to protect mankind from itself. Mudd helped them to capture him to be despicable, and would not allow him to leave. Mudd had to work with Kirk to disable the androids. Kirk left hiom with the robots to guard him - including a simulacrum of his shrewish wife....

MUDD, STELLA

Played by: Kay Elliot
Episode: "I, Mudd"

Stella Mudd was Harry Mudd's shrewish wife he had fled from years before. He created an Android (see separate entry for further details) in her image - with a cut-off so he could get the final word in at last. Kirk had the Android reprogrammed so that he couldn't and left Mudd with it for punishment.

MUGATO

Played by: Janos Prohaska
Episode: "A Private Little War"

The Mugato is a huge, ferocious ape-like creature native to the plnet Neural. It has white fur, and a single large horn in the middle of its forehead. The bite of the creature is almost always fatal, but can be staved off by the knowledge of the witch-women of the native race.

MULHALL, Dr. ANN

Played by: Diana Muldaur
Episode: "Return To Tomorrow"

Dr. Ann Mulhall was an assistant to McCoy assigned to the "Enterprise" for a while.

NATIRA

Played by: Kate Woodville
Episode: "For The World Is Hollow, And I Have Touched The Sky"

Natira was the High Priestess of the People of Yonada (see separate entry for futher details). She wed McCoy for a while.

NAVAL PERSONNEL

Story: "Star Trek IV - The Voyage Home"

During the "Enterprise" sequence, we are shown a number of Naval personnel.
These include: (1) FBI Agent
Played by: Jeff Lester
(2) Shore Patrolman
Played by: Joe Lando
(3) CDO
Played by: Newell Tarrant
(4) Technicians
Played by Mike Timoney, Jeffrey Martin
(5) Marine Sergeant
Played by : 1st sgt. Joseph Naradzay, USMC
(6) Marine Lieutenant
Played by: 1st Lt. Donald w. Zautcke, USMC

NAZIS

Episode: "Patterns of Force"

The inhabitants of Ekos set up their own Nazi Party. Its members included: (1) SS Major
Played by Gilbert Green
(2) SS Lieutenant
Played by: Ralph Maurer
(3) SS Trooper
Played by: Ed McCready
(4) Gestapo Lieutenant
Played by: Peter Canon
(5) Troopers:
Played by: Pul Baxley, Bill Baxley, Bill Blackburn
(6) Newscaster
Played by: Bartell LaRue

See also entries on: Daras, Melakon, John Gill Eneg
For further Information, see entry on Ekosians.

NELLIS, TOM

Played by: Dallas Mitchell
Episode: "Charlie X"

Tom Nellis was the navigator of the cargo ship "Antares." The crew of the ship rescued Charlie Evans from the lost world of Thasus, but became more distrubed by his inhuman behavior. When Charlie reached the "Enterprise," he destroyed the "Antares" in a fit of temper, killing the entire crew.

NESVIG

Played by: Morgan Jones
Episode: "Assignment: Earth"

Colonel Nesvig was head of security at Cape Canaveral.

NEURALS

Episode: "A Private Little War"

Various inhabitants of the planet Neural were seen, including:
Patrol Leader
Played by: Paul Baxley

See separate entries on: Tyree, Nona, Ytan, Apella.

Neural was generally a very peaceful world. The natives were split into two distinct types: hill people and town dwellers. The hill people are nomadic hunters, who occassionally gather food but prefer to hunt. They are, however, very gentle with others of their race and with outworlders. The women of the tribes would occassionally be witch-women. Such witches were very revered, because their knowledge of the properties of plants enable their
herbal skills to cure or bewitch.

The town dwellers, as their name implies, live in small towns and prefer to raise crops and livestock. For most of the world;s history, the two different cultures managed to exist peacefully. However the Klingons (see separate entry) changed this forever. Wishing to take control of the world, they began to arm the townsfolk and to turn them against the hill people. Under the terms of the Organian Peace Treaty (see Organians), the Klingons could not simply invade and conquer the planey.

Instead, they hoped to produce an economic situation where the towns folk would rely upon the materials supplied them by the Klingons, and thus become a dependency of the Klingon empire. Kirk, on learning of this, countered the move by arming the hill people with equal weapons, and betgan escalation of the combat in order to keep the sides fair. The situation on Neural is now very different from the peace Kirk had once found there. It is not known whether either side in this war will survive the "progress".

NIOBIANS

Episode: "All Our Yesterdays"

A number of the inhabitants of Beta Niobe were seen. These Included:
(1) Prosecutor
Played by: Kermit Murdock
(2) Fops
Played by: Ed Bakely, Al Cavens
(3) Woman
Played by: Anna Karen
(4) Jailer
Played by: Stan Barrett
(5) Constable
Played by: Johnny Haymer

See separate entries on: Zarabeth, Mr. Atoz.

The inhabitants of the world of Beta Niobe discovered that their sun was about to go nova. They had never discovered the means for space flight, but escaped the impending destruction of threir world using time travel. Everyone returned to some time in the past that they found congenial.

NOEL Dr. HELEN

Played by: Marianna Hill
Episode: "Dagger Of The Mind"

Dr. Helen Noel was a psychologist assigned to the "Enterprise" whose field of expertise was penal research. She and Kirk beamed down to the Tantalus Penal Colony to investigate Dr. Tristan Adams. Kirk had met her previously at a Christmas party, and found her attractive. Adams used his neural neutralizer to make Kirk fall deeply in love with her. Once Adams was defeated, Kirk was cured of the implainted feelings of love.

NOMAD

Played by: Vic Perrin
Episode: "The Changling"

In the year 2020 , the Nomad probe was buildt and launched from the Earth by Jackson Roykirk. It was programmed to scan for life-forms and record the data, in preparation for manned flights into space. Shortly after launching, the probe was lost, and presumed destroyed in a collision in space. Though Nomad had suffered an accident, it had against all odds collided with what it call the Other. This was an alien probe named Tan-Ru, whose mission had been to secure soil speciments and to sterilize them for return to its home world. Instead of destroying the two probes, the accident caused some fusion and confusion. The two probes joined, repaired themselves and became the new Nomad. In the damage, though,the two mission tapes had somehow been combined - Nomad was now programmed to scan for life, analize and then sterilize it.

Employing this new "directive", and the combined abilities it had gained from the Other, Nomad scanned the Malurian system. It found there billions of biological infestations - and sterilized the planets. Four inhabited worlds were su

ddenly rendered lifeless. When the Enterprise investigated, they found Nomad and brought it aboard. Nomad, with its faulty tapes, believed that Kirk was its creator, Roykirk. Its abilities were staggering - it both killed and resurected Scotty, and it wiped the knowledge rom Uhura's mind when it heard her singing. It had one aim in mind, however - to return to Earth and wipe it of biological infestations. Kirk finally literally talked the insane machine to death by convincing it that it was far less perfect thatn the biological units it was attempting to destory. Nomad self-destructed in a blaze of illogic.

NONA

Played by: Nancy Kovack
Episode: "A Private Little War"

Nona was a witch of the hill people of Neural (see separate entry for further details). She was married to Kirk's friend, Tyree, the leader of the tribe, but lusted after power. She was killed attempting to betray the tribe to the villagers.

NORMAN

Played by: Roger Tatro
Episode: "I, Mudd"

Norman was an Android (see separate entry for further details).

NUMBER ONE

Played by: Majel Barrett (as "M.Leigh Hudec")
Episode: "The Cage"

Number One was the cold, emotionless first officer under the "Enterprise," serving under Christopher Pike. When she left the ship, Spock became both science officer and first officer.

NURSE

(1) Played by: Joan Webster
Episode: "Space Seed"
(2) Played by: Judi Sherven
Episode: "Wolf In The Fold"
(3) Played by: Cindy Lou
Episode: "Return To Tomorrow"

ODONA

Played by: Sharon Acker
Episode: "The Mark Of Gideon"

Odona was an inhabitant of Gideon (see separate entry for further details). She was the daughter of the leader of the Council, Hodin.

O'HERLIHY

Played by: Jerry Ayres
Episode: "Arena"

O'Herlihy was a member of the tacticians aboard the "Enterprise."

Omegans

Appearances: "The Omega Glory"

The history of Omega IV parallels that of the Earth to a very large degree, save that in this world, events took a different turn in the 1990s. On Omega, a war broke out, and the Communist Chinese invaded the USA. A biological agent, a killer virus, was released in the course of the war, wiping out many of the inhabititants of Earth, and reducing the level of general civilization of the survivors. The Communists, namces shortened to Kohms, took over what they could of the US. They are countered by the Yangs (a cooruption of "Yanks"), and eventually beaten back.

In the midst of this fighting, the USS Exeter arrived, commanded by Tracy. His men beamed down and contracted the killer disease. He stayed to talk with the Kohms, who had an extended life-spand, while his crew beamed back, spreading the disease to the rest of the ship. The entire crew perished, turning into white powder. Tracy, on the planet below, survived. He realized that there was an immunizing agent there, and theorized that he could never leave.

Kirk, Spock and McCoy, investigating the strange deaths on the Exeter, arrived on Omega, and learned this story. McCoy proved that the immunizer worked after a mere few hours on this planet, and that it was safe for them to return home. Kirk managed to capture the crazed Tracy and to convince both Kohms and Yangs to work together to rebuild their shattered planet.

O'NEIL

Played by: Sean Morgan
Episodes: (1) "The Return Of The Archons"
(2) "The Tholian Web"

O'Neil was a member of the security team on the "Enterprise." He and Sulu beamed down to Beta 3 to investigate the culture, but were attacked and brainwashed by the Lawgivers. Both were later restored to normal.

Organians

Appearances: "Errand Of Mercy"

The world of Organia lies on the boundary of Federation space and the Klingon Empire (se separate entry).

Its piople have evolved far beyond the need of bodies, being something like glowing balls of light in their natural state. For the sake of visiting humanoids, they do assume conventional appearances, however, out of courtesy. They are a gentel, pacifistic piople, given to contemplation and exploration. They seek neither to influence nor to educate other races, and only ask that they be left in peace to live their own lives. However, due to the strategic nature of the world, both the Federation and the Klingons felt a complling need to solicit the friendship of the Organians for their cause.

For as long as they could, the Organians stood aloof from the battle of wits between Kirk and Kor, but they eventually were forced to interfere. Both parties were on the brink of warfare, which would certainly have disturbed the Organians' peace. They therefore defused all weapons for its terms, there can be no warfare between the races. In the case of disputed planets, whichever race can best utilize the world in question shall be given the planet. Members of either side who are peaceful must be allowed freedom of travel, and the rights to rest and provisioning when such are requested. Neither side particularly likes these terms, but the power of the Organians to enforce them simply forces bothe parties to accept the terms - at least on the surface. The Klingons especially never cease from their attempts to circumvent the treaty in any possible.

ORIONS

1) Orion Space Officer
Played by: Robert Philips
Episode: "The Cage"

2) Orion Trader
Played by: Joseph Mell
Episode: "The Cage"

See separate entry for Thelev.
appearances: "The Cage"
"Journey To Babel"
"The Time Trap"
"The Pirates Of Orion"

The system of Orion is one that is in considerable flux. The peoples of its worlds do not like off-worlders unduly, and they believe that other races are there to be exploited whenever this is possible. The traders of Orion are a notorious example of this, being only as moral in their business dealings as they are forced to be. The slavers, as their name implies, take capitives for resale within the system of Orion - since most of the Federation worlds have long since outlawed ownership of sentient beings. Federation worlds have long since outlawed ownership of sentient beings. The pirates of Orion are freebooters who prey on smaller ships and take whatever they can whenever opportunity presents itself.

Several different racial types exist within the Orion system. The dominant male are blue in coloration, leading one to speculate that they are in some way related to their closest neighbors, the Andorians (see separate entry). Since they are so close to the Andorian system. Orion pirates often undergo minor surgery to pass as Andorians for the purpose of spying. Such was the case with the dispute at Babel.

Another race is predominantly green-hued: This was once a race native to some world in the system, long ago enslaved. While the men of this race are unexceptional, the green slave-girls are notorious throughout the Galaxy for their erotic natures. They are extremely sensous dancers, and are reputed to have voracious sexual appetities and abilities. Such rumors are perfectly true, thus placing the slave-girls extremely high in demand. As has been noted, slavery is illegal in the Federation - yet it is hard to estimate how many slave-girls of this race exist in "free" space.

Orion refuses to get involved with the politics of other races, and maintains a strict neutrality between others. The merchants do this because they wish to trade with anyone they can; the pirates do it because they wish to rob everyone they can, impartially.

OXMYX, BELA

Played by: Anthony Caruso
Episode: "A Piece Of The Action"

Bela Oxmyx was the biggest mobster of Sigma Iota II (see separate entry for further details).

OZABA, Dr.

Played by: Davis Roberts
Episodes: "The Empath"

Dr. Ozaba was one of the two scientists on Minara II, observing conditions prior to its sun going nova. He and Dr. Linke were tortured to death by the Vians, Lal and Thann.

PALAMAS, CAROLINE

Played by: Leslie Parrish
Episode: "Who Mourns For Adonais?"

Lt. Caroline Palamas was an expert in archaelogy and anthropology. Scott fell in love with her, but she was not so certain about her feelings. When they met the Greek god Apollo, she found him forceful and yet attractive. She was forced, however, to rebuff his attentions in order that Kirk could defeat him and get them all to safety.

PALMER

Played by: Elizabeth Rogers
Episodes: (1) "The Doomsday Machine"
(2) "The Way To Eden"

Lt. Palmer was a communications officer on the "Enterprise."

Pandrons

Appearances: "BEM"

The Pandrons are a very arrogant species, believing that they are a superior life-form. The reason for this is that they are actually colony creatures - each Pandron is made of three interlocked beings. The top section resembles a head, the central one a thorax and arms, and the bottom one a trunk and legs. The co-operate to achieve maximum efficiency, but can split apart when they wish to.

PARMEN

Played by: Liam Sullivan
Episode: "Plato's Stepchildren"

Parmen was the sadistic leader of the Platonians (see separate entry for further details). He was married to Philana.

PERGIUM ENGINEER

Played by: George E. Allen
Episode: "The Devil In The Dark"

The engineer was in charge of repairs at the reactor plant in the Pergium mines of Janus VI.

PETRI

Played by: Jay Robinson
Episode: "Elaan Of Troyius"

Petri was an ambassador of Troyius (see separate entry for further details). He was assigned to teach civilized behavior to Elaan.

PHILANA

Played by: Barbara Babcock
Episode: "Plato's Stepchildren"

Philana was the wife of Parmen, leader of the Platonians (see separate entry for further details).

Phylosians

Appearances: "The Infinite Vulcan"

The Phylosians are the last members of their species. They are intelligent, ambulatory plants. Their civilization was accidentally destroyed by the arrival of Dr. Keniculus. He spread a disease to the race that caused most of them to die out. Appalled, he stayed to work on a permanent cure for them, whilst teaching them about the rest of the Galaxy. Both he and they believed that there was a dire need for peace-keeping force, and they determined to create one. Over 250 years passed, with Keniculus cloning himself over and over to keep alive his ideals. He attempted to use Spock as a mould for his peace-keepers, only to discover that there already was one - the Federation. A cloned Spock and Keniculus the Fifth remained on :Phylos to attempt to cure the Phylosians together.

PICARD, CAPT. JEAN-LUC

Played by: Patrick Stewart
Series regular

Before taking command of the maiden voyage of the Galaxy-class Enterprise (NCC-1701-D), Picard commanded the deep space vessel Stargazer during a lengthy 22-year mission. Besides his passion as a starship commander, he holds deep interests in archeology and 20th Century detective fiction. He frequently quotes Shakespeare. Picard was kidnapped from the Enterprise by the Borg, a race of cybernetic organisms who "assimilate" (destroy) all biological races. The Borg transformed Picard into one of them, calling him Locutus and used him as a "liason" to the Federation until Picard himself severed the mind-control.

PIKE, CAPTAIN CHRISTOPHER

Played by: Jeffrey Hunter
Episode: "The Cage"
Played by: sean Kenney
Episode: "The Menagerie"

Christopher Pike was the captain of the "Enterprise" immediately prior to James Kirk. His main friend was his ship's surgeon, Dr. Boyce. After seven years, he was promoted to Fleet Captasin. On a cadet inspection, the ship's baffle-plates ruptued. Pike saved several cadets' lives, but was dosed with delta radiation that degenerated all his muscles. he was confined to a motorized chair that kept him alive, but unable to communicate with the outside world. Spock braved his career by taking Pike back to the forbidden planet of Talos IV. The inhabitants there were able to give some expression to Pike's will for his last years of life.

PINTER

Played by: Dick Scotter
Episode: "This Side of Paradise"

Pinter was one of the people in Elias Sandoval's colony on Omicron Ceti III.

PIPER, Dr. MARK

Played by: Paul Fix
Episode: "Where No Man Has Gone Before"

After Dr. Boyce retired, Dr. Mark Piper became chief surgeon of the "Enterprise." Shortly into the five year mission, his advanced age made him resign the post, and he was replaced by Leonard McCoy.

PIPER, MISS

Played by: Julie Parrish
Episode: "The Menagerie"

Miss Piper was the secretary to Commodore Mendez, who is in charge of Star Base 11.

PITCAIRN

Played by: Clegg Hoyt
Episode: "The Cage"

Pitcairn was Transporter Chief of the "Enterprise" under Captain Christopher Pike.

PLASUS

Played by: Jeff Corey
Episode: "The Cloud Minders"

Plasus was the father of Droxine and the High Advisor of Stratos (see separate entry for further details).

Platonians

Appearances: "Plato's Stepchildren"

The Platonians (named after the philosophies of Plato, whom they greatly admire) are not native to the world which they now inhabit. Their home world's sun went nova, and the people who lived there fled into space to seek a new world. The Platonians - a segment of that race - found their world, and settled down. The world had a large supply of ht erare element kironide. This contains much power, and can be assimilated into humanoid bodies through the actions of the thyroid glands. as the level of the kironide within their bloodstream built up the Platonians discovered that they were developing tremendously potent mental abilities - including telepathy and telekinesis. They began a pruification program to breed what they considered to be perfect specimens of their race, weeding out poor genetic specimens. They discovered that they had an enor-

mously lenthened life-span - in the order of thousands of years - and and immunity to disease.

As they grew in mental power, the power slowly corrupted the Platonians. They moved from a desire to remove the poor genes from their race to a despising of any lesser races. They hid their world from other eyes - lesser eyes, to their minds. They also developed sadistic quirks, which they would work out on any throwbacks in their own race. Anyone born with thyroid problems could simply not assimilate the kironide and therefore lacked their mental abilities. Such throwbacks were allowed to survive to provide amusement for the Platonians, who revelled in using their powers to force their "clowns" to perform ludicrous acts.

One thing that they were not immune to, however, was accidents. When thir ruler, Parmen became infected after such an accident, McCoy, Kirk and Spock were brought to their world to heal him. McCoy managed this, and the Platonians realized that he would be useful to them. In an attempt to force him to stay, they controlled the actions of Kirk and Spock. The problem was that McCoy realized that the Platonians were bound to destroy the Enterprise to ensure that their location remained the secret that they desired. He discovered the ability of the thyroid to assimilate the kironide, injecting himself, Kirk and Spock with massive amounts of the element. This gave them greater mental powers thatn the Platonians, and they were able to utilize force to make their "hosts" see reason. Their supposedly high moral stance was shown to a shambles, and the Platonians forced to change their society - faced with greater force than their own, their moral supremacy theories curmbled, and they had little option but to obey.

POLICEMAN

Played by: Hal Baylor
Episode: "The City On The Edge Of Forever"

Whilst Kirk and Spock were in 1930 New York, they were caught stealing clothes by a patrolman on his beat. When Kirk's explanations failed to produce results, Spock was forced to nerve-pinch the poor man.

Preservers

Appearances: "The Paradise Syndrome"

Note: though the Preservers do not appear in this story, they are integral to the tale.

A mysterious race of beings known only as the Preservers travels the Galaxy collecting specimens of cultures doomed to extinction. They remove these specimens to worlds uncontaminated by their enemies, allowing them to grow in peace. One such group that have been transplanted and thrive now are a small group of Indians of the Navaho, Mohican and Delaware tribes. These peaceful fishers and gatherers would have been wiped out by the encroaching whites, but on this world, so like their own lakes, they survive.

Little is known of the Preservers themselves. They clearly have very advanced sciences, since they can utilize gravitational power to repel asteroids. The language is based on musical notes and harmonies.

PRESTON, PETER

Played by: Ike Eisenman
Story: "Star Trek II - The Wrath Of Khan"

Peter Preston was a member of the "Enterprise" engineering crew, and Scott's nephew. During the attack by Khan, Preston remained at his post, stopping a dangerous leak. his actions saved the ship, but proved to be ultimately fatal.

Providers

Appearances: "The Gamesters Of Triskelion"

The Providers are the final three survivors of the native race of Triskelion. When they realized that their race was doomed, three of the natives had their brains removed to life-support systems, hooked into computers. This allowed them vastly extended lifetimes, but it gave rise to problems of the loss of emotions and the onset of boredom. With the vas powers at their command, the Providers set about changing their world to relieve the montony. They kidnapped aliens that passed close to their planet, and enslaved them. These thralls they bred for fighting, and the Providers would then wager on the outcome of their bloody arena games. They could experience vicarious thrills and wager at the same time.

They believed that the humans from the Enterprise would provide excellent material, and thus kidnapped Kirk, Chekov and Uhura for breeding and fighting. They soon came to realize that the humans loved freedom too much to willingly submit to this cruel form of slavery and death. Kirk, realizing their natures, appealled to their love of gambling witha wager of his own: he would match their three gladiators. If he lost he'd stay willingly. If he won, they would have to free the thralls and teach tem and guide them to become a

civilization of their own. The gamblers could not refuse such an offer, and when Kirk won the fight, they kept they kept their word. Kirk assured them that they would find the challenge of creating and leading a new civilization far more challenging than simply playing blood sports. They have found that he is quite correct, and are exhilareted with their new purpose in life.

RAD, TONGO

Played by: Victor Brandt
Episode: "The Way To Eden"

Tongo Rad was the son of the Catullan ambassador to the Federation. Tongo dropped out and joined the utopian-seeking followers of Dr. Sevrin. He, like the others found their Eden - an acid-filed world that would have killed them.

RAEL

Played by: Jason Evers
Episode: "Wink Of An Eye"

Rael was one of the Scalosians (see separate entry for further details).

RAHDA

Played by: Naomi Pollack
Episode: "That Which Survives"

Rahda was a member of the "Enterprise" crew.

RAMART, CAPTAIN

Played by: Charles J. Stewart
Episode: "Charlie X"

Captain Ramart command the cargo ship "Antares" that discovered Charlie Evans stranded on the strange world of Thasus. Ramart and his crew rescued the boy, but were disturbed by his uncanny mental abilities and transfered him to the "Enterprise." Annoyed at Ramart, Charlie caused the "Antares" to explode, killing all aboard it.

RANCHER

Played by: Gregg Palmer
Episode: "Spectre Of The Gun"

The rancher was one of the illusions created by the Melkotian (see separate entry for further details).

RAND, JANICE

Played by: Grace Lee Whitney
Regular, first season
Stories: (1) "Star Trek - The Motion Picture"
(2) "Star Trek III - The Search For Spock"
(3) "Star Trek IV - The Voyage Home"

Janice Rand was original assigned to the Enter prise as Captain Kirk's yeoman. It was her duty to functin as his secretary, valey and aide. She transferred out from the ship, training as transporter chief. She returned, briefly, to the Enterprise during the V'Ger crisis, but is now stationed elsewhere.

RAY

Played by: Brian Tochi
Episode: "And The Children Shall Lead"

Ray was one of the children deceived by Gorgan.

RAYBURN

Played by. Bud Albright
Episode: "What Are Little Girls Made Of?"

Rayburn was a security guard from the "Enterprise," killed by the andoroid Ruk.

RAYNA

Played by: Louise Sorel
Episode: "Requiem For Methuselah"

Rayna was an android created byt he immortal Flint (see separate entry for further details). Flint wanted an

equally immortal companion, and had manufactured his ideal woman. Flint used Kirk to bring out Raymana's feelings of love and make her truly alive. Forced to chose between Flint and Kirk., Rayna was unable. In her dilemma, she died.

REGER

Played by: Harry Townes
Episode: "The Return Of THe Archons"

Reger was one of the villagers of Beta 3 immune to the pacifying effects of Landru. He helped Kirk for a while, until the Lawgivers captured Reger and made him part of the body. Knowing he would be forced to betray the humans, Reger had Kirk stun him. He had a daughter Tula.

RIDER

Played by: Richard Anthony
Episode: "Spectre Of The Gun"

The rider was one of the illusions created by the Melkotian (see separate entry for further details).

Rigelians

Appearances: "Star Trek - The Motion Picture"

The natives of Rigel Four are members of the Federation. They are one of the beings whose appearances from the first movie were cut. They are turtlelike beings, at home in the water. They move slowly, but have a tremendous amount of stamina. Their ex-skeletons make them difficult to harm, and are a warrior race.

Rigelians

Appearances: "The Cage"

The natives of Rigel VII are a blood-thirsty, savage race, who live solely for warfare. They have never developed more than a feudal society, for the various lords are simply uninterested in co-operation. They build large castles, and frequently raid their neighbors. Their armored warriors are among the fiercest fighters that the Galaxy knows.

Rigelian Hypnoid

Appearances: "Mudd's Passion"

This creature is a strange being, able to project hypnotically a false appearance. It is not known whether it is native to Rigel VII, or one of the many other worlds or moons of the Rigelian system.

RIKER, CMDR. WILLIAM

Played by: Jonathan Frakes
Series regular

William Riker, also known as "Will", serves as First Officer of the Enterprise. In that position, he is known as "Number One" by Captain Picard. Riker is an outgoing, friendly man, and uses this technique in his job. Besides commanding the ship in Picard's absence, Riker leads the landing parties, now known as "Away Teams", because Starfleet had decided not to put their captains in that much danger on planetary missions. Before joining the Enterprise, Riker had some romantic relationship with Deanna Troi, and occasionally working with her again on the same ship presents its challenges.

RILEY, KEVIN

Played by: Bruce Hyde
Episodes: (1) "The Naked Time"
(2) "The Conscience Of The KIng"

Kevin Riley was one of the crewmembers of the "Enterprise." When the crew was infected by the contamination of Psi 2000, Riley reverted to singing and impersonating one of the kings of old Ireland that he believed he was descended from. Later, when the Karidian Players came aboard the "Enterprise," he was almost killed, because he was one of the last people ever to have seen Kodos the butcher of Tarsus IV (Riley's home world) alive.

RIZZO

Played by: Jerry Ayres
Episode: "Obession"

Rizzo was a security guard killed by a vampire cloud (see separate entry for further details).

RODENT

Played by: John Harmon
Episode: "The City On The Edge Of Forever"

Rodent was a particularly unsavory denizen of New York city in 1930.

RODRIGUEZ, ESTEBAN

Played by: Perry Lopez
Episode: "Shore Leave"

Rodriguez was a member of the landing party checking out the Caretaker's world. He was caught up in the illusions it generated. He and Angela Martine were romantically ivolved.

ROJAN

Played by: Warren Stevens
Episode: "By Any Other Name"

Rojan was the leader of tyhe Kelvans (see separate entry for further details).

ROKA

Played by: Fred Williamson
Episode: "The Cloud Minders"

Roka was one of the revolutionary Trogs (see separate entry for further details).

ROMAINE, MIRA

Played by: Jan Shutan
Episode: "The Lights Of Zetar"

Lt. Mira Romaine was one of Scott's romantic partners. She was responsible for transfering information to the Memory Alph library planetoid. She became infected with the Lights of Zetar (see separate entry for further details).

ROMANS

Episode: "Bread And Circuses"

A small world parallel to Earth, still had the Romans in charge. The inhabitants of this world included:
(1) Policeman
Played by: William Brambley
(2) Announcer
Played by: Bart LaRue
(3) Master Of The Games
Played by: Jack Perkins

See also the entries on: Merik, Claudius, Septimus, Flavius, Maximus and Drusilla.

Planet 892-IV is another world with parallel history to Earth, at least to a point. In this world, however, the Roman Empire never fell. It continued to spread, and in its equivalent of the 20the Century now dominates the entire planet. The practice of slavery is still continued, as is the ancient blood-sport of gladiatorial combat. On 892-IV, this has been brought into the modern age by the televising of such fights for the masses, and is used as a ratings booster.

Faith in the ancient gods of Rome no longer really applies, and their names tend to be used as trademarks, on everything from cars to cigarrettes. Christianity was ruthlessly suppressesd for almost two thousand years, but is now getting its message across to that world. Perhaps in time, it will lead to the fall of the Roman civilization and the rise of a better one.

ROMULANS

A number of Romulans, mostly unnamed, have appeared in the show over the years.
These include:
(1) Romulan Commander
Played by: Mark Lenard
Episode: "Balance Of Terror"
(2) Scope Operator
Played by: Robert Chadwick
Episode: "Balance of Terror"
(3) Centurian
Played by: John Warburton
Episode: "Balance Of Terror"
(4) Crewmen
Played by: Walter Davis, Vince Deadrick

Episode: "Balance of Terror"
(5) Romulan Commander
Played by: Joanne Linville
Episode: "The Enterprise Incident"
(6) Technical Officer
Played by: Richard Compton
Episode: ""The Enterprise Incident"
(7) Technician
Played by: Robert Gentile
Episode: "The Enterprise Incident"
(8) Guard
Played by: Mike Howden
Episode: "The Enterprise Incident"
(9) Soldier
Played by: Gordon Coffey
Episode: "The Enterprise Incident"
10. Caithlin Dar , Romulan ambassador to Nimbus III
Played by: Cynthia Gouw
Star Trek V
11. Nanclus, Romulan ambassador to the Federation
Played by: Darryl Henriques
Star Trek VI

See also entries on Decius, Tal.
Appearances: "Balance Of Terror"
"The Deadly Years"
"The Enterprise Incident:"
"The Survivor"
"The Time Trap"
"The Practical Joker"
Star Trek V: The Final Frontier
Star Trek VI: The Undiscovered Country

A few thousand years ago, the Vulcans (see separate entry) were a warrior race. They developed rudimentary methods of space travel and began a very aggressive colonization process. Shortly after this, their culture experienced the massive shock that led to their adoption of absolute logic as their guide-line. However, the twin worlds of Romulus and Remus, colonized by the warrior Vulcans, developed in isolation on a different path. Instead of outlawing their emotional natures, as the Vulcan race had, the Romulans (as the twin worlds' inhabitants came to be known) made warfare an instituation,and regulated their aggressive natures. The entire Romulan society was structured about the military.

After a period in total isolation, the Romulans created a unique form of spaceship, patterned and painted after birds of prey. The ships were small, but efficient fighters, and on venturing out from their world to begin their own program of colonization, they ran into the human sphere or influence. The Romulans, as was their nature, attacked these ships, and warfare broke out. In those days, space warfare was still fairly primitive, and neither side could take prisoners, nor was subspace radio sufficiently developed to allow for the transmission of pictures Accordingly, neither side actually saw the other.

The R9omulans soon realized that the enemy's ships outclassed them, and they agreed to peace terms. This was conducted entirely over the radio, and set forth Neutral Zone between Romulan and Federation space. Both parties would police their sides of the Zone, and entry by either party into the Zone would be considered an act of war. The humans believed that this would lead to peace between them and the Romulans, whereas to the Romulans the peace was simply a matter of delay. As soon as they had developed a weapon that they believed would be powerful enough, they would break out of their restricted Zone and begin their war again.

For a hundred years, there was peace, of sorts. the Federation Outposts (asteroid bases) monitored the Neutral Zone, and the Romulans used their bird of prey ships to ensure that their space was not violated. In the meantime, the Romulan researches had developed what they believed to be a very efficient cloaking device, hiding their ships from radar and sensor scans. They also had a plasma cannon that they believed was superior to any that the Federation had. The Romulan command decided to test both weapons, arming a single ship with both, and sending it out to attack the Outposts. They knew that this would draw a starship into the area, and enable their ship and the Federation vessel to fight. should their ship win, then this would be the signal for the mass production of both weapons and the start of full-scale warfare once again.

The Commander of the bird of prey knew this. Though raised on centuries of military thinking, he was sufficiently intelligent to wonder if this was the correct course of action. Nevertheless, he would have to do his duty and perhaps start a war that might ignite the Galaxy. In the event, the Enterprise, under the command of Captain Kirk, proved able to work about the limitaitons of both the cloaking device and the plasma projector. Kirk's grasp of tactic ledc him to defeat and destroy the Romulan craft, thus averting disaster for the time being. The Romulan high command realized that their systems still needed much work, and went quietlyabout their research to improve both weapons.

The Federation, having been warned by Kirk of the cloaking device, managed to keep track of this research. The learned after two years that the device had beeen modified, and desired a working model so that they could study it for design flaws. Accordingly, an elaborate scheme was wset up using the Enterprise once again. Kirk feigned insanity, and Spock feigned murding him, to allow them acccess to the Romulan ship bearing the cloaking device. They managed to steal the device and, accidentally, the Romulan Commander.

Romulans, though tending to use males in their military, have no prejudice against women fighting. If they have the ability, female commanders are not uncommon. romulans, like Vulcans, have the pointed ears and upswept eyebrows, and also the strength of Vulcans. Both males and females therefore make extremely capable warriors. Both sexes are allowed military careeers, though fewer chose to pursue one.

Since they are of common stock, Vulcans and Romulans can interbreed - though according to official Vulcan thought such matings are impossible. Romulan/ Vulacan matings for pleasure are obviously extremely rare (since the Romulans remain isolated) - but the Romulans do take Vulcan Prisoners. They do this as a savage way of humilating their cousins. Vulcans consider the Romulans to be baraians because they induldge themselves in their emotions and practice warfare. Romulans therefore enjoy humilitating the "logic-lovers." By giving Vulcans certain drugs, the Romulans can inspire passion in the Vulcans, and then mate with them. Offspring of such forced matings are almost always produced. The child is then shown to the Vulcan father or mother to humiliate them, and then the child is simply abandoned.

Vulcans consider such children as non-existent, officially, and prefer to ignore them in athe unlikely event that they survive, they are left as feral creatures. One such half-bred was Saavik. When the Romulans abandoned her home world as being impossible to colonize, Saavik and the other half-breeds were left behind. A Vulcan expedition, sent to the world to scavenge any information on the Romulans left by the departed people, came across the feral children. The Vulcans simply ignored them, but Captain Spock, being half-human realized that this was not logical nor merciful. The children were not at fault in this matter, and he insisted on their rescue. To provide an example, he himself brought Saavik up, training her in science and self-control.

Saavik has proven that she has honor in the eyes of Vulcan. Though she could have her genes scanned and thus have her parent's house identified, she has chosen not to humilate the house concerned by doing this. This was much approved by the Vulcan race, and she has no idea whether her father or mother was her vulcan parent. By dint of the fact that she has achieved so much in her few years among them, the Vulcans have come to accept Saavik for what she is. Spock's family has unofficially adopted her, and both Sarek and Amanda enjoy her company and take pride in her achievements.

The Romulands continue to expand their knowledge and sphere of influence, ever seeking the final weapon that will give them the edge to attack and destroy the Federation. A relatively recent development has been their replacing the bird of prey craft with stolen Klingon designs. The bird of prey was a small, relatively inefficient craft, and the Klingon designs is far better for warfare. Naturally the far more sophisticated Federation designs would be prefered, but the Romulans have been unable to steal either the craft itself or the plans for one. Takin a Federation starship in one piece would bring much honor to any commander who could achieve such a coup.

ROSS

Played by: Terrance O'Connor
Story "Star Trek - The Motion Picture"

Chief Ross was a member of the crew of the "Enterprise."

ROSS, TERESA

Played by: Venita Wolf
Episode: "The Squire Of Gothos"

Teresa Ross was a member of the "Enterprise" crew abducted by Trelane because of her fine looks.

ROWE

Played by: Mike Howden
Episode: "I, Mudd"

Lt. Rowe was a member of the security team on the "Enterprise."

RUK

Played by: Ted Cassidy
Episode: "What Are Little Girls Made Of?"

The world of Exo-III was once a thriving place. The natives, desiring more relaxtion time and less involvement with menial chores, developed a line of androids to serve them. They believed that this would be a step forward, but the Old Ones (as they became known) had made a serious miscalculation. The androids were creatures of pure logi, and abhored any for of illogic. It became obvious to them that their creators were themselves extrememly illogical, and for their own survival, the androids felt that it was necessary to destroy their creators.

The entire race was annihilated swiftly, but the androids discovered that they had very little motivation to develop on their own. Accordingly, the android civilization began to decay. Conditions of the surface of the

world deteriorated, and the androids retreated to the depths of the planet as the surface became all ice and snow. For millenia, the androids simply died out, until there was a single survivor, one of the original creations, known as Ruk. Ruk was filled with a conviction that there would some day be an android civilization on his world, but over the millenia his memories of what had happened to the Old Ones had been suppressed. When the starship carrying a bio-chemist, Richard Corby, crashed, only Corby survived long enough for Ruk to save him. Corby was dying, but Ruk used his android machinery to make a duplicate of Corby's body, transfering his mind into it.

Vorby provided the incentive that Ruk and his race had lacked. He began planning the android takeover of the Galaxy, realizing that as a machine he was freed from the problems of the flesh, and all the waknesses it gave arise to. He made an android duplicate of Brown, his dead assistant, and also an android beauty, Andrea. Planning his new worlds, he managed to lead Ruk into trusting him. The arrival of Kirk and Corby's fiancee, Christine Chapel, dislocated those plans and precipitated disaster. Kirk proved to Andrea that she didn't know emotions; Corby was as dangerous as the Old Ones he had killed, but Corby managed to destroy Ruk. Andrea disposed of a duplicate Kirk, which refused to listen to her about her emotions. Brown was destroyed, and finally Andrea destroyed both herself and Corby, ending his crazed dreams of an android society.

RUSS

Played by: Tim Burns
Episode: "The Doomsday Machine"

Russ was a member of the "Enterprise" crew.

RUTH

Played by: Shirley Bonne
Episode: "Shore Leave"

Ruth was an old flame of Kirk's. He conjured her up again on the Caretaker's world, thatnks to its mechanisms for making reality of thoughts.

SAAVIK

Played by: (1) Kirstie Alley
Story: "Star Trek II - The Wrath Of Khan"
(2) Robin Curtis
Stories: "Star Trek III - The Search For Spock"
"Star Trek IV - The Voyage Home"

Saavik was a half-Vulcan, half Romulan child, left to die by both races until rescued by Spock. He raised and educated her, training her as skillful sceince officer. Like the Vulcans, she is partially telepathic and very strong, but she had great difficulty in mastering her emotions, so as to be acceptable. She helped to save Spock on Genesis, and helped him through ponn farr, and afterwards she remained on Vulcan with Spock's parents.

SALISH

Played by: Rudy Solari
Episode: "The Paradise Syndrome"

Salish was one of the Indians (see separate entry for further details). He was the son of the old medicine chief, and engaged to marry Miramanee, Goro's daughter. she fell in love with Kirk and married him instead, Salish fought Kirk and lost, then instigated the death of Miramanee in revenge.

SALT VAMPIRE

Played by: Sharon Gimpel
Episode: "The Man Trap"

Note: The monster suit used in this story actually is shown again as a decoratin in Tremane's house in "The Spuire Of Gothos." It simply a prop though, and not the vampire.

A small planet named M113 was the home of the final member of an alien species that was never named, but simply termed the "salt vampire" for its behavior. The race had died out over centuries, presumably from having killed all of the "food supply" off. The creature itself is a gnarled, hairy being, with suckers on its finger-tips. To survive, the vampire would hypnotize its victims into seeing someone or something familiar to them, lulling them into a state of security and helplesness. It would then attach its suckers to the victim's naked skin and drain all the the salt from the prey. The sudden loss of salt would inevitably kill the victim.

Just how intelligent this creature was is highly debatable. Professor Crater, who discovered the being, believed that it was of relatively high attainment, but bothe

Kirk and Spock considered it be a simple predator. It showed a certain degree of cunning and adaption to the humans it preyed upon, but this was most likely simply due to the way it "camoflagued" itself to seem harmless to them. Certainly, it was not intelligent enough to eat at intervald, and in response to what it saw as an unlimited food supply (ther crew of the Enterprise), it simply began to gorge itself. Finally, it underestimated its hypnotic effect. McCoy though believing that the creature was Crater's wife, killed it when it attacked Kirk to feast.

The question than remains unanswered is whether the vampire could have built the civilization that lies in ruins on M113. If it was only as inteligent as its prey, the answer must be that it could never have managed such a feat of construction. This would then necessitate there having been through lack of salt. In which case, are the vampires native to M113? There seem to be tow options: If they were native, they must have evolved after the intelligent race of this world; otherwise, they had to have been from another planet, brought to the planet M113 by star ship. In purpose of warfare? In the second case, if they were brought to M113 from another world, are there then more of them still at large in the Universe? SAM Played by: Dick Dial Episode: "The Devil In The Dark" Sam was one of the Pergium miners on Janus VI, under Vanderberg.

SAMURAI

Played by: Sebastian Tom
Episode: "Shore Leave"

One of a variety of illusions made real on the Caretaker's world, this one taken from Sulu's fertile imagination.

SANDOVAL ELIAS

Played by: Frank Overton
Episode: "This Side Of Paradise"

Elias Sandoval was the leader of a small prototype colony on Omicron Ceti III. The colony became infected by spores (see separate entry), though eventually cured. They were all moved to a safer planet.

SAN FRANCISCANS

Story: "Star Trek IV - The Voyage Home"
During the story, a number of inhabitants of San Francisco are shown.
These include:
(1) Lady On Tour
Played by: Voila Stimpson
(2) Garbagemen
Played by: Phil Rubenstein, John Miranda
(3) Antique Store Owner
Played by: Joe Knowland
(4) Waiter
Played by: Bob Sarlatte
(5) Cafe Owner
Played by: Everett Lee
(6) Joe
Played by: Richard Harder
(7) Nichols
Played by Alex Hentelhoff
(8) Pilot
Played by: Tony Edwards
(9) Patient
Played by: Eve Smith
(10) Interns
Played by: Tom Mustin, Greg Karas
(11) Doctors
Played by: Raymond Singer, David Ellenstein, Judy Levitt
(12) Usher
Played by: Teresa E. Victor
(13) Jogger
Played by: James Menges
(14) Punk on Bus
Played by: Kirk Thatcher

See separate entries on: Dr. Gillian Taylor Bob Briggs, Naval Personnel.

SAR SIX

Played by: Robert Sampson
Episode: "A Taste Of Armageddon"

Sar Six was a member of the council of Eminiar Seven, which was headed by Anan Seven.

SARATOGA CREW

Story: "Star Trek IV - The Voyage Home"
Various members of the "Saratoga" are shown.
These include:
(1) Science Officer
Played by: Mike Brislane
(2) Captain
Played by: Vijay Amritraj

(3) Helmsman
Played by: Nick Ramus

SAREK

Played by: Mark Lenard
Episodes: (1) "Journey To Bable"
(2) "Star Trek III - The Search For Spock"
(3) "Star Trek IV - The Voyage Home"

sarek of Vulcan is one of his world's most noted ambassadors. He married Amanda Grayson of Earth late in life. The couple have one child, Spock. For years, Sarek refused to acknoledge his son's existence, disapproving of Spock's choice to join Starfleet. The two become reconciled later.

SARGON

Played by: James Doohan
Episode: "Return To Tomorrow"

See the entry on Arretans.

Sarpedons

Appearances: "All Our Yesterdays"

Note: the sun of Sarpedon, Beta Niobe, is mentioned in the animated episode "The Counter-Clock Incident".

The world of Sarpedon was a very healthy and scientific place to live in its final years. The natives, however, had no worlds close to their own, and thus never developed space flight. The discovery that their sun, Beta Niobe, was going to go nova caused a great deal of constrenation and panic, but this was settled fairly quickly for the natives of Sarpedon had another means of escaping their inevitable doom: into the past.

Time travel had been known for a number of years. A tyranical leader named Zorcon had used the time travelling apparatus to exile his political foes into different periods in the deep past - a particularily nasty form of solitary confinement. When he was overthrown and a fairer ruling body placed in power, a library was built to scan and record the past using the apparatus. Now, however, the time travel facilities would prove to be life saving. The entire population of Sarpedon would be physically moved into different eras of the past.

This escape through time was achieved before the inevitable explosion of their sun. Each person would select the time-period that they prefered, then be treated to make them immune to the diseases and conditions of that time. They could never return safely to the present - not that there was anything worth returning, since Sarpedon is now a dead cinder hung in space. Kirk, Spock and McCoy were accidentally transmitted into the past of Sarpedon in their efforts to understand where the race had gone to. Since they had been unprocessed, they had to return to the present or perish. The three of them - Kirk in their medaevel period and McCoy and Spock deep in the prehistoric past - had a certain amount of trouble, but did return to library and escaped the world before the nova explosion.

SAYANA

Played by: Shari Nims
Episode: "The Apple"

Sayana was one of the Feeders of Vaal (see separate entry for further details). She and Makora became the first of the feeders to learn about sex.

Scalosians

Appearances: "Wink Of An Eye"

Scalos was a world that once was much like the Earth - until their native race polluted beyond endurance. What happened then was that a strange new drug was produced that affected all of its race, vastly accelerating their metabolism and spped. They lived their lives as far greater rates than before. Not only that, but all the males became sterile, so it looked as though the Scalosians were doomed to extinction.

A partial solution was discovered to the problem. Outside males could breed with the females and thus prolong the race. The Scalosians then set up a beacon to call for help, luring unwary travellers to their world. The same that affected the Scalosians was then used on their victimes, accelerating them to the same tempo as the natives. The problem is that while this drug was fine for the Scalosians, on outworlders it also increased their susceptibility to damage. The slightest cut in the skin would lead to rapid tissue degeneration and the death of the victim.

Whn the Scalosians discovered the Enterprise had answered their call, they saw this as a tremendous opportunity, for it contained hundreds of males - enough for their needs for centuries, with careful handling. They plan to keep the ship frozen, thawing out males as they are needed. Kirk, accelerated to their rate, buys time for the ship, and Spock manages to synthesize both the acceleratio drug and an antidote. They then defeat the Scalosians and slow everyone down to normal speed. Despite their hostility, Kirk promises these people Federation aid to overcome their sterility problem.

SCHMITTER

Played by: Biff Elliott
Episode: "The Devil In The Dark"

Schmitter was one of the Pergium miners on Janus VI, working under Vanderberg. He was killed by the Horta.

SCOTT, MONTGOMERY

Played by: James Doohan
Series regular

Montgomery Scott was the chief engineer of th Enterprise during her five year mission. A brilliant technician, he and Spock evolved many new techniques during their years together. After the mission, he was assigned to refurbishing the ship. An attempt later to transfer him out of the Enterprise failed, and he is back where he enjoys being the most - on the Enterprise.

SECURITY GUARDS

These tend, by the nature of their jobs, to be pretty transient.
Included are:
1) Played by: Eddie Paskey
Episode: "Where No Man Has Gone Before"
2) Played by: Jerry Foxworth
Episode: "Mudd's Women"
3) Played by: David L. Ross
Episodes: (1) "Miri"
(2) "Return Of The Archons"
(3) "The Trouble with Tribbles"
4) Played by Brett Dunham
Episode: "The Menagerie"
5) Played by: Joan Johnson
Episode: "Space Seed"
6) Played by: Bobby Bass
Episode: "Space Seed
7) Played by: Jon Cavett
Episode: "The Devil In The Dark"
8) Played by: Ron Veto
Episode: "The Alternative Factor"
9) Played by: Vince Canenti
episode: "The Alternative Factor"
10) Played by: Tom Lupo
Episode: "The Alternative Factor"
11) Played by: Bill Blackburn
Episode: "The Alternative Factor"
12) Played by: Michael Barrier
Episode: "The City On The Edge Of Forever"
13) Played by: Arnold Lessing
Episode: "The Changling"
14) Played by: Paul Prokop
Episode: "Mirror, Mirror"
15) Played by: Paul Baxley
Episode: "Assignment: Earth"
16) Played by: Dick Durock
Episode: "Elaan Of Troyius"
17) Played by: Charles Beck
Episode: "Elaan Of Troyius
18) Played by: Arell Blanton
Episode: The Savage Curtain"
19) Played by: John Bayer
Episode: :"Turnabout Intruder"
20) Played by Rod Perry
Story: "Star Trek - The Motion Picture"
21) Played by: John Dresden
Story: "Star Trek - The Motion Picture"
22) Played by: Joshua Gallegos
Story: "Star Trek - The Motion Picture"

Schlat

Appearances: "Yesteryear"

The sehlat is a large carnivore native to Vulcan. It has shaggy fur and six-inch teeth, yet can be domesticated. Young Vulcan children often keep sehlats as pets, as they can be fiercely loyal and protective.

SEPTIMUS

Played by: Ian Wolfe
Episode: "Bread And Circuses"

Septimus was the aged leader of the runaway slaves who were attempting to spread the message of Christianity to the Roman world (see separate entry for further details).

SEVEN, GARY

Played by: Robert Landing
Episode: "Assignment: Earth"

Gary Seven was a human taken from the Earth whilst young, and brought up on some alien world. He was then returned to Earthe in the Twentieth Century to help the planet through a difficult phase. Little is known of his sponsors, save that Isis (see separate entry) may be one of them.

SEVRIN

Played by: Skip Homeier
Episode: "The Way To Eden"

Doctor Sevrin was a being who hated technology, for he had become infected with a deadly disease that was artificial. He was a carrier, and not allowed to stray from technologically advanced worlds for fear he would infect other races. Sevrin hated this, and tried to convince himself that it was untrue. Hating technology, he preached a return to simplicity, as embodied in his own beliefs in a paradisical world called Eden. He and his followers managed to reach that world, to discover that it was more like hell than paradise. Sevrin perished there, eating an apple filled with acid.

SEVRIN'S FOLLOWERS

Played by: Deborah Downey, Phyllis Douglas
Episode: "The Way To Eden"

See also entries on: Adam, Irina, Tongo Rad.

SHAHNA

Played by Angelique Pettyjohn
Episode: "The Gamesters Of Triskelion"

Shahna was one of the thralls employed by the Providers (see separate entry for further details). She was assigned to train Kirk, but he managed to win through her emotions and interest her in matters other than fighting.

Shamin Priests

Appearances: "Star Trek - The Motion Picture"

Note: the Shamin Priests are one of a number of races whose appearances in the first film were eliminated.

They are members of the Federation, and vaguely avain in nature.

SHAW, AREEL

Played by: Joan Marshall
Episode: "Court Martial"

Areel Shaw was one of Kirk's old girl-friends. She served as the prosecuting attorney when Kirk was charged with murdering his old friend, Benjamin Finney.

SHEA

Played by: Carl Byrd
Episode: "By Any Other Name"

Lt. Shea was a security officer on the beam-down that met the Kelvans.

SHRAS

Played by: Reggie Nalder
Episode: "Journey To Babel"

Shras was an Andorian ambassador (see separate entry for further details).

SINGH

Played by: Blaisdell Makee
Episode: "The Changling"

Singh was a member of the "Enterprise" crew.

SIRAH

Played by: Irene Kelley
Episode: "The Omega Glory"

Sirah was the wife of Cloud William, of Omega IV (see separate entry for further details).

Skorr

Appearances: "The Jihad"

The Skorr are bird-like creatures from a planet named Skorr. They eveolved from predatory ancestors, and became a very militaristic species. Two hundred years ago, a revered religious leader, Alar, talked them into accepting hte way of peace, but this is a tenous thing. After his death, his personality was recorded onto an artifact known as the Soul of Skorr, to rrmind the Skorr of Alar's philosophies. As long as the Soul is retained, this will keep the Skorr in line. Should the Soul ever vanish, the Skorr are likely to return to their original warrior ways, and declare war on the rest of the Galaxy.

Slavers

Appearances: "The Slaver Weapon"

The Slavers were an unknown species who ruled the entire Galaxy something like a billion years ago. Then, somehow, they were completely annihilated. No-one knows for certain what they looked like, but they would seem to have been lizard-like beings. They had amazingly scientific society, and when they expired, they left behind a number of "Slaver Boxes". These are boxes in stasis fields, which contain anything - or nothing. Sometimes the most amazing things are found in these boxes, and sometimes there are bombs about to explode.

The only way to find such boxes are by pure accident, or by using another Slaver box as a detector. Two boxes in fairly close proximity to one another will glow.

SMITH, YEOMAN

Played by: Andrea Droom
Episode: "Where No Man Has Gone Before"

Yeoman Smith was Kirk's first assistant, before she was replaced by Janice Rand.

SONAK

Played by: Jon Kamal
Story: "Star Trek - The Motion Picture"

Lt. Commander Sonak was a full Vulcan science officer, destined to replace Spock on the "Enterprise." He was, however, killed during a transporter malfunction whilst attempting to beam aboard.

SPINELLI

Played by: Blaisdell Markee
Episode: "Space Seed"

A member of the "Enterprise" crew.

SPOCK

Played by: Leonard Nimoy
Series regular
Played by: Carl Steven, Vadia Potenza, Stephen Manley, Joe W. Davis
Star Trek III: The Search for Spock

Spock was the son of Sarek of Vulcan and Amanda Grayson. He joined Starfleet, to his father's disapproval, though they later reconciled. A brilliant scientist and logician, Spock was promoted to the captaincy of the Enterprise after the departures of Captain Decker and Admiral Kirk. He died saving the Enterprise from the Genesis effect. His mind was retained by McCoy and rejoined to a recreated body on the Genesis planet. He returned as science officer of the Enterprise. Spock later retired from Starfleet and joined the Federation diplomatic corps. Ambassador Spock went to Romulus to negotiate for Romulan-Vulcan reunification. The Enterprise commanded by Captain Picard came to his aide, but Spock chose to remain on Romulus.

Spores

Appearances: "This Side Of Paradise"

Technically, the spores of Omicron Ceti III are neither

aliens nor monsters, but they are some form of life that can affect humans. The spores are produced by plants, and can infect animal life. They are a benign parastical form, curing all ills in their hosts. They can regenerate body structure to repair damage, and they produce tranquility of mind and contentment. The only way to destory their effects, as Kirk discovered, is to produce strong feelings of anger in an infected person. Such surges kill the beningn spores and free the host. It is questionable as to whether or not this freedom is necessarily a good thing.

STARFLEET PERSONNEL

Over the years, a number of Starfleet Personnel have been shown.

These include"
(1)"Mr. Adventure"
Played by: Scott McGinnis
Story: "Star Trek III - The Search For Spock"
(2)Civilian Agent
Played by: Conroy Gedeon
Story: "Star Trek III _ The Search For Spock"
(3) Guards
Played by: Gary Faga, Dougglas Alan Shanklin
Story: "Star Trek III - The Search For Spock"
(4) Federation Council President
Played by: Robert Ellenstein
Story: "Star Trek IV - The Voyage Home"
(5)Communications Officer
Played by: Michael Snyder
Story: :"Star Trek IV - The Voyage Home"
(6)Display Officer
Played by: Michael Berryman
Story: "Star Trek IV - The Voyage Home"
(7)Alien Communications Officer
Played by: Jane Wiedlin
Story: "Star Trek IV - The Voyage Home"
(8)Controllers
Played by: Thaddeus Golas, Martin Pistone
Story: "Star Trek IV - The Voyage Home"
9. St. John Talbot, Nimbus III ambassador
Played by: David Warner
Story: "Star Trek V: The Final Frontier"
10. Starfleet chief of staff
Played by: Harve Bennett
Story: "Star Trek V: The Final Frontier"
11. Starfleet officer
Played by: Melanie Shatner
Story: "Star Trek V: The Final Frontier"
12. Federation president
Played by: Kurtwood Smith
Story: "Star Trek VI: The Undiscovered Country"
13. Adm. Cartwright
Played by: Brock Peters
Story: "Star Trek VI: The Undiscovered Country"
14. Excelsior communication officer
Played by: Grace Lee Whitney
Story: "Star Trek VI: The Undiscovered Country"
15. Excelsior officers
Played by: Christian Slater, Angelo Tiffe, and Jeremy Roberts
Story: "Star Trek VI: The Undiscovered Country"

STARNES, PROFESSOR

Played by: James Wellman
Episode: :"And the Children Shall Lead"

Professor Starnes was the leader of the science team on Triacus. He and the rest of the adults committed suicide at the instigation of Gorgan.

STARNES, TOMMY

Played by: Craig Hundley
Episode: "And the Children Shall Lead"

Tommy Starnes was the son of Professor Starnes, and one of the children deceived by Gorgan.

STEVE

Played by: Paul Comi
Episode: "Balance Of Terror"

Stiles was a navigator of the "Enterprise." His family had fought in the Romulan war, and he was convinced another was inevitable. When the Romulans turned out to be off-shoots of the Vulcans, Stiles made several nasty remarks about Spock, betraying his inner prejudices. When Spock finally saved Stiles' life, the navigator learned his lesson about judging without the facts.

STOCKER

Played by: Charles Drake
Episode: "The Deadly Years"

Commodore Stocker was appointed head of Star Base

10. On the way there in the "Enterprise," he was forced to assume command when a plague of aging struck the senior officers. His inexperience in the field severly endangered the crew when he attempted to cross the Romunlan neutral zone. He was more than happy to relinquish command back to Kirk.

STONE

Played by: Percy Rodriguez
Episode: "Court Martial"

Postmaster Stone was in charge of Star Base 11 when Kirk was tried on charges of killing his old, Benjamin Finney. He replaced Commodore Mendez in that post.

STONN

Played by: Lawrence Montaigne
Episode: "Amok Time"

Stonn was the lover of T'Pring, the woman Spock was supposed to marry on Vulcan. T'Pring prefered Stonn because he was more controllable than Spock, and thus better for her ambitions.

STRATOSIANS

Episode: "The Cloud Minders"
Various inhabitants were shown, including:
Cooud Guards
Played by: Kirk Raymone, Jimmy Fields, Harve Selsby

See also separate entries on: Plasus, Droxine, Vanna.

The inhabitants of Stratos long ago lived on the surface of their world. As they achieved industrial society, the race began to diverge. Miners, who worked below the surface, tended to have lower IQ's and acted very emotionally. As the centuries wore on, this began to seem to the surface-dwelling Stratosians to be a racial matter, and that the Trogs (as they named theworkers) were actually an inferior race. The surface dwellers planned and constructed a beautiful city that floated in the clouds, far above the surface of their world. Though the Trogs did the actual work, the only people permitted to dwell in the city of Stratos were the ones with the higher intellects. Some workers for servants were selected from the Trogs, and some Trogs were born and raised in the city. These Trogs proved to have surprisingly high IQs and - not surprisingly- and intense dislike of the established social order.

Clashes between the Trog agitators and the elders of Stratos grew worse and worse all the time. Finally, when Kirk and Spock arrived for a much-needed shipment of minerals, the activists attempted to use the aliens as bargaining tools. Kirk became embroiled in the controversy, and McCoy discovered that the reason for the Trogs' low IQ had nothing to do with heredity - there was an invisible, ordpless gas in the mines that retarded their development. This was why Trogs born in Stratos were so much more intelligent - they were not exposed to the gas. McCoy developed a small air filter to remove the problem for the miners, and Kirk extracted a promise from the Stratosians that the Trogs would become full members of the Ardanan race.

The dwellers of Stratos were lovers of science, harmony and art. Their calm, ordered society is now being changed by the infusion of the Trogs - but not for the worse.

STYLES

Played by: James B. Sikking
Story: "Star Trek III - The Search For Spock"

Captain Styles was the ultra-neat, by-the-book, intensely proud commander of the "Excelsior."

SULU

Played by: George Takei
Series regular

Sulu was assigned to the Enterprise originally as part of the science team but later reassigned as her helmsman. He has a dash of romantic blood. He is proficient in combat and fiercely loyal to his ship. After all his years on the Enterprise, Starfleet promoted and reassigned him to captain the Excelsior starship.

SURAK

Played by: Barry Atwater
Epsidoe: "The Savage Curtain"

Surak was the Vulcan leader responsible for their adoption of the Rule for Logic. See separate entry for further information.

SURVIVORS

Played by: Anthony Jochim, Leonard Mudie
Episode: "The Cage"

Survivors of the ill-fated exploratory party led by Dr. Haskins from the American Continental Institute that crashed onto Talos IV. Actually, only Vina survived; the rest of the "survivors" were images produced by the telepathic Talosians.

SYBO

Played by: Pilar Seurat
Episode: "Wolf In The Fold"

Sybo was an empath, married to Jaris, prefect of Argelias II (see separate entry for further details).

SYBOK

Played by: Laurence Luckinbill
Star Trek V: The Final Frontier

Sybok is half-brother of Spock from Sarek's first marriage prior to Amanda. Rather than follow the traditional Vulcan path of logic, Sybok embraced an alternate mysticism which includes an unusual form of mind control. The ultimate goal of this mysticism is to reach God at ShaKaRee. In this quest, Sybok takes hostages on Nimbus III and then comandeers the Enterprise. They travel to ShaKaRee, where a mysterious "God-like" being does exist, but is evil in nature. Sybok realizes the foolishness of his ways and attempts to kill the God-creature with his mind-control, but dies in the process.

SYLVIA

Played by: Antoinette Bower
Episode: "Cats-Paw"

Sylvia was one of the two Transmuters (see separate entry for further details).

SYLVIA

Played by: Bonnie Beecher
Episode: "Spectre Of The Gun"

Sylvia was one of the illusions created by the Melkotian (see separate entry for further details.

TAL

Played by: Jack Donner
Episode: "The Enter prise Incident"

A Romulan Sub-Commander.

TALOSIANS

Played by: Georgia Schmidt, Serena Sand, Meg Wyllie
Episode: "The Cage"

The natives of Talos IV are highly evolved creatures. Though humanoid in appearance their vastly-increased brain size has resulted in the heads being oversized. Veins stand out on their naked skulls. Their brains are so advanced that they communicate primarily by telepathy with one another at high speed. Their evolution into this state of genius has caused them much emotional loss, however. Emotions are raw, unprocessed thoughts that they have eliminated from their lives, and yet regret losing. They look down on less evolved humanoid species as being very little different from the animals about them. Their magnified brain-power makes it simple for the Talosians to implant realistic-seeming illusions into the minds of such beings.

Their loss of emotions concerned them, as they rapidly became bored with their environment. They decided to build a menagerie and to populate it with human beings after the crash-landing of an Earth ship onto their world. They had only one survivor to work with, a young girl called Vina. Because of their lack of knowledge, they managed to save her life and reassembled her - but not as the beautiful creature that she once was. Instead, she became twisted and deformed, scarred and ugly. To protect her mind, they gave her the illusion of beauty and mobility again.. They then set about trapping a mate for her - selecting the young Captain Christopher Pike for that purpose.

Pike refused to acceed to their plans as Vina had done, and discovered that they could not read his mind if he had volent thoughts - such strong emotions effectively blocking their comprehension. Though he could only see what they allowed him to see, he managed to force the Keeper to reveal what was real behind

all of the fraud. The Talosians realized that humans simply were too fond of freedom to be kept as "breeding stock" for the pleasure of an alien race. They allowed Pike to leave eventually, though retaining Vina and allowing her the pleasure of the illusion of her beauty.

Years later, when Pike was injured in a terrible accident and confined in a wrecked body, Spock returned the Enterprise to Talos IV and the Talosians, now a wiser and more gentle race for having had contact with the humans, took Pike with them, giving him the illusion of his youth and virility back for the remainder of his days. Clearly, the Talosians had learned compassion and concern from the humans - and realized that simple intellect without caring was worthless.

TAMAR

Played by: Jon Lormer
Episode: "The Return Of The Archons"

Tamar was a member of the resistance fighting against the power of Landru and his Lawgivers. Tamar mocked Landru's power, but was betrayed by Hacom to the Lwgivers, who killed the old man.

TAMOON

Played by: Jane Ross
Episode: "The Gamesters Of Triskelion"

Tamoon was one of the thralls of the Providers (see separate entry for further details). She was assigned to train Chekov, and developed a (literal perhaps) crush on him.

TAMULA

Played by: Miko Mayama
Episode: "A Taste of Armageddon"

Tamula was an ensign on the "Enterprise," one of the party captured on Eminiar VII. When Kirk and rest escaped, Tamula was left to guard Mea Three until Eminiar's war was over.

TANKIS

Played by: Judy McConnell
Episode: "Wolf In The Fold"

Yeoman Tankis was a member of the crew of the "Enterprise."

TARK

Played by: Joseph Bernard
Episode: "Wolf In The Fold"

Tark was a native of Argelias II (see separate entry for further details). He was the father of Kara.

Taureans

Appearances: "The Lorelei Signal"

A small colony of people attempted to settle on the planet Taurus (no connection with Taurus II, for which see the next entry). Something n the world, however, drained their life energies. The women discovered that with small devices, they could syphon off life-energies from men, and so extend their own lives by 27 years. At the end of that time, they had to lure further males to their world, which they did through a signal. This was specifically designed to appeal only to men, women hearing nothing at all. When the men arrived, they would be drained of thier life-forces, and these were used to recharge the women. When the Taureans attempted this on the Enterprise crew, they snared many of the males, but the females managed to turn the tables. They restored the drained males, and Kirk arranged for the Federation to collect the Taureans and transport them to a less deadly world.

Taurus Primitives

Appearances: "The Galileo Seven"

Taurus II is a small world near the heart of the quasar-like Murasaki 312. The only native creatures as yet detected by visitors are huge, hairy creatures standing about twelve feet high. Their level of intelligence is hard to assertain, since they appear to possess clothing

and weapons of primitive kind. Yet they do not seem to have any real grasp of language, though thhey do band together to hunt. What manner of creatures they might hunt is unknown, but it clearly must be something both huge and ferocious enough for them to need some primitive form of communal life.

Since the only recorded visitors to this planet were the seven crewmembers of the shuttle "Galileo, " and since they were forced to land under adverse conditions, no scientivic study of these primitives has ever been made. Hence, very little is knon about them or their behavior.

TAYLOR, Dr. GILHAN

Played by: Catherine Hicks
Story: "Star Trek IV - The Voyage Home"

Dr. Gillian Taylor was an expert on whales, working at the Cetacean Institute under Bob Briggs. Frustated by the failure to protect the whales, she helped Kirk to take her two favorite whales into the future. This both saved and also gave the whales a new chance at survival. Gillian went with Kirk when he returned to the future, and was assigned a job on a science ship, helping this time to ensure that the whales survived.

TECHNICIAN

Played by: Libby Erwin
Episode: "The Lights Of Zetar"

The technician was one of the people on the library planetoid of Memory Alpha who was killed by the Lights of Zetar (see separate entry for further details).

TELLARITE

Played by: Gary Downey
Episode: "Whom Gods Destroy"

See also separate entry on Gav.
Appearances: "Journey To Babel"
"Whom Gods Destroy"
"The Time Trap"

Tellarites are lesser members of the Federation of Plantets. They look rather like bipedal pigs with beards, and are noted for being argumentative, rude and arrogant. There was a Tellarite in the assylum on Elba II with the insane Garth of Izar (see entry on Antosians). Among the inhabitants of the strange region of space known as the Delta Triangle was a ship full of Tellarites.

TEPO

Played by: John Harmon
Episode: "A Piece Of The Action"

Tepo was one of the mobsters on Sigma Iota II (see separate entry for further details).

Terratins

Appearances: "The Terratin Incident"

In the very early years of space flight, some human colony ships simply vanished and were never found. One or two of these ships actually made planetfall. One of those was on a world named Terra Ten. Over the centuries, the people built a magnificent city, but strange radiations from the planet shrank the natives of the world down to one sixteenth of an inch. Their name became corrupted to Terratin. Their planet proved to be geologically unstable, and they managed to contactj the Enterprise for help in transporting to a new, safer world - Verdanis.

TERRELL, CLARK

Played by: Paul Winfield
Story: "Star trek II - The Wrath Of Khan"

Captain Terrell was the commander of the scout ship "Reliant." He and Chekov were captured by Khan and subjected to having Ceti eels placed into their ears to render them docile. Terrel was later ordered to kill Kirk, but could not do it. To avoid the agony the refusal caused him, he commінted suicide with his own phaser.

THANN

Played by: Willard Sage
Episode: "The Empath"

Thann was a Vian (see separate entry for further details).

THARN

Played by: Vic Perrin
Episode: "Mirror, Mirror"

Tharn was the ruler of the Halcons. (See separate entry for further details.)

THASIAN

Played by: Abraham Sofaer
Episode: "Charlie X" Appearances: "Charlie X"

Thasus is a strange world, one long listed as officially devoid of intelligent life. However, Thasians do exist, being creatures of pure mentality. Without bodies, they are free intellects, and can cross boundaries of space and time. However, being without bodies has meant that they have lost many emotions, and are devoid of the possiblilities of warmth the contact. This does not concern them overly, but has caused a problem with their human "adopted child.: The craft carrying three-year old Charlie Evans crashed on Thasus, leaving only Charlie alive. There was now way that Charlie could survive without help, and the Thasians freely gave it. They taught Charlie how to survive by unlocking the inherent potential of his mind. He was taught to manipulate reality, to unlock doors into other dimensions, and to control matter.

This was vital for him to survive on Thasus, but Charlie was found and "rescued" by an Earth ship. Charlie had never learned to interact with those of lesser abilities than himself, and he soon began to realize that his abilities far outstrepped those of other humans. This god-like power he possessed, coupled with his emotional immaturity, went to his head. He seized control of the Enterprise, forcing its crew to acceed to his demands. The Thasians realized that though they had made Charlie able to survive with them, he was totally unsuited for interaction with his own species. They reached out to take him back to them, to Charlie;s horror. Their remote intellects offered him neither warmth nor love - but this was unavoidable. The Thasians could never allow so storng a creature as Charlie to intrude into human space. They had saved his life - and condemned him to utter despair in return. As a result of this realization the Thasians have cut off all contacr with lesser races, never wishing to cause such unwitting harm again.

THELEV

Played by: Willaim O'Connell
Episode: "Journey To Babel"

Theleve was supposedly an Andorian ambassador, but was actually an Orion spy (see relevant entries in separate entry for further details).

THERAPISTS

Played by: Eli Behar, Walt Davis
Episodes: "Dagger Of The Mind"

Two of the workers at the Tantalus Penal Colony, controlled by Dr. Tristan Adams.

Thetans

Appearances: "BEM"

The natives of Delta Theta III are tribal savages. They are not exactly sentient yet, but are being guided on their way by a strange being, a disembodied energy entity. It believes that the Thetans are capable of such advancement. The Federation has agreed to place the planet under interdict to avoid interference with this being's attempts to spark intelligence among the native race.

Tholians

Appearances: "The Tholian Web"

The Tholians are a very territorial species, and not at all willing to meed or communicate with other races. Virtually nothing is known of them, save that they "see" in a different part of the electromagnetic specturm than most races do. This means that their true appearance is very odd to human eyes. They have a sophisticated science, of unknown form, that seems highly effective.

THOMPSON

Played by Julie Cobb
Episode: "By Any Other Name"

Yeoman Thompson was a member of the "Enterprise" crew who was killed by the Kelvan leader, Rojan.

Tiburans

Appearances: "The Savage Curtain"

The people of Tiburan are for the most part a savage folk. They have however begun to experiment in sciențivic ways. One leader, Zora, is particularly noted for her cruelty. She ran savage genetic experiments on her own tribe. such is the abhorance in which she is held that he name is famed Galaxy-wide as one of the most evil beings of all time.

TIMOTHY

Played by: Winston DeLugo
Episode: "Court Martial"

Mr. Timothy was a member of the "Enterprise" crew.

TOMAR

Played by: Robert Fortier
Episode: By Any Other Name"

Tomar was one of the Kelvans (see separate entry for further details). Scott managed to get him blind drunk.

TOMLINSON, ROBERT

Played by: Stephen Mines
Episode: "Balance Of Terror"

Tomsinson was the head of the phaser crew of the "Enterprise." He was about to wed his pretty assistant, Angela Martine, when a Romulan attack broke out. In the subsequent battle, Tomlinson was killed.

TORG

Played by: Stephen Liska
Story: "Star Trek III - The Search For Spock"Torg was Kruge's second in command. He was killed boarding the "Enterprise".

TORMOLEN, JOE

Played by: Stewart Moss
Episode: "The Naked Time"

Joe Tormolen was one of the "Enterprise" crew who beamed down to Psi 2000 to investigate the deaths of the scientific team stationed there. He became infected by the water there, which caused great depressions. Back on the "Enterprise, " he became very despondent, believing men should never venture into space. He stabbed himself with a knife, and was rushed to sickbay. Though his wound wasn't all that serious, he died simply because he was too depressed to get better.

T'PAU

Played by: Celia Lovsky
Episode: "Amok Time"

T;Pau was the matriarch of Spock's family, and one of Vulcan's most revered Elders. She is the only person ever to have refused a seat on the Federation Council.

T'PRING

Played by: Arlene Martel
Episode: "Amok Time"

T'Pring was the Vulcan woman that Spock was mindlinked to marry. She was too independant to accept being in his shadow, and preferred Stonn. Accordingly, she asks Kirk to be her champion against Spock, knowing that if Kirk wins, he wouldn;t want her. T'Pring was a supremely pragmatic female.

TRACY, KAREN

Played by: Virginia Aldridge
Episode: "Wolf In The Fold"

Karen Tracy was a member of the "Enterprise" crew. She was a specialist with a psychotricorder, and became

the second victim of Rejak.

TRACY, RONALD

Played by: Morgan Woodward
Episode: "The Omega Glory"

Captain Ronald Tracy was the captain of the "USS Exeter," one of the sister ships to the "Enterprise." His crew were all wiped out on Omega IV by a deadly virus. Tracy survived only because he stayed on the surface instead of returning to his ship, and the natural agents in the air cured him. Having lost his crew, he became obsessed with the supposed immortality that some of the Omegans possessed. When Kirk opposed him, Tracy attempted to have the natives kill him. Instead, Kirk won and arrested Tracy to stand court-martial for his actions.

TRADER

Played by: Guy Raymond
Episode: "The trouble with Tribbles"

The trader was the proprietor of the bar on Deep Space STation K7. He was an opportunist and something of a con-artist — more than a match for a dishonest trader like Cyrano Jones.

TRANSMUTERS

Appearances: "Catspaw"

Beings from another Galaxy, two Transmuters known as Sylvia and Korob are sent to Purus in Federation space to discover whether their race could conquer the Federation and colonize our Galaxy. They have a machine, the Transmuter, than can alter their physical appearances, and also give them vast amounts of power at their fingertips. They normally appear to be tiny creatures that could never survive in a normal atmospher, and when a landing party comes into range, they capture the humans, adopt forms that seem familiar to them and then begin to test them. They take from the minds of Sulu and Scott the deep dark fears of magic and terror, and set up a castle filled with horrors. They capture Kirk, Spock and McCoy and set about examining them.

Sylvia is dissatisfied with the lack of senations experienced by her race, and enjoys the control of feelings that she has in her female form. She tries seduction on Kirk, but he simply uses her to get information. She is giving way too much to emotions, and Korob is afraid that she is unhinged by what she is experiencing. He helps the crew to escape, and Kirk smashes the wand used to channel the power of the Transmuter. This destroys the artificial environment the aliens had established, and they revert to their natural forms and perish.

TREFAYNE

Played by: David Hillary Hughes
Episode: "Errand of Mercy"

One of the ruling Council of Organia. See separate entry for further details.

TRELANE

Played by: William Campbell
Episode: "The Squire of Gothos"

Vast disembodied creatures exist all over the Universe, beings of pure mentality. One such race gave rise to the chld-creature Trelane. Its parents, wishing Trelane to discover the methods and joys of the manipulation of matter, allowed him to play on a world that they formed in Quadrant 904, not realizing that they were near any inhabited worlds. They then left Trelane to amuse himself. Trelane used his limited (by the standards of his own people only) powers to scan the Quadrant, and discovered with joy the primitive world of Earth. Being a child, he did not realize that what he was seeing was hundreds of years in the past, having no idea of the problems of light delay over astronomical distances. The primitive nature of the humans and their barbaric customs pleased him, and he promptly used his abilities to reform part of his playworld to correspond to an English castle, and he himself adopted the dress and mannerisms of a Squire.

The Enterprise happened upon this anomalous planet, affording much delight to Trelane, who recognized its crew as being humans — inhabitants of his favorite planet, here to play with! Being a child, his ideas of play were frankly violent, selfish and rude. Like many children, he threw temper trantrums when denied his wishes, and finally, realizing that he was more powerful than Kirk or the others, simply began to abuse his power to torture and overpower them. At this point, his parents realized that their offspring was causing problems, and returned to take him home again. In a display of casual ability, they returned all things to their rightful order and removed Trelane — he had played enough for the time being...

TRELANE'S PARENTS

Played by: Barbara Babcock, James Doohan
Episode: "The Squire of Gothos"

TRIBBLES

Appearances: "The Trouble with Tribbles"
"More Tribbles, More Troubles"

Tribbles are small creatures that are all fur and fecundity. Little balls of colored fur, they are a gentle species that respond to affection with a warm purring sound which is appealing to humans but repulsive to Klingons (see separate entry). Apart from purring, Tribbles do only two things: eat and breed. Tribbles have a voracious appetite, especially for grains, and will eat almost continually. However, this does not cause a Tribble to get fat — what happens instead is that they breed.

McCoy hazarded a guess that Tribbles are born pregnant, which is close to the truth. Tribbles are asexual creatures that simply begin breeding almost as soon as they are born, and have eaten sufficient to begin growth of babies. As soon as those babies are born, they start eating — and begin forming further young. In their native environment (wherever that is) sufficient predators exist to keep the Tribble population fairly stable. In uncontrolled environments, however, Tribbles simply suffer an incredible population explosion. Though harmless in and of themselves — in fact, they are very pleasant pets since they consume all that they ingest — they wreak havoc simply by eating everything in sight, and getting into everything.

The Klingons, desting the Tribbles, developed a spider-like creature to devour the Tribbles, called a glommer. Cyrano Jones, who had caused the initial problems with the Tribbles by spreading them into human space, stole the glommer for his own use. He also managed to breed what he thought was a safe Tribble — one that simply grew when fed. It turned out that he was wrong about this, since the large Tribble wasn't a single individual, but a colony that would split apart into hundreds of smaller Tribbles.

TROGS

Episode: "The Cloud Minders"

Various Trogs were seen, including:
Prisoner
Played by: Garth Pillsbury

See also entries on: Vanna, Midro, Roka

For further information, see the entry on Stratosians.

TROI, LT. CMDR. DEANNA

Played by: Marina Sirtis
Series regular

Deanna Troi is "ship's counselor" aboard the Enterprise, which basically makes her "ship's psychologist", offering assistance to the captain and crew alike. Troi is half human, half Betazoid. The Betazoid race is telepathic, but Troi's human elements make her only "empathic", able only to read emotions of others. This talent is useful in her job. Her mother is the meddlesome but loving Lwaxana. Before coming to the Enterprise, she was involved in a romance with Will Riker.

TROYIANS

Appearances: "Elaan of Troyius"

The two wor
lds of Troyius and Elas (see separate entry on Elasians) were at war for centuries, until both sides evolved the scientific prowess that would enable them to totally obliterate the other. Both parties then realized that their best solution would be to declare peace. Accordingly, the ruler of Troyius agreed to marry the Dohlman of Elas to cement the peace. This was despite the distaste that all Troyians felt for the savage Elasians.

Troyians are lovers of art and science, whilst the Elasians honor and respect only warfare. Troyians thus consider the other race to be crude, unsophisticated barbarians, barely one step up from animals. Since the Elasians consider the Troyians to be effete fools, the length of the war is hardly surprising. However, Elaan, Dohlman of the Elasians, finally learned to accept that civilization had some advantages, and reluctantly agreed to see through the terms of the treaty — as opposed to simply knifing her husband-to-be in the back the first opportunity that arose.

TULA

Played by: Brioni Farrell
Episode: "The Return of the Archons"

Tula was the daughter of Reger. She joined in the Festival of Landru, actually an extended orgy of sex and violence.

TYLER, JOSE

Played by: Peter Duryea
Episode: "The Cage"

Jose "Joe" Tyler was the navigator on the "Enterprise" under Christopher Pike.

TYREE

Played by: Michael Whitney
Episode: "A Private Little War"

Tyree was the leader of the hill people of Neural (see separate entry for further details). He was Kirk's friend from a previous trip there.

UHURA

Played by: Nichell Nichols
Series Regular

Uhura was the communcations officer for the Enterprise. A bright, cheerful lady, she was also an accomplished and admired singer. She is currently assigned to the second Enterprise.

UHURA'S CREWMAN

Played by: Vince Howard
Episode: "The Man Trap"

The salt vampire of M113 read Uhura's mind when aboard the "Enterprise," and fabricated a crewmember that would be Uhura's ideal. Its attack on Uhurais aborted, however.

VAAL

Appearances: "The Apple"

The people of Gamma Triangulae VI decided that they would have to have a perfect society, and built a computer to control their planetary environment completely. This computer they naed Vaal. It could control the weather, and would grow food for them. In return, the people are Feeders of Vaal. There are unstable rocks on the planet that explode, and Vaal gains his energy from these. Because of the amount of control he exerts over the planetary biosphere, Vaal needs regual fuel supplies. The Feeders he keeps in what Vaal considers to be a perfect state. They never age, nor grow sick, nor die. To maintain a small, stable population, he has forbidden the Feeders to have sex.

Kirk and his men stumble into the setup, and Kirk believes that Vaal is repressing the growth of these people, since they seem to have no ambition nor drive. He is attacked by Vaal, and retaliates by withholding the power stones. Vaal finally runs out of stored power and is destroyed. The Feeders are freed to evolve without control, to become their own people — and to indulge in death, disease and sex again.

LT. VALERIS

Played by: Kim Cattrall
Star Trek VI

Valeris is a protege of Spock that was posted to the Enterprise during the Klingon peace mission. Only later was it revealed that she was one of the co-conspirators attempting to sabotage the conference.

VALKRIS

Played by: Cathie Shirriff

Story: "Star Trek III — The Search for Spock" Valkris was the Klingon agent used by Kruge to get him information on the Genesis Project. She informed him that she had seen the material, and knew he would be forced to kill her for it.

VANDERBERG

Played by: Ken Lynch
Episode: "The Devil in the Dark"

Vanderberg was the administrative head of the Pergium mining colony on Janus VI. His miners were being killed by the Horta, and he called in help from the "Enterprise." Kirk and Spock managed to communicate with the creature, and discovered that it was only protecting its young. They negotiated a mutually profitable relationship between the Hora and Vanderberg, who was sorry for the problems he and his men had accidentally caused.

van GELDER, DR. SIMON

Played by: Morgan Woodward
Episode: "Dagger of the Mind"

Dr. Simon van Gelder was the director of the Tantalus Penal Colony. His assistant, Dr. Tristan Adams, de-

veloped a machine called the neural neutralizer, which isolated a person's brain from outside stimuli, leaving him open to the slightest suggestion. Adams used the machine of van Gelder, driving him insane. Van Gelder managed to escape to the "Enterprise," his insanity alerting Kirk that tere was a problem on the colony. Spock and McCoy between them pieced together the story and helped cure van Gelder. When Adams died from his own machine, van Gelder destroyed the device and restored order to the Penal Colony.

VANNA

Played by: Charlene Polite
Episode: "The Cloud Minders"

Vanna was the revolutionary leader of the Trogs, fighting the cloud city of Stratos (see separate entry for further details).

Vedala

Appearances: "The Jihad"

The Vedala are a very ancient race, and developed space travel centuries before any other living race. They are incredibly shy, however, and virtually never have contact with other species. They ten to travel on converted asteroids, now established witha force shield and cloaking device to prevent other races from ever finding them. Only very rarely, and in cases of emergency, will they ever contact other races.

Vendoran

Appearances: "The Survivor"

The Vendorans are tall beings with many tentacles, and the strange ability to change into anything they choose. They have very little concept of morality, and tend to absorb what personality they have from anyone who has been in close contact with them for a while. Vendor is offlimits under Federation edicts, due to the problems that Vendorans cause. It is, however, sufficiently close to Romulan space for the Romulans occassionally to use Vendorans to spy on the Federation. The drawback is that while Vendorans are loyal to the Romulans when they are close to the Romulans, as soon as they spend some time with other species, they switch their loyalties also. This makes them very poor spies over any extended periods.

V'Ger

Appearances: "Star Trek - The Motion Picture"

Voyager 6 was launched by NASA in the late 20th Century, to seek out new worlds for possibile colonization, and to transmit the data back to Earth. However, not too long into the mission, Voyager entered the field of a black hole, and was flung thousands of light years away. NASA assumed it had been destroyed, but it hadn't quite. It was badly damaged when it returned to real space, but sill "alive." It emerged near to a world composed of sentient machines. They recovered Voyager, and scanned it.

The machines could tell its purpose, and realized that it was vastly underequipped for the mission. They began to rebuild it, adding in tremendous potential that it had never possed before. To return to Earth and report, it would need better scanning gear, defenses, propulsion... The machines rebuilt Voyager as V'Ger, because many of its records hadbeen destroyed in the accident. Their enthusiasm for the project resulted in a huge entity, literally miles across, which had become self-aware. V'Ger started back towards the far-distant home it vaguely recalled, and scanned as it passed along, recording everyghing in data form inside its own being. As it travelled, it felt a vast longing - fo9r something it could not understand . Its purpose of reporting its data was still there, but it need much, much more than that. It sought its creator, and wanted to understand both logic and purpose. There hadj to reasons for all things, and it wanted to understand them. Because it was a maehine, V'Ger believed that its creator was a machine. It simply could not understand that small biological units might also be living beings.. The ships that they travelled the stars in seemed far more likely.

Entering Klingon space, V'Ger encountered small, almost insignifican attacks. It calmly destroyed the gnats, and moved on. Three Romulan cruisers had been annihilated. It's ultimate destination loomed ahead when it encountered the retarded "being" it perceived as the Enterprise. It could not understand, though, why this being allowed itself to be infested with useless biologicals, so it captured, analyzed and duplicated one of these beings as a probe unit for itself. This probe unit, Ilia, retained some of its fleshly attributes, and as V'Ger analyzed the data from it, it gradually realized that these biological units had in fact been its original creators. Appalled, V'Ger decided that the only way to understand such insanity was to join with a biological units had in fact been its original creators. Appalled, V'Ger decided taht the only way to understand such insanity was to join with a biological unit. Decker volunteered, and he, Ilia and V'Ger become one new being with unknown powers. together, this new creation vanished.

Vians

Apparances: "The Empath"

Minara II is a star that is home to several races. One of these is a vey advanced society, the Vians. They have intellectual abilities that far out strip their moral senses. Realizing that their sun is about to go nova, they abandon their home world, and prepare to depart for the stars. They can save one, but only one, of the the other races - and have to decide which of them is the worthiest. To do this, they take Gem, an Empath (see separate entry) and force her to make the decision as to whether or not her compassion for others can outweigh her fear. Gem proves that it can, when she is forced to save McCoy from death by risking her life. Kirk shames the Vians into that Gem has more compassion than they have, and they agreee to rescue her along with their own.

VINA

Played by: Susan Oliver
Episode: "The Cage"

Vina was the sole survivor of the ill-fated American Contintntal Institute expedition that crash landed on Talos IV. The natives discovered her close to death and rebuilt her. Not knowing human anatomy, they botched the job, leaving her scared and ugly. The Talosians have immenst mental powers, and gave her the illusion of beauty back. When they wished to breed humans, they selected Captain Christopher Pike for her. Pike's will defeated them, but they allowed Vina the illusion of his company. After Pike's accident, he returned himself to Vina and joined her in her mental freedom.

VULCANS

In the series, a number of different Vulcans have been featured.
These include:
(1) Vulcan Executioner
Played by: Russ Peek
Episode: "Amok Time"
(2) Vulcan Litterbearers
Played by: Mark Russell, Gary Wright, Joe Paz, Charles Palmer
Episode: "Amok Time"
(3) Vulcan Bell & Banner Carriers
Played by Frank Vinci, Mauri Russell, Dave Perna
Episode: "Amok Time"
(4) Vulcan Masters
Played by: Edna Gover, Paul Weber, Norman Stuart
Story: "Star Strek - The Motion Picture"
(5) Child
Played by: Katherine Blum
Story: "Star Trek III - The Search For Spock"
(6) High Priestess
Played by: Judith Anderson
Story: "Star Trek III - The Search For Spock"

See separate entries on: T'Pring, T'Pau, Stonn, Sarek, Surak.
Appearances: As a race: "Amok Time'
"Yesteryear"
"The Time Trap"
"Star Trek - The Motion Picture"
"The Search For Spock"
"The voyage Home"
Spock: all voyages
Sarek: "Journey To Babel"
"Yesteryear"
"The Search For Spock"
"The Voyage Home"
Surak: "The Savage Curtain"

The Vulcans were the race first contacted byt he humans as they expanded into space. The two races form the core of the Federation, for despite their differences, they remain firm friends and possess much in common.

In the past, the Vulcans were a warlike race, dedicated to warfare and glorying in combat. This constant lust for fighting brought the fledgling society to the brink of chaos, even as it began to colonize the stars. One offshoot of this colonization plan is the Romulan race (see separate entry). It becam clear to the Vulcans, however, that their rage and warfare would tear their civilization apart, and a new way for them had to be found. One philosopher, revered now above all others, came up with the only answer: the way of total devotion to logic. It was the emotions that were the cause of lust, savagery and anger, therefore the emotions had to be suppressed. The Vulcans realized that this was the only way that their race could survive, by controlling the emotions.

This had to begin from birth and the race dedicated itself to the task. Each child was brought up in control of his or her emotions. Vulcans possess emotions, contrary to many beliefs, but they are never allowed control of the personality. Vulcans allow only logic to be their guide. Subjecting themselves to the rigorous discipline of logic to be their guide. Subjecting themselves to the rigorous discipline of logic, the Vulcans rapidly matured

as a society. All warfare ceased, as did all crime, as the entire race adapted to this new way. Military training was still the norm for all Vulcans, for they knew that not all races would embrace peace as willingly as they themselves had. However, their system of logic dictated the philosophy of IDIC: Infinite Diversity in Infinite Combination. To the Vulcans, everything is worth the knowing, and every race has its own inner beauty. It is the belief of live and let live taken to its deepest degree: Vulcans believe that all races should be different, because each difference adds to the glory of the Universe.

Naturally, the Vulcans, revering logic as they do, hold the study of science to be the greatest pursuit. The Vulcan Academy of Science is known throughout the Galaxy for its studies and for the wealth of research done there. Though the Vulcans are members of the Federation, they do not make good administrators - they prefer to be scientists, linguists and diplomats, leaving the administrative posts to more aggressive species like the humans. The Vulcans, being logical, do not worry about taking orders; they know that they excell at science, and that the humans seem better equipped to policy decisions.

Despite their burial of their emotions, ;the Vulcans have not done away entirely with it. They can allow themselves to experience emotions should they chose to do so - and almost all of them feel love of beauty, and the affection of family and friends. It is done quietly and without the display that humans tend to indulge in, but the affection is not less strong for all of that. There is one way that they cannot chose their emotions, however: ponn farr. The sex drive, though sublimated in male Vulcans, is still strong, and expresses itself in a violent outburst every seven years. At this time, the Vulcan male must mate or die. The need for a female of his race is too great to be denied, and if he is unable to engage in sexual congress, the strains of emotion within his body will literally kill him. Vulcans are ashamed of this reversion to the primitive, and few outworlders know of this.

Vulcans do however attempt to add logic even to this. Since a Vulcan male in the grip of ponn farr must mate, the obvious result of such desire would be that of raping the first female he came across. To prevent such anarchy and violence, Vulcan parents chose brides for their sons before they reach puberty. Vulcan mental powers are then used to fix the image of the bride-to-be in the youth's mind, so that even in the grip of ponn farr, there will be only the one person that he will seek - his mate. There are problems with such a system - for example, in the case of Spock. His chosen was T'Pring, but T'Pring did not wish to mate with Spock. Her own ambition was for a less famed and more pliable mate. Instead, she invoked ritual law. If the female has another choice for her mate, the two males must meet in combat to the death. Since the male in ponn farr is too far gone from logic to fight in other way, the fights must be until one or other is killed..

This system of mating does not preclude other, more logical ways. Sometimes the bride-to-be has died, for example, or a Vulcan is widowed. In such cases, a Vulcan male may wed any other Vulcan. In case of Sarek, he shose a human, Amanda Grayson. Their mixed-breed son, Spock, was a result of this very unusual union, and Spock shares traits of both races, though his Vulcan heritage is stronger. (This discussion is not deliberately excluding the will of the females - they do not suffer from ponn farr and thus can select their mates at any time.) Though Vulcan males are forced to mate every seven years, this does not mean that they cannot perform sexually between such attacks - though many off-worlders assume that this is so..

Vulcan dedication to science includes the science of the mind, and they have developed strong telepathic powers. They can mind-meld - a joining of their own with that of another being for an exchange of information, or to help the other being to gain control of its own mind. They can communicate telepathically with one another over short distances. With non-telepathic species they can best suggest thoughts into the minds of that person.

Their scientific method has also extended into the field of combat. They are well trained in their native historic fighting impliments, but prefer a form of unarmed combat, turning their own powerful bodies into weapons. They know many ways to kill but prefer to render other beings unconscious with the "nerve pinch." This is partly a physical attack on a nerve center, and partly a telepathic stunning of the victim. It is virtually instantaneous, and totally painless. humans cannot utilize the nerve pinch since they cannot deal the mental attack with the pinch.

Vulcan is a harsh world, with a hot, bright sun, and dusty atmosphere. The Vulcan race is hardy. Their strength is much greater than that of most other races. Their bodies are more rugged and impervious to injury. Their blood is copper-bases, rather than iron-based like humans. As a result, their features have a slight greenish tinge to them. Their internal organs are arranged differently to humans, and their blood pressure is lower. Vulcans can control their bodily functions to a degree, and they can survive conditions that would kill a human. They require less sleep than humans, and feel no need to relax or play.

Imbiding of alcoholic beverages to them is senseless. Nor do they indulge in other forms of poisoning their bodies. - they do not smoke, nor do they take non-medicinal drugs.

Vulcans are also occassionally known by theiry archaic anglicized names as Vulcanians.

The official policy of Vulcan is that peace cannot be kept through force of arms, only through understanding. This means that the Vulcans as a whole do not join the military of the Federation. One exception to this case was the starship Intrepid, which was manned entirely by Vulcans. The ship was destroyed in contact with a gigantic amoeboid invader of our Galaxy (see separate entry).

Vulcans and Romulans can still interbreed, though Vulcans would never willingly mate with such savages as they feel the Romulans are. Knowing this, the Romulans frequently force Vulcan captives to mate with a Romulan and then witness the birth of the offspring as a means of shaming and humiliating their captives. When such children are found by Vulcans, they are ignored as being impossible and left to die. Saavik was rescued by Spock from such a fate; for all his Vulcan heritage, Spock's humanity would not allow a feral child to die. Whatever shame her parentage may hav ecaused, none of it is the fault of the child. Thanks to Spock's training, his family has now accepted Saavik on her own merits, overlooking the stigma of her birth.

At the age of seven, the young Vulcan must undergo a rite of passage known as the kahs-wan. This is a survival test that the Vulcans take - they must spend ten days in the desert alone, without taking food, water or weapons with them. They must live offf the land, or admit to failure.

Vulcan is by and large a harsh world, and the predators there are quire ferocious. Cities tend to at oases in the deserts, and are surrounded by stockades. Nowadays, with force shields and such like, the stockades are mostly kept as a ritual gesture to the past.

With their telepathic abilities, naturally the Vulcans are very interested in the powers of the mind. The Vulcan Academy of Science investigates this one way, but there is a strain of mystical belief on Vulcan that is well developed. Some of its adherents are known as the Masters, from their mastery of their own minds. Their discipline, known as Kolinhar, is only achieved after the most arduous mental training. It represents the sloughing off of the bodily urges and fears, and what is considered to a union with the Oneness, an achievement of the perfection of logic.

Another branch of this takes the form of a priesthood, which tends to be feminine. Vulcan, as a whole, is Matriarchy, with women in many of the positions of authority and power. The priesthood believes not exactly in God, but in the presence of a Universal Mind, with whom it is possible to achieve contact. They have a number of mystical ceremonies to achieve this fusion. On a slightly lower level, they have achieved a version of racial immortality because of their telepathic natures.

Shortly before a Vulcan dies, he or she mind-melds with their closet friend. They pass on their essence of being, their katra, to this other person. The katra is then taken to the Hall of Ancient Wisdom, where it is retransfered to a kind of central storage. The dead person's knowledge and experience thus become a part of the heritag of the race, available to anyone who wishes to tap it.

Very, very rarely, a process of refusion of mind and body can be attempted. This dangerous cermony, fal tor pan, has only been attempted once within recorded history - with Spock and the body that the Genesis Effect regrew for him. In this ceremony, the mind is taken back from the host, and refused with the body of the original. It is difficult and dangerous proceedure for both people, and even when successful, many memories and mental abilities are frequently damaged or lost forever. WAITRESS Played by: Sharon Thomas Story: "Star Trek III - The Search for Spock" The waitress in the Spacedock bar frequented by Dr. McCoy.

WALLACE, Dr. JANET

Played by: Sarah Marshall
Episode: "The Deadly Years"

Dr. Janet Wallace was an expert in endocrynology and one of Kirk's many girl-friends. She helped McCoy to isolate a cure for the aging disease that struck the command crew on Gamma Hydra IV.

WASHBURN

Played by: Richard Compton
Episode: "The Doomsday Machine"

Washburn was a member of the "Enterprise" crew.

WATKINS

Played by: Kenneth Washington
Episode: "That Which Survives:

Watkins was Scott's engineering assistant on the "Enterprise". He was killed by Losira.

WATSON

Played by: Victor Brandt
Episode: "Elaan of Troyius"

Watson was a member of the "Enterprise" crew.

WESLEY

Played by: Barry Russo
Episode: "The Ultimate Computer"

Commodore Wesley was a member of Starfleet Command, and an old friend of Kirk's.

WESTERVLIET

Played by: Byron Morrow
Episode: "For the World is Hollow, and I Have Touched the Sky"

Admiral Westervliet was a senior member of Starfleet Command.

WHITE RABBIT

Played by: Bill Blackburn
Episode: "Shore Leave"

One of a number of illusions conjured up by the life-giving processes of the Caretaker's world.

WILSON

See crewmembers

WITCHES

Played by: Rhodie Cogan, Gail Bonney, Maryesther Denver
Episode: "Catspaw"

The three witches were illusions conjured up by Sylvia and Korob in an attempt to terrify Kirk and his landing party.

LT. WORF

Played by: Michael Dorn
Series regular

Worf, serving as Enterprise's security chief after the death of Lt. Tasha Yar, is the first Klingon in Starfleet. Worf is honorable, yet has been willing to fight first, ask questions later. He was adopted by Earth Russian parents. He has a Klingon brother, Kern. Worf is the father of Alexander, a child he fathered with K'Ehleyr. When civil war broke out in the Empire, Worf resigned his Starfleet commission to fight for Gawron. When order was restored, he rejoined the Enterprise. Working with humans and being a father has given Worf deeper insights into what a "warrior" really is.

COL. WORF

Played by: Michael Dorn
Star Trek VI

Col. Worf is the grandfather of Lt. Worf. The elder Worf was a lawyer in the Klingon Empire. It fell to the senior Worf to defend Captain Kirk and Dr. McCoy in their Klingon trial. While other Klingons were turning the trial into a "monkey court", Worf attempted to defend his clients honorably and under due process.

WU

Played by: Lloyd Kino
Episode: "The Omega Glory"

Wu was a leader of the Kohms of Omega IV (see "Star Trek — The Aliens and Monsters File" for further details).

X. CHARLIE

See CHARLIE EVANS.

YAR, LT. TASHA

Played by: Denise Crosby
Former series regular

Yar grew up on an Earth colony filled with rape gangs and lawlessness. It was there that she first developed her quick wit and fighting ability. She joined Starfleet to escape her world and to do good when all she had seen was corruption and death. She was 28 when she was hand-picked by Picard as his security chief aboard the Enterprise. There, she finally found a family, befriending the crew. She even seduced Data. Tragically, she was killed by Armus, the "skin of evil" during his sadistic encounter with the Enterprise. When a temporal distortion occurs, changing history, she is brought back. In the alternate history, she was never killed, but the Federation is at war with the Klingons. She joins the Enterprise-C in its attempt to put back the true course of history.

YONANDAN

Played by: Jon Lormer
Episode: "For the World is Hollow, and I Have Touched the Sky"

The elderly Yonandan was the person who discovered that his world was inside an asteroid, and he was killed by the Oracle for this discovery.

Yonandans

Appearances: "For the World is Hollow and I Have Touched the Sky"

Ten thousand years ago, the star of the people known as the Fabrini (see separate entry) went nova. The Fabrini were an advanced civilization, and they prepared for the survival of their race. They built generation starships inside of hollow asteroids, and sent them on the voyages to distant stars, propelled by primitive drive systems. Such journeys would take many millenia, but at least their race would survive. One such asteroid ship contained the People of Yonada.

This ship was run by a computer known as the Oracle. Because of the high premium placed on the lives of the inhabitants, each of them was fitted with a small monitoring device, linking them to the Orace. This enabled their status to be continually scanned, and in the event of problems, they could be helped. Over the course of the centuries, the Oracle malfunctioned, and the implants ceased to be a method of scanning, and were transformed into a method of mind control. The Oracle helped to hide the truth about its origins, and the fact that the world of Yonada was an asteroid on a voyage. Instead, it gave rise to a presthood, and became itself a deity to these people.

For further centires, this was accepted as the truth, and the Oracle led the People away from the preparations that they should make for their inevitable colonization of a planet. The asteroid was detected by the Enterprise and communications established. Though the Oracle realized that these intruders were dangerous, Kirk and his companions managed to get to the main bank of the computer, and Spock was able to reprogram it to continue with its original functions and enable the People to find a new home.

YUTAN

Played by: Gary Pillar
Episode: "A Private Little War"

Yutan was an inhabitant of Neural (see separate entry for further details).

ZABO

Played by: Steve Marlo
Episode: "A Piece of the Action"

Zabo was one of the hoods on Sigma Iota II (see separate entry for further details).

ZAHRA

Played by: Maurishka
Episode: "Operation: Annihilate"

Yeoman Zahra was a member of the landing party to Deneva.

ZARABETH

Played by: Mariette Hartley
Episode: "All Our Yesterdays"

Zarabeth was an inhabitant of Beta Niobe (see "Star Trek — The Aliens and Monsters File" for further details). Her family had led a revolt against the tryant, Zorcon. In retaliation when the attempt failed, Zorcon exiled Zarabeth to the ice age of her world, never to return. When Spock and McCoy were stranded there also, she fell in love with Spock. She did not wish to lose him, but eventually had to let him go, and remain in her lonely exile.

Zaranites

Appearances: "Star Trek — The Motion Picture"

Note: The Zaranites are one of a number of races whose appearance in the first film was cut.

They are insectoids, with large brains, and straight antennae projecting from the manible areas.

Zeons

Appearances: "Patterns of Force"

See entry on Ekosians.

Zetarans

Appearances: "The Lights of Zetar"

Zetar as a world died long ages ago, but the final hundred survivors of that planet refused to accept their fate and perish with it. Instead, in some strange way they became a single, unified being, a glowing cluster of lifhts, that aim someday to return to corporeal form. For eons, they wandered the Galaxy, attempting to find new hosts. Their vast mentalities opened the way to other civilizations, and finally they approached Memory Alpha, one of the libraries of the Federation. They attempted to take over the bodies of the librarians, but failed. The minds of the races there rejected the attempted invasion, and all of the inhabitants died.

The light-lifeforms managed to make another contact, of Mira Romaine on the Enterprise. Somehow, they became linked to her. In their true form, they could attack the ship, but they still wanted only to return to the flish. Their aggression and siregard for other life-forms left Kirk with no options but to destroy them. Mira was subjected to high pressures, and the lights destroyed — without harming Mira.

ZORA

Played by: Carol Daniels de Meni
Episode: "The Savage Curtain"

Zora was a cruel leader of the tribles of Tiburan (see separate entry for further details). An illusion of her was created by the Excalbians for Kirk and Spock to fight.

ABBOTT, JOHN

Actor
Appearancess: "Errand of Mercy"
Role: Ayelbourne

John Abbott was born in 1905 in London. He originally trained to be a commercial artist before transferring to acting. He moved to Hollywood in 1941, and has appeared in numerous films and tv shows. Films include: "Mrs. Miniver" (1942), "Gigi" (1958), and "The Black Bird" (1975).

ACKER, SHARON

Actress
Appearancess: "The Mark of Gideon"
Role: Odona

Sharon Acker was born in 1936 in England. She has been mostly on tv, including the series "The Senator" (1970-71), "The New Perry Mason" (1973-74) and "Executive Suite" (1976-77). Films include: "Lucky Jim" (1957), "Point Blank" (1967) and "Threshold" (1983).

ADAMS, MARC

Actor
Appearancess: "The Conscience of the King"
Role: Hamlet

ADAMS, PHIL

Stunt Man
Appearancess: "Amok Time"
Role: Kirk's Double

Phil Adams has done stunt work in many tv series, including "The Wackiest Ship in the Army.: His movies include "The Christmas Coal Mine Miracle" (1977).

ADAMS, STANLEY

Actor, Writer
Appearancess: "The Trouble with Tribbles"
"More Tribbles, More Trouble"
Role: Cyrano Jones
Script: "The Mark of Gideon"

Stanley Adams was born in 1915. Aside from his "Star Trek" role, he is best known for his part in "Lost in Space's" infamously worst episode, "The Great Vegetable Rebellion." Films include "The Atomic Kid" (1954) and "Nevada Smith" (1966). He killed himself in a fit of depression in 1977.

AHART, KATHY

Actress
Appearancess: "Space Seed"
Role: Crew Woman

ALBRIGHT, BUD

Actor
Appearancess: "What Are Little Girls Made Of?"
Role: Rayburn

Bud Albright's tv credits include the movie "Drive Hard, Drive Fast" (1973).

ALDREDGE, VIRGINIA

Actress
Appearancess: "Wolf in the Fold"
Role: Karen Tracy

Virginia Aldredge's films include "Riot in a Juvenile Prison" (1959).

ALEXANDER, DAVID

Director
Appearancess: "Plato's Stepchildren"
"The Way to Eden"

David Alexander's other tv credits include "The Man From UNCLE."

ALLEN, GEORGE E.

Actor
Appearancess: "Devil in the Dark"
Role: First Engineer

ALLEN, PHILIP RICHARD

Actor
Appearancess: "The Search For Spock"
Role: Captain Esteban

Philip Richard Allen's films include "Mommie Dearest" (1981). His tv work inclues shows like "Get Chris-

tie Love!"

ALLEY, KIRSTIE

Actress
Appearancess: "The Wrath of Khan"
Role: Saavik

After making her film debut with "The Wrath of Khan," Kirstie Alley declined to repeat her role for the subsequent filsm. She made one tv series, the abominable "Masquerade" (1983-84), and numerous tv movies that include "A Bunny's Tale" (1985) and "North and South" (1985). She is now making her name famous as the new owner of tv's "Cheers." She was born in 1955 in Wichita, Kansas, and is married to Parker Stevenson ("Simon & Simon").

ANDERSON, BARBARA

Actress
Appearancess: "Conscience of the King"
Role: Lenore Karidian

Barbara Anderson is best known for her part in "Ironside" (1967-1971). She also appeared in "Mission Impossible" during its final year (1972-73). She won an Emmy in 1968 for her "Ironside" work. Her tv movies include "Visions..." (1972), "The Six Million Dollar Man" (1973), "Strange Homecoming" (1974), and "Doctors' Private Liveds: (1978).

ANDERSON, JUDITH

Actress
Appearances: Star Trek III
Role: Vulcan High Priestess

Judith Anderson was born in Australia in 1898 and made her first stage appearance in the US in 1918. She made her film debut in 1933, and has appeared many times since. She was named a Dame Commander of the British Empire in 1960 for her outstanding film work. That same year she won an Emmy for her role as Lady Macbeth in a television production of Macbeth. Films include Rebecca (1940), The Ten Commandments (1956), and A Man Called Horse (1970). Search for Spock was her first film in more than a decade. Since then she took a role on the NBC soap opera Santa Barbara. She died in 1992.

ANDES, KEITH

Actor
Appearancess: "The Apple"
Role: Akuta

Keith Andes was born in Ocean City, NJ in 1920. He spent several years in radio and stage work before turning to movies and tv roles. Films include: "Clash By Night" (1952), and "Tora! Tora! Tora!" (1970). He appeared in the tv series "Glynis" (1963-65) and "Search" (1972-73).

ANDRECE, ALYCE & RHAE

Actresses
Appearancess: "I, Mudd"
Role: Alices

The Andrece twins also appeared in the "Batman" episode "Nora Clavicle And The Ladies' Crime Club."

ANDREWS, BUNNY

Music Editor
Star Trek VI

ANDREWS, TIGE

Actor
Appearancess: "Friday's Child"
Role: Kras

Born Tiger Androwaous in 1923, Tige Andrews was the star of "The Mod Squad" (1968-73) and a regular on "The Detectives" (1959-62). His films include: "Mr. Roberts" (1955), "The Last Tycoon" (1976), "Raid on Entebbe" (1977) and "The Return of the Mod Squad" (1979).

ANSARA, MICHAEL

Actor
Appearancess: "The Day of the Dove"
Role: Kang

One of tv's most familiar faces, Michael Ansara was born in Lowell, MASS, of Lebanese ancestors in 1922. He married Barbara Eden in 1958. He came to fame playing Cochise in the tv series "Broken Arrow" (1956-58) and appeared in the lead in "The Law Of The Plainsman" (1959-62). He returned to sf laying Kane in the

first season of "Buck Rogers in the 25th Century" (1979-80). Films include: "Voyage To The Bottom Of The Sea" (1960), "Guns Of The Magnificent Seven" (1969) and "The Manitou" (1978).

ANTHONY, LARRY

Actor
Appearancess: "Dagger Of The Mind"
Role: Ensign Berkeley

Larry Anthony appeared in a number of tv shows in the Sixties, including "The Man From UNCLE."

ANTHONY, RICHARD

Actor
Appearancess: "Spectre Of The Gun"
Role: Rider

ANTONIO, LOU

Actor
Appearancess: "Let That Be Your Last Battlefield"
Role: Lokai

Lou Antonio was a regular on "The Snoop Sisters" (1973) "Dog And Cat" (1977) and "Makin' It" (1979). He has also directed tv shows. Films include: "Hawaii" (1966) and "Partners In Crime" (1973). He has turned more recently to producing, including films like "Mickey And Maude" (1984).

ARMEN, MARGARET

Writer
Scripts: "The Gamesters of Triskelion"
"The Paradise Syndrome"
"The Cloud Minders"
"The Lorelei Signal"
"The Ambergris Element"

Margaret Armen had written stories for shows like "The Rifleman" and "The Big Valley" before her "Star Trek" scripts. Since then, she has written for "Barnaby Jones" and other series.

ARMRITRAJ, VIJAY

Actor
Appearancess: The Voyage Home"
Role: Starship Captain

Vijay Armritraj was born in India. He was intially a tennis star, winning the Davis Cup, before turning to acting. He made his movie debut in "Octopussy" (1983). Other roles include an episode of "Fantasy Island."

ARMSTRONG, DAVE

Actor
Appearancess: "Operation - Annihilate!"
Role: Kartan

Dave Armstrong's films include "Sex And The Married Woman" (1977). He appeared several times on "The Man From UNCLE."

ARNDT, JOHN

Actor
Appearancess: (1) "Miri"
(2) "Dagger Of The Mind"
(3) "Balance Of Terror"
(4) "Space Seed" Role: Crewman
(named as "Fileds" in "Balance of Terror")

AROESTE, JEAN LISETTE

Writer
Scripts: "Is There In Truth No Beauty?"
"All Our Yesterdays"

ASIMOV, ISAAC

Special Consultant
Star Trek: The Motion Picture

Prolific science fiction writer Isaac Asimov served as special science consultant for Star Trek: The Motion Picture. He was born in Russia in 1920, but came to the US at the age of 4. He was an original writer for Astounding Science Fiction magazine, and wrote over 400 books on many subjects. He died in 1992.

ATIENZA, FRANK

Actor
Appearancess: "The Omega Glory"
Role: Executioner

ATWATER, BARRY

Actor
Appearancess: "The Savage Curtain"
Role: Surak

Films include: "Nightmare" (1956) and especially "The Night Stalker" (1972), where he played the vampire that Kolchak stalked. He appeared as a frequent guest on "The Loretta Young Show." He has acted in many shows of the early Sixties, from "The Man From UNCLE," "Voyage To The Bottom Of The Sea" and "One Step Beyond." His death in the mid-seventies was a great loss.

AYRES, JERRY

Actor
Appearancess: (1) "Arena"
(2) "Obsession"
Roles: . (1) O'Herlihy
(2) Rizzo

Jerry Ayres' tv roles include the tv movies "Message To My Daughter" (1973), "Attack On Terror — The FBI versus The Ku Klux Klan" (1975) and "Disaster On The Coastliner" (1979).

BABCOCK, BARBARA

Actress
Appearancess:
(1) "The Squire of Gothos"
(2) "A Taste Of Armaggedon"
(3) "Assignment: Earth"
(4) "Plato's Stepchildren"
Roles: (1) Voice of the Mother
(2) Mea Three
(3) Voice of Isis
(4) Philana

Films include: "Heaven With A Gun" (1968), "Salem's Lot" (1979), "Back Roads" (1981) and "Lords of Discipline" (1983). She was a regular on "Dallas" (1978-82), "The Four Seasons" (1984) and as a semiregular on "Hill Street Blues" (1981) on which she won an Emmy in 1981.

BACHELIN, FRANZ

Art Director
Appearances: "The Cage"

BAKEY, ED

Actor
Appearancess: "All Of Yesterdays"
Role: First Fop

Ed Bakey's films include "Dead And Buried" (1981), "Zapped!" (1982) and "The Philadelphia Experiment" (1984). He has appeared on shows like "Cannon" and "The Guns Of Will Sonnett."

BAL, JEANNE

Actress
Appearancess: "The Man Trap"
Role: Nancy Crater

Jeanne Bal was a regular on "Love And Marriage" (1959-60), "Bachelor Father" (1961), "Mr. Novak" (1963-64) and hosted "NBC Playhouse" during summer, 1960.

BALDAVIN, BARBARA

Actress
Appearancess:
(1) "Balance Of Terror"
(2) "Shore Leave"
(3) "Space Seed"
(4) Turnabout Intruder"
Role: (1) and (2) angela
(3) Baker
(4) Communications Officer

Barbara Baldavin was a regular on "Medical Center" (1971-76). She also guested on series like "The Bionic Woman."

BANKS, EMILY

Actress
Appearancess: "Shore Leave"
Role: Tonia Barrows

Emily Banks was a regular on "The Tim Conway Show" (1970). Her films include "When Hell Was In Session" (1979).

BAR-DAVID, S.

Writer

One of the two names that Shimon Wincelberg wrote under. See entry for Wincelberg, Shimon.

BARNETT, GREGORY

Stunt Man
Appearancess: Star Trek IV, Star Trek V
Role: Spock's Double

BARRETT, MAJEL

Actress
Series Regular, Seasons One to Three
Voice Artist, Animated series
Appeared in "The Cage" under he name M. Leigh Hudec
"Star Trik - The Motion Picture"
"The Voyage Home"
Role: Nurse Christine Chapel

Majel Barrett was born Majel Leigh Hudec in Columb, OH. She married producer Gene Roddenberry, and the couple have a son. She has appeared in a few of Gene Roddenberry's other productions, and her irruglar tv appearances include "Beyond Westworld" and "The Next Step Beyond." Recently, she played Deanna Toi's mother on "Star Trk - The Next Generation."

BARRETT, STAN

Actor
Appearancess: "All Our Yesterdays"
Role: The jailer

Stan Barrett's films include "Sky Heist" (1975) and "Harry & Son" (1984).

BARRIER, MICHAEL

Actor
Appearancess:
(1) "The Squire of Gothos"
(2) "This Side of Paradise"
(3) "The City On The Edge Of Forever"
(4) "Catspaw"
Roles: (1) (2) and (4) DeSalle
(3) Guard

Michael Barrier's other tv work includes "Voyage To The Bottom Of The Sea."

BASCH, HARRY

Actor
Appearancess: "What Are Little Girls Made Of?"
Role: Dr. Brown

Harry Basch was a regular on "Falcon Crest" (1982-84). His films include "Scalplock" (1966), "The Love War" (1970) and "Law And Order" (1976).

BASS, BOBBY

Actor
Appearancess: (1) "Space Seed"
(2) "This Side of Paradise"
(3) Errand of Mercy"
Role: (1) and (2) Crewman
(3) Klingon Guard

Bobby Bass' films include "Blood Beach" (1981), "Megaforce" (1982) and "Star 80" (1983).

BATANIDES, ARTHUR

Actor
Appearancess; "That Which Survives"
Role: D'Amato

Arthur Batanides' films include "Cry Tough" (1959), "The Feminist And The Fuzz" (1971) and "The Heist" (1973). His tv appearances include "Lost In Space," "The Man From UNCLE" and "The Rifleman."

BATES, RUSSELL

Writer
Script: "How Sharper Than A Serpent's Tooth"

BAXLEY, PAUL

Stunt man
Appearancess:
(1) "What Are Little Girls Made Of?"
(2) "Shore Leave"
(3) Amok Time"
(4) "The Trouble With Tribbles"
(5) "A Private Little War"
(6) "Patterns Of Force"

(7) "Assignment: Earth"
Roles: (1) (3) Kirk's Double
(2) Black Knight
(4) Ensign Freeman
(5) Patrol Leader
(6) First Trooper
(7) Security Chief

Paul Baxley worked on many Sixties shows, including "The Man From UNCLE."

BAYER, JOHN

Actor
Appearancess: "Turnabout Intruder"
Role: Guard

BAYLOR, HAL

Actor
Appearancess: "The City On The Edge Of Forever"
Role: Policeman

Hal Baylor was a regular on "The Life And Legend Of Wyatt Earp" (1955-56). He appeared in the tv film "The Macahans" (1976), and shows such as "The Rifleman."

BECK, CHARLES

Actor
Appearancess: "Elaan Of Troyius"
Role: Guard

BEECHER, BONNIE

Actress
Apperances: "Spectre Of The Gun"
Role: Sylvia

BEGGS, HAGEN

Actor
Appearancess; (1) "The Menagerie"
(2) "Court Martial"
Role: Lt. Hansen

Hagen Beggs' films include "I Love A Mystery" (1973), "Hey, I'm Alive" (1975) and "Star 80" (1983).

BEHAR, ELI

Actor
Appearancess: "Dagger Of The Mind"
Role: Therapist

BELLAH, JOHN

Actor
Appearancess: (1) "Charlie X"
(2) "The Naked Time"
Role: Crewman

John Bellah's films include "The Amazing Howard Hughes" (1977), "A Few Days In Weasel Creek" (1981) and "Ghost Dancing" (1983). He also appeared in shows like "The Man From UNCLE."

BELLI, CESAR

Actor
Appearancess: "And The Children Shall Lead"
Role: Steve

Son of attorney Melvin Belli.

BELLI, MELVIN

Attorney/actor
Appearancess: "And The Children Shall Lead"
Role: Gorgan

Melvin Belli was born in Sonora, CA in 1907. He was admitted to the bar in 1933, developing a flamboyant trial manner. This included a malpractice case, where he won after handing the jury his client's artificial leg as evidence. His defense of the "Black-Gloved Rapist" Frank Avilez was not so successful, though he did get his client's sentence reduced from 440 years to 220. His period of fame was the highest when he defended Jack Ruby. Ruby had shot down Lee Harvey Oswald after Oswalk had killed President Kennedy. The publicity that Belli garnered from the case led to his brief acting career. Aside from "Star Trek", he appeared in the films "Wild In The Streets" (1968) and "Gimme Shelter" (1970), the game show "Whodunnit/" (1979) and the tv movie "Lady Of The House" (1978). After a period of relative quit, he has now emerged again torepresent Jim and Tammy Bakker in their current fight over their troubled PTL Christian network.

BENNETT, HARVE

Producer/Writer
Script: "The Wrath of Khan"
"The Search For Spock"
"The Voyagle Home"
Executive Producer:
"The Wrath of Khan"
"The Search For Spoke"
"The Voyage Home"
Voice:
"The Search For Spock"
Role: Flight Recorder

Harve Bennett had won an Emmy as executive producer of A Woman Called Golda. He produced such well-known tv series as The Six Million Dollar Man, The Bionic Woman, The Gemini Man, and The Powers of Matthew Starr. He joined Star Trek as a writer and executive producer for Star Trek II. He came back in those capacities for the next three Trek films. He didn't take part in the sixth Trek film. He appeared in Star Trek III as the voice of the ship flight recorder and in a walk-on as a Starfleet chief of staff in Star Trek V.

BERGERE, LEE

Actor
Appearancess: "The Savage Curtain"
Role: Abraham Lincoln

Lee Bergere was a regular on "Hot 1 Baltimore" (1975) and "Dynasty" (1981-82). His films include "Evening in Byzantium" (1978). TV appearances include "The Man From UNCLE" and "One Step Beyond."

BERGMANN, ALAN

Actor
Apperances: "The Empath"
Role: Lal

Alan Bergmann's films include "Welcome Home, Johnny Bristol" (1972). His tv appearances include "Cannon".

BERMAN, RICK

Executive Producer
Star Trek: The Next Generation

Before beginning work on TNG, Berman worked on such successful series as MacGyver, Cheers, and Family Ties. He also worked on the informational series What On Earth and Primal Mind. He was executive producer of The Big Blue Marble from 1977-1982, winning an Emmy for that show. He is also creator of Deep Space Nine, with Michael Piller.

BERNARD, ARTHUR

Actor
Appearancess: "A Private Little War"
Role: Apella

Arthur Bernard's films include "My Father's House" (1975) and "The Girl, The Gold Watch And Everything" (1980).

BERNARD, JOSEPH

Actor
Appearancess: "Wold In The Fold"
Role: Tark

Joseph Bernard's films include "The Immortal" (1969), "The Challenge) (1970), "The Winds Of Kitty Hawk" (1978), and "The Man Who Loved Women" (1983).

BERRYMAN, MICHAEL

Actor
Appearances: "The Voyage Home"
Role: Stafleet Display Officer

Michael Berryman's other films include "Doc Savage Man of Bronze" (1975), "Deadly Blessing" (1981) and "Invitation To Hell" (1984).

BESCH, BIBI

Actress
Appearances: Star Trek II: The Wrath of Khan
Role: Dr. Carol Marcus

Bibi Besch is primarily a tv actress, from such short series as Secret of Midland Heights (1980-81) and The Hamptons (1983). Her career began around 1976 with appearances on shows such as Police Appearances and The Six Million Dollar Man. Her films include Victory at Entebbe (1976) and The Lonely Lady (1983). More recently she guest starred on the hit series Northern Exposure and won a 1992 Emmy Award.

BILLY, MICHELE AMEEN

Actress
Appearancess: "Star Trek - The Motion Picture"
Role: Epsilon Lt.

Ms. Billy was assistant to Harold Livingstone, making a cameo appearance in the Epsilon sequence.

BINNEY, GEOFFREY

Actor
Appearancess: "Wink Of An Eye"
Role: Compton

Geoffrey Binney's films include "The Appearances Of Pretty Boy Floyd: (1974), "Once An Eagle" (1977) and "Swan Song" (1980).

BISSELL, WHIT

Actor
Appearancess: "The Trouble With Tribbles"
Role: Lurry

Whitney Bissell was born in New York City in 1919. He began acting as a boy, and had amassed numerous credits before entering films in 1943, and then into a large number of tv roles. His only series was "The Time Tinnel." Films include: "Creature From The Black Lagoon" (1954), "Invasion Of The Body Snatchers" (1956), "The Tim Machine" (1960) and "Soylent Green" (1973). He died in 1981.

BIXBY, JEROME

Writer
Scripts: "Mirror, Mirror"
"By Any Other Name"
"Day Of The Dove"
"Requiem For Methuselah:

Jerome Bixby is a fairly well-known sf author, who co-wrote the initial screenplay for "Fantastic Voyage." His most famous Appearances, adapted twice by "The Twilight Zone," is "It's A Good Life."

BLACK, JOHN D.F.

Writer/Producer
Script: "The Naked Time"
Producer: Season One

John Black has written extensively for tv. His tv movie scripts include "Thief" (1971), which won the Edgar Award from the Mystery Writers of America and was nominated for an Emmy, the original "Wonder Woman" (1974) with Cathy Lee Crosby, "A Shadow In The Streets" (1975) [which he also produced] and "The Clone Master" (1978) [which he again produced]. He wrote for shows such as "Wagon Train" and "Laredo," producing superior stores every time. Though "The Naked Time" was his only script for "Star Trek," his careful workmanship is evident in the tone of the first season, which he helped to set.

BLACKBURN, BILL

Stunt double
Appearancess: (1) "Shore Leave"
(2) "A Taste of Armageedon"
(3) "The Alternative Factor"
(4) "A Piece Of The Action"
(5) "Patterns Of Force"
Roles: (1) The White Rabbit
(2) Extra
(3) Guard
(4) Lt. Hadley
(5) Storm Trooper

BLALOCK, STEVE

Stunt Man
Appearancess: "The Search For Spock"

BLANTON, ARELL

Actor
Apprearances: "The Savage Curtain"
Role: Chief Security Guard

Arell Blanton's films include "Pennies From Heaven" (1981). As Arello Blanton now works on soft-porn films like "Chesty Anderson - US Navy" (1984).

BLOCK, ROBERT

Writer
Scripts: "What Are Little Girls Made Of?"
"Catspaw"
"Wolf In The Fold"

Robert Bloch was born in Chicago in 1917. A prolific writer, he churned out sf, horror and mystery tales in abundance. When Alfred Hitchcock filmed his famour novel "Psycho" in 1960, it inspired Block to turn to tv and film writing. Films include: "The Caginet Of Caligari" (1962) and "The House That Dripped Blood" (1971). His contributions to tv include scripts for "Alfred Hitchcock Presents," "Thriller" and "Ghost Appearances."

BLOOM, JOHN

Actor
Appearances: Star Trek VI
Role: "behemoth" alien

The "behemoth" alien in Star Trek VI.

BLUM, KATHERINE

Actress
Appearancess: "The Search For Spock"
Role: Vulcan Child

BOLDER, CAL

Actor
Appearancess: "Friday's Child"
Role: Keel

Cal Bolder was one of a group of bit-part actors that appeared on mnay shows in the Sixties, frequently uncreditied. His appearances include "The Man From UNCLE."

BONNE, SHIRLEY

Actress
Appearancess: "Shore Leave"
Role: Ruth

Shirley Bonne was a regular on "My Sister Eileen" (1960-61).

BONNEY, GAIL

Actress
Appearancess: "Catspaw"
Role: Second Witch

Gail Bonney's tv films include "The Priest Killer" (1971), "The Devil's Daughter" (1973), "Death Scream" (1975) and "Kingston: The Power Play" (1976). Her tv spots include "One Step Beyond."

BOOTH, JIMMIE

Actor
Appearancess: "Star Trek - The Motion Picture"
Role: Klingon

BOUCHET, BARBARA

Actress
Appearancess: "By Any Other Name"
Role: Kelinda

Barbara Gutscher was born in Reichenberg, Germany, in 1943. She came to the US as a child, and became a tv model in commercials before turning to acting. Films include: "Casino Royale" (1966) and "Sweet Charity) (1969).

BOWER, ANTOINETTE

Actress
Appearancess: "Catspaw"
Role: Sylvia

Films include: "The Scorpio Letters" (1967), "A Death Of Innocence" (1971), "First You Cry" (1978), "Blood Song" (1981), "The Thorn Birds" (1983) and "The Evil That Men Do" (1984). She guest-starred on numerous shows in the Sixties, including "The Man From UNCLE" and "Perry Mason."

BRADSHAW, BOOKER

Actor/Writer
Appearancess: (1) "A Private Little War"
(2) "That Which Survives"
Role: Doctor M'Benga

Booker Bradhaw both acts and from time to time writes scripts for shows like "Get Christie Love!" and "Planet Of The Apes". He provided one of the voices for "Galaxy Express: (1982).

BRALVER, ROBERT

Stunt Man
Appearancess: (1) "Friday's Child"
(2) "Star Trek - The Motion Picture"
Role: (1) Grant

(2) Stunt Double

Bob Bralver has worked on many tv shows doing stunts, including Harve Bennett's "The Bionic Woman," and "The Man From UNCLE." He was the stunt driver responsible for the car work in "Knight Rider."

BRAMLEY, WILLIAM

Actor
Appearancess: "Bread and Circuses"
Role: Policeman

William Bramley still makes occasional films, like "Jaws 3-D" (1983) and "The Wild Life" (1984). TV appearances include "The Girl From UNCLE," "Iron Horse," "Petrocelli" and "Barnaby Jones."

BRANDT, VICTOR

Actor
Appearancess: (1) Elaan of Troyius"
(2) "The Way To Eden"
Role: (1) Watson
(2) Tongo Road

Victor Brandt was a regular on "Nobody's Perfect" (1980). His films include "Strange Homecoming" (1974), "The Deadly Triangle" (1977), "Zuma Beach" (1978) and "Wacko" (1983).

BRANNEN, RALPH

Actor
Appearancess: "Star Trk - The Motion Picture"
Role: Crewman

BRENNER, FAYE

Script Supervisor
Star Trek VI: The Undiscovered Country

BRETON, BROOKE

Associate Producer
Production" "The Voyage Home"

BRIAN, DAVID

Actor
appearances: "Patterns Of Force"
Role: John Gill

David Brian was born in New York City in 1914, and became a song and dance man in Vaudeville. After serving in the Coast Guard in World War II, he made his film debut in 1949. He starred in "Mr. District Attourney" (1954-55) and "The Immortal" (1970). Films include: "Million Dollar Mermaid" (1952) and "How The West Was Won" (1962).

BRIGGS, JACK

Property Master
Appearances: "The Cage"

BRILL, CHARLIE

Actor
Appearancess: "The Trouble With Tribbles"
Role: Arne Darvin

Charlie Brill was a regular on "Rowan & Martin's Laugh-in" (1968-69) and "Supertrain" (1979). His films include "Young Love, First Love" (1979) and "Your Place or Mine" (1983).

BRISLANE, MIKE

Actor
Appearancess: "The Voyage Home"
Role: Saratoga Science Officer

BROCCO, PETER

Actor
Appearancess: "Errand Of Mercy"
Role: Claymare

Peter Brocco's films include "Alias Smith and Jones" (1971), "Raid On Entebbe" (1977), "Jeckyll And Hide - Together Again" (1982) and "Twilight Zone - The Movie" (1983). He seems to have been permanently playing old men onshows like "Chase," "Voyage To The Bottom Of The Sea" and "The Man From UNCLE."

BRODY, LARRY

Writer
Script: "The Magics of Megas'Tu"

Larry Brody wrote the tv movies "The Night The City Screamed" (1980) and "Farrell For The People" (1982). His scripts are usually for crime shows, such as "Barnaby Jones" and "Cannon."

BROOKS, ROLLAND M.

Art Director
Season One

BROOKS, STEPHEN

Actor
Appearancess: "Obsession"
Role: Garrovick

Stephen Brooks was a regular on "The Nurses" (1963-64), "The FBI" (1965-67), and "The Interns" (1970-71).

BROWN, MARCIA

Actress
Appearancess: "Shore Leave"
Role: Alice

BROWN, MARK ROBERT

Actor
Appearancess: "And The Children Shall Lead"
Role: Don

BROWN, ROBERT

Actor
Appearancess: "The Alternative Factor"
Role: Lazarus

Robert Brown was the star of "Here Come The Brides" (1968-70) and "Primus" (1971).

BROWN, ROGER AARON

Actor
Appearancess: "Star Trek - The Motion Picture"
Role: Epsilon Technician

Roger Aaron Brown's films include "McNaughton's Daughter" (1976), "Death On The Freeway" (1979), "Don't Cry, It's Only Thunder" (1982) and "Sins Of The Past" (1984).

BROWNE, KATHIE

Actress
Appearancess: "Wink Of An Eye"
Rople: Deela

Kathie Browne was a regular on "Slattery's People" (1965) and "Hondo" (1967). Her films include "Berlin Affair" (1970). She is married to Darren McGavin ("The Night Stalker").

BRUCK, KARL

Actor
Appearancess: "The Conscience Of The King"
Role: King Duncan

Karl Bruck's films include "Escape Of The Birdmen" (1971) and "Escape From The Planet Of The Apes" (1971). He was born in Vienna, Austria, in 1906. His family was killed during the holocaust, and he fled to the United States. He appeared often on tv shows, such as "The Girl From UNCLE" and was a regular on the soap "The Young And The Restless" for ten years. He died in 1987.

BURDETTE, MARLYS

Actress
Appearancess: "A Piece Of The Action"
Role: Krako's Gun Moll

BURNS, JUDY

Writer
Script: "The Tholian Web"

Judy Burns has written for a number of shows, including "Toma."

BURNS, TIM

Actor
Appearancess: "The Doomsday Machine"

Role: Russ

Tim Burns' films include "Gargoyles" (1972) and "Monkey Grip" (1983).

BURNSIDE, JOHN

Actor
Appearancess: "A Taste Of Armaggedon"
Role: Extra

BURTON, LEVAR

Actor
Role: Geordi LaForge
Series regular

LeVar Burton studied in a seminary before becoming an actor. He won a scholarship to USC to study drama. During this time, he landed his breakthrough role as Kunta Kinte in the epic Roots. For that, he earned an Emmy nomination. He later appeared in Looking for Mr. Goodbar, The Hunter, and The Supernaturals. He hosted Reading Rainbow for children on PBS.

BUTRICK, MERRITT

Actor
Appearances: Star Trek II, Star Trek III
Role: Dr. David Marcus

Besides appearing as Dr. David Marcus in Star Trek II and III, he is known for his role of Johnny Slash on the series Square Pegs (1982-'83). His films include Zapped! and When Your Lover Leaves. He died of AIDS in 1990.

BUTLER, ROBERT

Director
Appearances: "The Cage" (Original Pilot)

Robert Butler is most notable for tv work. His occasional films include: "The Computer Wore Tennis Shoes" (1969) and "Now You See Him, Now You Don't" (1971), both for Disney. He won an Emmy as director of the year (1973) for his work on the tv series "The Blue Knight." He won again in 1980 for his work on "Hill Street Blues." He was the co-creator of "Remington Steele."

BYERS, RALPH

Actor
Appearancess: "Star Trek - The Motion Picture"
Role: Crewman

Ralph Byers' films include "Blind Ambition" (1979) and "The Cradle Will Fall" (1983).

BYRD, CARL

Actor
Apparances: "By Any Other Name"
Role: Lt. Shea

Carl Byrd's films include "The Phantom Of Hollywood" (1974) and "Night Cries" (1978).

CADIENTE, DAVE

Actor
Appearancess: "The Search For Spock"
Role: Klingon Sergeant

CALENTI, VINCE

Actor
Appearancess: "The Alternative Factor"
Role: Security Guard

CALL, ANTHONY

Actor
Appearancess: "The Corbomite Maneuver"
Role: Dave Bailey

CAMPBELL, WILLIAM

Actor
appearances: (1) "The Squire of Gothos"
(2) "The Trouble With Tribbles"
Roles: (1) Trelane
(2) Koloth

William Campbell was born in Newark, NJ in 1926. He went to Hollywood in 1950, and has appeared in numerous tv shows and movies. Films include "The Secret Invasion" (1964) and "Pretty Maids All In A Row" (1971). Television appearances include shows like "Gunsmoke". He starred in the syndicated series "Cannonball" (1958).

CANON, PETER

Actor
Appearancess: "Patterns Of Force"
Role: Gestap Lt.

Peter Canon has played small roles in tv shows over the years, including "The Wackiest Ship In THe Army."

CAPRA, FRANK (III)

Second Assistant Director
Production: "The Voyage Home"

Grandson of famous director Frank Capra. His other films include "Zapped!" (1982).

CARABATSOS, STEPHEN W.

Writer/Producer
Scripts: "Court Martial"
"Operation - Annihilate!"
Producer: last portion of first season

CARLYLE, RICHARD

Actor
appearances: "The Squire of Gothos"
Role: Karl Jaeger

Richard Carlyle was the star of "Crime Photographer" in 1951 for three months. His films include "Say Goodbye, Maggie Cole" (1972), "The Spell" (1977) and "Marciano" (1979). TV appearances include "One Step Beyond" and "Cannon."

CARMEL, ROGER C.

Actor
Appearancess: (1) Mudd's Women"
(2) "I, Mudd"
(3) "Mudd's Passion"
Role: Harcourt Fenton Mudd (Harry Mudd)

Born 1929, Roger C. Carmel appeared in numerous tv shows. He was a regular on "The Mother-In-Law" (1967-68) and "Fitz and Bones" (1981). His films include "Anatomy Of A Seduction" (1979) and "Hardly Working" (1981). As well as his acting credits, Carmel also provided the voice for Smokey the Bear and more recently that of Senor Naugles in ads for the California restaurant chain. He was found dead in his apartment on November 11, 1986 by his landlord, after he hadn't been seen for two days. He had apparently died of a drug overdose, as cocaine implements were found about his body. During the Sixties his six foot three inch, 260 pound frame with the prominent moustachios were a familiar sight on most tv shows, ranging from"I Spy" and "The Man From UNCLE" to "The Alfred Hitchcock Show" and "Voyage To The Bottom Of The Sea."

CARR, PAUL

Actor
Appearancess: "Where No Man Has Gone Before"
Role: Lee Kelso

Paul Carr is one of those television actors who never seems to have stopped working, yet never quite left a mark on the tv audience. His nervous young man roles graced shows like "The Rifleman" and "Voyage To The Bottom Of The Sea" (he was extremely good in that show's best episode, "Doomsday"). His mid-range includes shows like "The Green Hornet" and "The Six Million Dollar Man." He was wasted in guest spots on"Buck Rogers In The 25th Centry," and though he seems to have slowed down a little of late, his infrequent appearances graced "Today's FBI" and "HIghway to Heaven." A fine, reliable actor all around.

CARSON, FRED

Actor
Appearancess: "Operation - Annihlate"
Role: First Denevan

Fred Carson's films include "The Cable Car Murder" (1971) and "Deadly Harvest (1972).

CARUSO, ANTHONY

Actor
Appearancess: "A Piece Of The Action"
Role: Bela Oxmyx

Anthony Caruso was born about 1915, and started as a singer, which he gave up to go into acting. He played many gangster roles in his career. His films include "Tarzan And The Leopard Woman" (1946), "Baby Face Nelson" (1957) and "Mean Johnny Barrows" (1976). TV appearances include "The Girl from UNCLE," "The Guns of Will Sonnett", and "Adventures of Superman".

CASSIDY, TED

Actor
Appearancess: (1) "What Are Litle Girls Made Of?"
(2) "The Corbomite Maneuver"
(3) "Arena"
Roles: (1) Ruk
(2) Voice of the False Balok
(3) Vloice of the Gorn

Ted Cassidy was born in 1932, and grew to well over six feet tall. His immense size and resonant voice made him almost too easy to cast as hulking manaces and/or idiots. He played such roles in shows from "Laredo" to his most famous part as Lurch in "The Addams Family" (1964-66). His few films include "Mackenna's Gold" (1968) and "The Last Remake of Beau Geste" (1977). He hated being confused with Richard Keil. He died in 1979 of complications following protracted surgery.

CATRON JERRY

Actor
Appearancess: (1) "Operation - Annihilate"
(2) "The Doomsday Machine"
Roles (1) Second Denevian
(2) Montgomery

Jerry Catron was a regular (and generally uncredited) bit player on "Voyage To The Bottom Of The Sea," generally playing hunchmen and monsters.

CATTRALL, KIM

Actress
Appearancess: Star Trek VI
Role: Valeris

Kim Cattrall played the conspiring Vulcan officer Valeris in Star Trek VI. She is a model who debuted in the film Mannequin with Andrew McCarthy.

CAVENS, AL

Actor
Appearancess: "All Our Yesterdays"
Role: Second Fop

CAVETT, JON

Actor
Appearancess: "Devil In The Dark"
Role: Guard

CHADWICK, ROBERT

Actor
Appearancess: "Balance Of Terror"
Role: Romulan Scope Operator

CHILBERG, JOHN E.

Art Director
Production: "The Search For Spock"

CHOMSKY, MARVIN

Director
Appearancess: "And The Children Shall Lead"
"Day Of The Dove"
"All Our Yesterdays"

Marvin Chomsky was born in 1929. His tv films include "ASsault On The Wayne" (1970) with Leonard Nimoy and the highly-praised "holocaust" (1978). He won an Emmy for this in 1977, and his second in 1978 for "Attica". His third was in 1981 for "Inside The Third Reich."

CLARK, BOBBY

Actor
Appearancess: "Arena"
Role: the Gorn

Bobby Clark's frame and ability served to cast him frequently as thugs and gunment, on shows like Bonanza" and "Gunsmoke."

COBB, JULIE

Actress
Appearancess: "By Any Other Name"
Role: Yeoman Thompson

Julie Cobb was a regular on "The DA" (1971-72), "A Year At The Top" (1977) and "Charles In Charge" (1984). Her films include "The Death Squad" (1974), "Salem's Lot" (1979) and "Brave New World" (1980).

COFFEY, GORDON

Actor
Appearancess: "The Enterprise Incident"
Role: Romulan Soldier

COGAN, RHODIE

Actress
Appearancess: "Catspaw"
Role: First Witch

Rhodie Cogan was in "Stand By Your Man" (1981).

COLICOS, JOHN

Actor
Appearancess: "Errand Of Mercy"
Role: Kor

John Colicos was born in Canada in 1928. He has been mostly on tv, including shows like "Battlestar Galactica". His occasional films include "Anne Of The Thousand Days" (1970), and "The Postman Always Rings Twice" (1981).

COLLINS, JOAN

Actress
Appearancess: "The City On The Edge of Forever"
Role: Edith Keeler

Joan Collins was born in London in 1933, and made her first film in 1952. After several years of hopping the Atlantic and various husbands, she landed her role on "Dynasty" and made her fortune at last. She also did a "Playboy" centerfold when she claimed to be fifty, though she had passed the actual year by two at the time. Her sister, Jackie, writes best-selling trashy novels. Films include: "Land Of The Pharoahs" (1955), "Tales From The Crypt" (1972) and "The Bitch" (1979). Her role in "Star Trek" is one of her two best performances - the other being "The Man From UNCLE" episode "The Galatea Affair."

COLLINS, SHELDON

Actor
Appearancess: "A Piece Of The Action"
Role: Young Boy

COLLINS, STEPHEN

Actor
Appearancess: "Star Trek - The Motion Picture"
Role: Commander Willard Dicker

Stephen Collins was born in Demoines, IO, in 1947. A shy child, he took to acting to overcome this. After several seasons on Broadway, he moved to Hollywood in 1974. After appearances on shows like "The Waltons" and "Charlie's Angels", he made a few tv films. He starred in the "Raiders Of The Lost Ark" tv rip-off, "Tales Of The Gold Monkey" (1982-83). Other films include "Choke Canyon" (1986) and "The Two Mrs. Grenvilles" (1987).

COLLIS, JACK T.

Production Designer
Production: "The Voyage Home"

Jack Collis' other films include "The Four Seasons" (1981), "Paternity" (1981), "Tex" (1982), "Night Shift" (1982), "National Lampoon's Vacation" (1983) and "Splash!" (1984).

COMI, PAUL

Actor
Appearancess: "Balance Of Terror"
Role: Centurian

Paul Comi appeared in "Ripcord" (1961-62). His films include "Warlock" (1959), "Pork Chop Hill" (1959) and "Cry Rape!" (1973). He guest-starred on numerous tv series, including "Voyage To The Bottom Of The Sea," "Barnaby Jones" and "Shannon."

COMPTON, RICHARD

Actor
Appearancess: (1) "The Doomsday Machine"
(2) "The Enterprise Incident"
Roles: (1) Washburn
(2) Technical Officer

CONRAD, BART

Actor
Appearancess: "Court Martial"
Role: Captain Krasnowsky

Bart Conrad appeared on shows like "Perry Mason" in small roles.

COOK, ELISHA

Actor
Appearancess: "Court Martial"
Role: Samuel T. Cogley

Elisha Cook, Jr., was born in San Francisco in 1906. He entered acting in his early teens, and made his first film in 1929. He soon became type-case as a hood, and made his memorable presence felt in the star-laden "The Maltese Falcon" (1941). Other firlms include "The Big Sleep" (1946), "Shane" (1953) and "Rosemary's Baby" (1968). In more recent years, he gained slightly better roles on tv, including appearances in "The Man From UNCLE" and "The Bionic Woman."

COOMBS, GARY

Stunt Man
appearances: (1) "The Galileo Seven"
(2) "Arena"
(3) "Errand of Mercy"
Rules: (1) Stunts
(2) The Gorn
(3) Klingon Guard

COON, GENE L.

Writer/Producer
Scripts (some as "Lee Cronin")
"Arena"
"Space Seed"
"A Taste Of Armaggedon"
"Devil In The Dark"
"Errand Of Mercy"
"The Apple"
"Metamorphosis"
"A Piece Of The Action"
"Bread And Circuses"
"Spock's Brain"
"Spectre Of The Gun"
"Wink Of An Eye"
"Let That Be Your Last Battlefield"
Producer: first season

Gene Coon's other scripts include the films "No Name On The Bullet" (1959) and "The Killers" (1964), Ronald Reagan's last acting role on the big screen. He also wrote for tv series such as "Mr. Lucky", "Wagon Train," and "Laredo". He died shortly after working with Gene Roddenberry on "The Questor Tapes" (1974).

COPAGE, JOHN

Actor
Appearancess: "The Doomsday Machine"
Role: Elliott

John Copage's other appearances include "The Man From UNCLE."

CORBETT, GLENN

Actor
Appearancess: "Metamorphosis"
Role: Zefrem Cochrane

Glen Corbett was born in 1934. His films include "The Priate of Blood River" (1962) and "Midway" (1976). On tv, he starred in "It's a Man's World" (1962-63), "Route 66" (1963-64), "The Road West" (1966-67) and "Dallas" (1983).

COREY, JEFF

Actor
Appearancess: "The Cloud Minders"
Role: Plasus

Jeff Corey was born in New York City in 1914. He switched from selling sewing machines to acting in the Thirties, to films in the Forties, to teaching acting in the Fifties and back to acting in the Sixties. (The "retirement" in the Fifties was not voluntary - he was one of the actors blacklisted during the McCarthy era.) His films include: "The Man Who Wouldn't Die" (1942), "Seconds" (1966) and "Beneath the Plant of the Apes" (1970).

CORRELL, CHARLES

Director of Photography
Production: "The Search For Spock"

Not to be confused with the actor who created the controversial "Amos 'n Andy." This Charles Correll's other films include "Cheech and Chong's Nice Dreams" (1981) and "The Joy of Sex" (1984).

COUCH, WILLIAM

Stunt Man
Appearancess: "Star Trek - The Motion Picture"

Bill Couch did stunt work on films like "Dead and Buried" (1981) and "Brainstorm" (1983). He worked on "The Man from UNCLE" and similar tv shows in the Sixties.

COURAGE, ALEXANDER

Composer Scores: Theme
"The Man Trap"
"Where No Man has Gone Before"
"The Naked Time"
"Miri"
"Dagger of the Mind"
"Menagerie"
"The Galileo Seven"
"The Squire of Gothos"
"Arena"
"Tomorrow Is Yesterday"
"Court Martial"
"Return of the Archons"
"Space Seed"
"A Taste of armaggedon"
"This Side of Paradise"
"Devil in the Dark"
"Errand of Mercy"
"The Alternative Factor"
"The City on the Edge of Forever"
"Operation - Annihilate!"
"The Enterprise Incident"
"Plato's Stepchildren"
"Wink of an Eye"
"The Lights of Zetar"

Alexander Courage was born in Philadelphia in 1919. After working as a band leader, he moved to radio arranging in 1948, then on to MGM. With the growth of television, he switched to the new medium and was the first choice of Gene Roddenberry to score both the "Star Trek" pilots, and then the most single episodes of the show. He also worked on "Voyage to the Bottom of the Sea" and "Lost in Space" at the same time. He is best known as an arranger for musicals, and his works include the film versions of "Porgy and Bess" (1959), "Doctor Doolittle" (1967) and "Fiddler on the Roof" (1971).

COURTNEY, CHUCK

Actor
Appearancess: "Patterns of Force"
Role: David

CRAIG, YVONNE

Actress
Appearancess: "Whom Gods Destroy"
Role: Marta

Yvonne Craig was born in 1941, and is probably best recalled by tv viewers as Batgirl. She has appeared in many shows of the Sixties, having made early appearances in "Mr. Lucky" (in a script written by Gene Coon), "Voyage to the Bottom of the Sea" and "The Man From UNCLE". Her few films include "Gidget" (1959), "Kissin' Cousins" (1964) and "In Like Flint" (1967).

CRAWFORD, JOHN

Actor
Appearancess: "The Galileo Seven"
Role: Commissioner Ferris

John Crawford was born in 1926, and acted onboth sides of the Atlantic in a variety of roles. Films include "I was a Communist for the FBT" (1952), "Satan's Satellites" (1958) [with Leonard Nimoy] and "Jason and the Argonauts" (1963). His numerous tv appearances include "Voyage to the Bottom of the Sea,' and a long stint on "The Waltons" (1972-81).

CRAWFORD, OLIVER

Writer Scripts: "The Galileo Seven:
"Let That Be Your Last Battlefield"
"The Cloud Minders"

Oliver Crawford wrote rather sparingly in the early Sixties. His other shows include a single script each for "Voyage to the Bottom of the Sea", "The Rifleman", "The Bionic Woman", and "Perry Mason."

CRIST, PAUL

Actress
Appearancess: "Star Trek - The Motion Picture"
Role: Crewmember

CROCKETT, DICK

~
Stunt Director
Appearancess: (1) "Where No Man Has Gone Before"
(2) "The Gamesters of Triskelion"
Rules: (1) Kirk's double
(2) Andorian thrall

Dick Crockett worked on films like "It Happened To Jane" (1959) and "Operation Petticoat" (1959), as well as in tv shows suchas "The Man From UNCLE," and "One Step Beyond." He was the stunt director on "Peter Gunn," and made a number of appearances playing.......a stunt director. They used such appearances so that he could explain the mechanics of various stuns, including the "correct" way to fall down a flight of stairs!

CRONIN, LEE

Writer

Pen-name for Gene L. Coon. See his entry for details.

CROSBY, DENISE

Actress
Roles: Tasha Yar, Sela
Series regular first season and "Yesterday's Enterprise" as Tasha Yar

Denise Crosby is the granddaughter of singing star Bing Crosby. Her films prior to joining The Next Generation include 48 Hours, Miracle Mile, and The Eliminators. On television, she appeared on L.A. Law, Days of Our Lives, and The Flash. She left TNG after the first season to pursue other projects, but returned as Yar in the episode "Yesterday's Enterprise". She later returned as the Romulan, Sela.

CRUCIS, JUD

Writer
Scripts: "The Counter-Clock Incident"

CULVER, JOHN

Writer
Scripts: "The Counter-Clock Incident"

CUMMINGS, BOB

Actor
Appearancess: "The Search For Spock"
Role: Klingon Gunner

CURTIS, ROBIN

Actress
Appearancess: "The Search For Spock"
"The Voyage Home" Role: Saavik

Robin Curtis has appeared in the tv movie "In Love With An Older Woman" (1982) and shows such as "Knight Rider" and "MacGiver."

DALEY, JAMES

Actor
Appearancess: "Requiem For Methuselah"
Role: Flint

DALTON, LEZLIE

Actress
Appearancess: "By Any Other Name"
Role: Drea

Lezlie Dalton was one of "The New Daughters Of Joshua Cabe" (1976).

DANIELS, JERRY

Actor
Appearancess: "The Apple"
Role: Marple

DANIELS, MARC

Director/Writer
Script: "One Of Our Planets Is Missing"
Appearancess: "The Man Trap"
"The Naked Time"
"The Menagerie"
"Court Martial"
"Space Seed"
"Who Mourns For Adonais?"
"The Changeling"
"Mirror, Mirror"

"The Doomsday Machine"
"I, Mudd"
"A Private Little War"
"By Any Other Name"
"Assignment" Earth"
"Spock's Brain"

Marc Daniels has been extremely prolific in tv directing. He returned to direct Roddenberry's pilot "Planet Earth" (1972). Other shows include several episodes of "The Man From UNCLE."

DANTE, MICHAEL

Actor
Appearancess: "Friday's Child"
Role: Maab

Michael Dante was born Ralph Vitti in Sanmford, CT in 1935. His films include" Kid Galahad" (1962), "Willard" (1971) and "Shining Star" (1977). He was a regular on the series "Custer" (1967), playing one of his many Indian characters. Virtually none of the tv westerns have managed without his help from time to time.

DARBY, KIM

Actress
Appearancess: "Miri"
Role: Miri

Kim Darby was born Deborah Zervy in Hollywood, 1948. Since her parents were snog-and-dance troupers, she grew up in the enviroment, becoming a child actress. Her tv appearances were many, and her feature film shot was "True Gret" (1969). She appeared in the tv film "The People" with William Shatner.

DARIS, JAMES

Actor
Appearancess: "Spock's Brain"
Role: Savage

James Daris's films include "Sky Heist" (1975).

DAUGHERTY, HERSCHEL

Director
Appearancess: "Operation - Annihilate"
"The Savage Curtain"

Primarily a tv director, Herchel Daugherty's work includes "Winchester "73" (1967). "The Victim" (1972). "She Cried Murder" (1973) and "Twice In A Lifetime" (1974). He directed both "The Man From UNCLE" and "The Girl from UNCLE" Appearancess.

DA VINCI, FRANK

Actor
Appearancess: "The Naked Time"
Role: Lt. Brent

DAVIS, JOE W.

Actor
Appearanc: "The Search For Spock"
Role: Spock (age 25)

DAVIS, WALT

Actor
Appearancess: (1) "Dagger Of The Mind"
(2) "Ballance Of Terror"
(3) "Errand Of Mercy"
Roles: (1) Therapist
(2) Romulan Crewman
(3) Klingon Soldier

Walt Davis's films include "Pursuit" (1972). "Outrage! (1973). "B.J. & The Bear" (1978) and "Kennedy" (1983). His numerous guest spots in tv include "Alias Smith And Jones, " "The Feather And Father Gang" and "The Bionic Woman."

DAWSON, BOB

Special Effects Supervisor
Production: "The Wrath Of Khan"
"The Search For Spock"

DEADRICK, VINCE

Actor
Appearancess: (1) "What Are Little Girls Made Of?"
(2) "Balance Of Terror"
Roles: (1) Matthews
(2) romulan Crewman

Vince Deadrick was in "Tron" (1982) and "Romancing The Stone" (1984). TV parts include "The Man From UNCLE."

DELANO, LEE

Actor
appearances: "A Piece Of The Action"
Lee Delano's films include "Blood Sport" (1973), "In The Glitter Palace" (1977), "HiAppearances Of The World Part One" (1981) and "Splash!" (1984). Another "Man from Uncle" bit-part player.

DELUGO, WINSTON

Actor
Appearancess: Court Martial":
Role: Timothy

DE MENI, CAROL DANIELS

Actress
Appearancess: "The Savage Curtain"
Role: Zora

DEMPSEY, MARK

Actor
Appearancess: "Tomorrow Is Yesterday"
Role: Air Force Captain

DEMYAN, LINCOLN

Actor
appearances: "Assignment: Earth"
Role: Sgt. Lipton

Lincoln Demyan appeared in "Longstreet" (1971) and "Man On A String
(1972). His tv appearances include "Branded".

DENBERG, SUSAN

Actress
appearances: "Mudd's Women"
Role: Magda Kovas

Susan Denberg appeared sporadically on tv in the Sixties, including shows like "The Wackiest Ship In The Army."

DENVER, MARYESTHER

Actress
Appearancess: "Catspaw"
Role: Third Witch

Maryesther Denver's - um - unique looks gained her roles in films like "Born To Be Loved" (1959) and "Nightmare" (1974) as well as in tv shows like "The Girl From UNCLE.'

DERR, RICHARD

Actor
appearances: (1) "The Alternative Factor"
(2) "The Mark Of Gideon"
Roles: (1) commodore Barlow
(2) Admiral Fitzgerald

Richard Derr's films include "Terror Is A Man" (1959), "The Victim"
(1972) and "Firefox" (1982). His many tv appearances include "Perry Mason, " Barnaby Jones" and "Cannon."

DEVENNEY, SCOTT

Actor
Appearancess: "The Voyage Home"
Role: Bob Briggs

DESOTO, ROSANA

Actress
Appearances: Star Trek VI
Role: Azetbur

Played Klingon chancellor Azetbur in Star Trek VI.

DIAL, DICK

Stuntman
Appearancess: (1) "Devil In The Dark"
(2) "The Apple"
Roles: (1) Sam
(2) Kaplan

Dick Dial worked on most of the Sixties tv shows including (inevitably) "The Man From UNCLE."

DIERKOP, CHARLES

Actor
Appearancess: "Wolf In The fold"
Role: Morla

Charles Dierkop's tv career includes "Police Woman" (1974-78). His films include "City Beneath The Sea" (1971), "Captains Courageous" (1977),
"The Deerslayer" (1978) and "Silent Night, Lonely Night" (1984).

DITMARS, IVAN

Composer
Appearances: "Requiem For Methusaleh"

DOBKIN, LAWRENCE

Director
Appearancess: "Charlie X"

Lawrence Dobkin was an actor ("Tokyo After Dark" [1959], "The Streets Of San Francisco"), writer and director. He acted in all three capacities on some shows, such as "The Rifleman."

DOLINSKY, MEYER

Writer
Script: "Plato's Stepchildren"

Meyer Dolinsky's other scripts include "The Manhunter" (1968) and "SST - Disaster In The Sky" (1977).

DONAHUE, ELINOR

Actress
Appearancess: "Metamorphosis"
Role: Nancy Hedford

Elinor Donahue is a very familiar tv face. She was a regular on :"Father Knows Best" (1954-63). "The Andy Griffith Show" (1960-61). Many Happy Returns" (9164-65). "The Odd Couple" (1972-74), and "Mulligan's Stew" (1977). She is returning shortly in "The New Adventures Of Beans Baxter" (9187)

DONNER JACK

Actor
Appearancess: "The Enterprise Incident"
Role" Sub-Commander Tal

DOOHAN, JAMES

Actor
Series Regular
Role: Montogomery Scott
Note: Also played many of the voice-over parts for both the live and animated series.

James Doohan was born in Vancouver, Canada, in 1920. After service in the Second World War, where he was wounded in the D-Day landings, he trained as an actor in New York City. In his native Canada, he made over 4,000 radio appearances, due to his extremely adaptable voice, before moving to Hollywood. A string of small parts on shows like "The Virginian", "The Man From UNCLE" and "The Rogues" led to his getting two offers for series at the same time - as Scotty on "Star trek" and as the chief engineer on "Voyage To The Bottom Of The Sea." Since "Star Trek," he played on "Jason Of Star Command" and in films like Roddenberry's "Pretty Maids All In A Row."

DORN, MICHAEL

Actor
Roles: Lt. Worf, Col. Worf
Series regular and "Star Trek VI"

Dorn's first experience in show business was in a rock group. He grew up in Pasadena, California and landed his first job as a series regular on CHIPs. After that series ended, he returned to acting classes and won roles on Hotel, Knots Landing, and Falcon Crest. Dorn made an appearance as "Colonel Worf", the Klingon lawyer in Star Trek VI.

DORNISCH, WILLIAM P.

Film Editor
Production: "The Wrath Of Khan"

DOUGLAS, PHYLLIS

Actress
Appearancess: (1) "The Galileo Seven"
(2) "The Way To Eden"

Roles: (1) Yeoman Meers
(2) Girl

DOWNEY, DEBORAH

Actress
Appearancess: "The Way To Eden"
Role: Girl

DOWNEY, GARY

Actor
Appearancess: "Whom Gods Destroy"
Role: Tellarite

DRAKE, CHARLES

Actor
Appearancess: "The Deadly Years"
Role: Commodore Stocker

DRESDEN, JOHN

Actor
Appearancess: "Star Trek - The Motion Picture"
Role: Security Officer

John Dresden's films include "Raw Force" (1982) and "Portrait Of A Hitman" (1984). He has also guest-starred on shows like "Barnaby Jones."

DROMM, ANDREA

Actress
Appearancess: "Where No Man Has Gone Before"
Role: Yeoman Smith

DYNARSKI, GENE

Actor
Appearancess: (1) "Mudd's Women"
(2) "The Mark Of Gideon"
Roles" (1) Ben Childress
(2) Krodak

Gene Dynarski was in Spielberg's "Duel" (1983). His other films invclude "The Sound Of Anger" (1968)., "Double Indemnity" (1973) and "Sins Of The Past" (9184). His tv guest sposts include "Voyage To The Botton Of The Sea" and "Iron Horse."

EASTON, ROBERT

Actor
Appearances: Star Trek VI
Role: Klingon judge

Robert Easton played the Klingon judge in Star Trek VI.

EDWARDS, TONY

Actor
Appearancess: "The Voyage Home"
Role:: Helicopter Pilot
Tony Edwards was in "Starman" (1984).

EFROS, MEL

Unit Production Manager/Co-producer
Star Trek V

EHRLICH, MAX

Writer
Script: "The Apple"

Max Ehrlich also wrote a single script for "Voyage To The Bottom Of The Sea."

EISENMANN, IKE

Actor
Appearancess: "The Wrath Of Khan"
Role:"Peter Preston

Ike Eisenmann made initial appearances on tv in shows like "Gunsmoke," then made his mark in Disney's "Escape To Witch Mountain" (1974). More recently, he starred i the short-lived "Fantastic Journey" (1977) and guest spots, such as "T.J. Hooker" and "Voyagers!"

EITNER, DON

Actor
Appearancess: (1) "Charlie X"
(2) "The Enemy Within"
Roles: (1) Navigator
(2) Kirk's Double

Don Eitner's other shows include "Lost In Space."

ELIAS, LOU

Actor
Appearancess: "And The Children Shall Lead"
Role: Technician

ELLENSTEIN, DAVID

Actor
Appearancess: "The Voyage Home"
Role: Doctor

ELLENSTEIN, ROBERT

Actor
Appearancess: "The Voyage Home"
Role: Federation Council Presiden

Robert Ellenstein is a veteran tv actor, with occasional movie roles. He had appeared in various shows, such as "The Man From UNCLE," "One Step Beyond" and "Bonanza" He recently appeared in an episode of "Star Trek - The Next Generation."

ELLIOTT, BIFF

Actor
Appearancess: "Devil In The Dark"
Role: Schmitter

Biff Elliott's films include "Pork Chop Hill": (1959). He guested on a number of tv shows, including "Voyage To The Bottom Of The Sea," "Planet Of The Apes," "Cannon" and "The Feather and Father Gang."

ELLIOTT, KAY

Actress
Appearancess: "I, Mudd"
Role: Stella Mudd

Kay Elliot's other guest sposts include "The Man From UNCLE."

ELLINSON, HARLAN

Writer
Script: "The City On The Edge Of Forever"

Harlan Ellison is one of science fiction's foremost writers, but his forays into the world of tv have all been bitter disappointments to him. His script for "City On The Edge Of Forever" was changed to elimate drug references; his Appearances for "Voyage To The Bottom Of The Sea" was reduced to simplistic levels; his creation of "The Starlost" was so radically altered that he publically disassociated himslef from the project. Both the latter bear his credit as "Cordwainer Bird" - his mark of disapproval. Other tv scripts have been more to his liking from "The Man from UNCLE" to "Burke's Law." His two scripts for " The Outer Limits" are classics ("Demon With A Glass Hand" and "Soldier"). His most recent involvement was with the Twilight Zone" series, to which he contributed both scripts and advice. The inevitable parting of the ways came when CBS executives refused to allow him to direct one of his own scripts, which they (and only they) considered "inappropriate."

ERMAN, JOHN

Director
Appearances: "The Empath"

John Erman is a successful tv director. His tv movies include "Green Eyes" (1977), "Moviola: This Year's Blonde" (1980), "Another Woman's Child" (1983) and " A Streetcar Named Desire" (1984). He won an Emmy for his direction of "Who Will Love My Children?" in 1982. he began his careeer as a production assistant on shows like "Stoney Burke."

ERWIN, LEE

Writer
Script: "Whom Gods Destroy"

Lee Irwin wrote the screenplay for "The Flying fontaines: (1959).

ERWIN, LIBBY

Actress
Appearancess: "The Lights Of Zetar"
Role: Technician

ESPINOZA, RICHARD

Second Assistant Director
Production: "The Wrath Of Khan"

Richard Espinoza was assistant director on "Vice Squad" (1982) and "Yellowbeard" (1983).

EVANS, RICHARD

Actor
Appearancess: "Patterns Of Force"
Role: Isak

Richard Evans' films include "Welcome Home, Johnny Bristol" (1972), "Honky Tonk" (1974) and "When Hell Was In Session" (1979). He was a regular on "Peyton Place" (1965).

EVERS, JASON

Actor
Appearancess: "Wink Of An Eye"

Jason Evers was born Herbert Evers in 1922. He has had a vast amount of tv exposure, including being the irregular target of "The Guns Of Will Sonnett" (1967-69). Other shows include "The Wrangler" (1960) and "Channing" (1963-64). His many guest-spots include "Gunsmoke" and "Fantastic Journey."

EWING, DIANA

Actress
Appearancess: "The Cloud Minders"
Role: Droxine

Diana Ewing appeared in "Washington: Behind Closed Doors"" (1977).

FAGA, GARY

Actor
Appearancess: (1) "Star Trek - The Motion Picture"
(2) "The Search For Spock"
Role: (1) Airlock Technician
(2) Prison Guard

Gary Faga's films include "Bogie" (1980) and "Emergency Room" (1983).

FARLEY, JAMES

Actor
Appearancess: "Arena"
Role: Lang

FARLEY, MORGAN

Actor
Appearancess: (1) "Return Of The Archons"
(2) "The Omega Glory"
Roles: (1) Hacom
(2) Maraak Scholar

Morgan Farley's films inlclude "A Killing Affair" (1977), "Orphan Train" (1979) and "Charlie And The Great Balloon Race" (1981).

FARRELL, BRIONI

Actress
Appearancess: "Return Of The Archons"
Role: Tula

Brioni Farrell appeared in "Keefer" (1978) and "My Tutor" (1983). She has guested on tv shows like "The Man From UNCLE" and "The Bionic Woman".

FERDIN, PAMELA

Actress
Appearancess: "And The Children Shall Lead"
Role: Mary

FERRER, MIGUEL

Actor
Appearancess: "The Search For Spock"
Role: First Officer of "Excelsior"

Miguel Ferrer appeared in "Heartbreaker" (1983) and "Lovelines" (1984). He is the son of actor Jose Ferrer.

FIEDLER, JOHN

Actor
Appearancess: "Wolf In The Fold"
Role: Hengist

John Fiedler's films include "True Grit" (1970), "Double Indemnity" (1973). "Woman Of The Year" (1976), and "The Cannonball Run" (1981). His tv series were "The Bob Newhart Show" (9173-78), "Kolchak - The Night Stalker" (1974-75) and "Buffalo Bill" (1983-84).

FIEDLING, JERRY

Composer
Appearancess: "The Trouble With Tribbles"
"Spectre Of The Gun"

Jerry Fielding was born in Pittsburgh, PA, in 1922. He began scoring films and television in the early 1960's. Notable scores are for "The Wild Bunch" (1969), "The Enforcer" (1976) and "The Gauntley" (1977). For television, he scored "The Bionic Woman:" and "Hogan's Heroes" among many. He conducted his orchestra on camera for "The Lively Ones" (1962-63. He died in 1980.

FIELDS, JIMMY

Actor
Appearancess: "The Cloud Minders"
Role: Cloud Guard

FINELLI, DARIO

Writer
Script: "Albatross"

FINNERMAN, GERALD PERRY (JERRY)

Director of Photography
All but 14 episodes

Jerry Finnerman was born in 1931 and is a noted cinematographer in tv. His other works include "Planet Of The Apes," "The Feather And Father Gang" and most recently "Moonlighting." Work in films includes "The Call Me MIster Tibbs" (9170) and "The Dream Merchants" (1980).

FIX, PAUL

Actor
Appearancess: "Where No Man Has Gone Before"
Role: Dr. Mark Piper

Paul Fix was born in Dobbs Ferry, NY, in 1901. In his life, he appeared in over 300 films, including "After The Thin Man" (1936), "The High And The Mighty" (1954) and "Night Of The Lepus" (19721) with DeForest Kelley. He is best recalled for a vast amount of tv work, however, generally playing doctors or sheriffs. His only regular series was "The Rifleman" (1958)-63). He died in 1983.

FLANAGAN, KELLIE

Actress
Appearancess: "Miri"
Role: Girl

FLETCHER, ROBERT

Costume Designer
Productions: "Star Trek - The MOtion Picture"
"The Wrath Of Khan"
"The Search For Spock"
"The Voyage Home"

Robert Fletcher has also worked on "Caveman" (1981) and "The Last Starfighter" (1984).

FONTANA, DOROTHY (D.C.)

Writer/Producer/Script Supervisor
Scripts: "Charlie X"
"Tomorrow Is Yesterday"
"This Side Of Paradise"
"Journey To Babel"
"Friday's Child"
"By Any Other Name"
"The Ultimate Computer"

Dorothy C. Fontana has had a long career in tv writing. She is also an experienced Appearances editor having working on shows like "Logan's Run" and "Fantastic Journey." More recently she wrote for "Buck Rogers" (changeing her credit after dissatisfaction with the end result) and "Dallas." She has written the pilot script for the new "Star Trek - The Next Generation." She novelized "The Questor Tapes" for Ballantine books, from Gene Roddenberry and Gene Coon's script.

FOREST, MICHAEL

Actor
Appearancess: "Who Morns For Adonias?"
Role: Apollo

Michael Forest's films include "The Silent Gun" (1969). His tv career encompasses many shows, including "Gunsmoke,"Branded" and "The Rifleman."

FORTIER, ROBERT

Actor
Appearancess: "By Any Other Name"

FORREST, BRAD

Actor
Appearancess: "That Which Survives"
Role: Ensign

FOSTER, ALAN DEAN

Writer
Scripts: "Star Trek - The Motion Picture"

Alan Dean Foster is a successful lightweights of author. His involvement with "Star Trek" began when he novelized the scripts of the animated servies into the popular "Star Trek Log" books. His other novelizations include" Aliens," "The Last Starfighter" and "Clash Of The Titans."

FOXWORTH, JERRY

Actor
Appearancess: "Mudd's Women"
Role:"Security Guard"

FRAKES, JONATHAN

Actor
Role: William Riker
Series regular

Jonathan Frakes grew up in Pennsylvania and attended Penn State and then Harvard. Before TNG, Frakes found work on Falcon Crest, Paper Dolls, and Bare Essence. He was a regular on the soap opera, The Doctors for a year.

FRANCIS, AL

Director of Photography
Appearancess: "Day Of The Dove"
"For The World Is Hollow And I Have Touched The Sky"
"The Tholian Web"
"Plato's Stepchildren"
"Wink Of An Eye"
"Whom Gods Destroy"
"Let That Be Your Last Battlefield"
"The Mark Of Gideon"
"The Lights Of Zetar"
"The Way to Eden"
"The Cloud Minders"
"The Savage Curtain"
"All Our Yesterdays"

FRANKHAM, DAVID

Actor Appearancess: "Is There In Truth No Beauty?"

David Frankham's films include "The Return Of The Fly" (1959), "Winter Kill" (1974), "Eleanor, First Lady Of The World" (1982) and "Wrong Is Right" (1982).

FRIED, GERALD

Composer Appearancess: "Shore Leave"
"Amok Time"
"The apple"
"Catspaw"
"Journal To Babel"
"Friday's Child"
"Wolf In The Fold"
"The Paradise Syndrome"

Gerald Fried was born in 1926. His many credits include extensive work on "The Man From UNCLE,:' and films such as "The Cabinet Of Caligare" (1962), "Soylent Green" (1973) and "Roots" (1976).

FRIEDMAN, MAL

Actor
Appearancess: "The Apple"
Role: Hendroff

GAGE, BEN

Actor
Appearancess: "Friday's Child"
Role: Akaar

Ben Gage's films include "The Big Operator" (!959) and "The Big Rip Off" (1975). He guested in many shows in the Sixties, includeing "Iron Horse."

GALLEGOS, JOSHUA

Actor
Appearancess: "Star Trek - The Motion Picture"
Role: Security Officer

Joshua Gallegos's other films include "Survival Of Diana" (1979) and "The Mystic Warrior" (1984).

GARION, BUDDY

Actor Appearancess: "A Piece Of The Action"
Role: Krako's Hood

Buddy Garion appeared in "The Death Squad" (1974).

GARR, TERRI

Actress
Appearancess: "Assignment Earth"
Role: Roberta Lincoln

Terri Garr and graduated to movies after a generally unsuccessful fling on tv. "Young Frankenstein" (1976) finally made her famous, since when she has appeared in films like "The Black Stallion" (1979), "Tootsie" (1982) and "Mr. Mom" (1983). Her series were "The Ken Berry Wow Show" (1972), "The Burns And Schrieber Comedy Hour" (1973), "The Girl With Something Extra" (1973)-74), and "The Sonny and Cher Comedy Hour" (1973-74).

GARRETSON, KATY E.

Second Asst. Director
Star Trek VI

GATES, BARBARA

Actress
Appearancess: "The Changeling"
Role: Crewwoman

Barbara Gates appeared in "The Young Country" (1970).

GATREAUX, DAVID

Actor
Appearancess: "Star Trek _ The Motion Picture"
Role: Commander Branch

David Gatreaux was originally signed on to play Mr. Spock's BVulcan replacement, Xon, in the proposed "Star Trek II" tv series. When this fell through and Nimoy agreed to do the film, Gatreaux was given a smaller part in consolation.

GEARY, RICHARD

Actor
Appearancess: "Whom Gods Destroy"
Role: Andorian

Richard Geary worked extensively on "Perry Mason," and guested on shows like "The Girl From UNCLE.'

GEDEON, CONROY

Actor
Appearancess: "The Search For Spock"
Role: Agent In Bar

GEHRING, TED

Actor
Appearancess: "Assignment: Earth"
Role: Police Officer

Much seen on tv, Ted Gehring's tv movies include "The Intruders" (1970), "The Rockford Files" (1974), "Captains And The Kings" (1976) and "The Night The Bridge Fell Down" (1983). He was a regular on "The Family Holvak" (1975-1977), "Little House On The Prairie" (1975-76), "Alice" (9179-81) and "Dallas" (1980-81. His theatrical movies include "The Legend Of The Lone Ranger" (1981).

GENTILE, ROBERT

Actor
Appearancess: "The Enterprise Incident"
Role: Technician

GEORGE, VICTORIA

Actress
Appearancess: "The Gamesters Of Triskelion"
Role: Ensign Jana Haines

GERROLD, DAVID

Writer
Scripts: "The Trouble With Tribbles"
"The Cloud Minders"
"More Tribbles, More Troubles"
"BEM'
Books:
"The Worlds of Star Trek"
"The Trouble With Tribbles"

David Gerrold's first script sale was to "Star Trek," and is fully ducumented in his book on the subject. After several novels, he also contributed scripts to "Logan's Run" and the new "Twilight Zone." More Recently, he was selected as Appearances editor on "Star Trek - The Next Generation." After a short while, his association with the series ceased.

GILMAN, SAM

Actor
Appearancess: "Spectre Of The Gun"
Role: Doc Holliday

Sam Gilman appeared in "The Tribe"(1974). He was a regular on "Shane" (9166) and guested on many westerns, including "The Rifleman."

GIMPEL, SHARON

Actress
Appearancess: "The Man Trap"
Role: The Creature

GLASS, SEAMON

Actor
Appearancess: "Mudd's Women"
Role: Benton

Seamon Glass's films include "The Other Side Of Hell" (1978), "She's Dressed To Kill" (1979), "Gideon's Trumpet" (1980) and "Partners" (9182). His other tv appearances includes "Buck Rogers in the 25th Centruy."

GLOVER, KRISTIN

Camera Operator
Star Trek VI

GOLAS, THADDEUS

Actor
Appearancess: "The Voyage Home"
Role: Controller

GOLDBERG, WHOOPI

Actress
Role: Guinan
Series regular

Whoopi Goldberg was a successful comedian and actress before appearing as Guinan. Before her entertainment career, Goldberg was a mother and waitress. She won her big break with an Oscar nomination for the film The Color Purple. Since then, she appeared in Jumpin' Jack Flash, Burglar, and Clara's Heart. She also won acclaim for her involvement in the homelessness crisis by appearing in the Comic Relief. She won an Oscar for the Oda Mae character in 1989's Ghost.

GOLDSMITH, JERRY

Composer
Star Trek: The Motion Picture, The Next Generation

Jerry Goldsmith was born in Los Angeles in 1930. He studied under Miklos Rosza, and began scoring films and tv in the Fifties. His work included Gunsmoke and Playhouse 90. He received an Academy Award for The Omen. For Star Trek, he scored Star Trek: The Motion Picture and The Next Generation.

GOLDEN, MURRAY

Director
Appearances: "Requiem For Methuselah"

Murray Golden has worked sparingly, his credits including a single episode of "The Rifelman" and several episodes of the "The Wackiest Ship In The Army."

GOLDSMITH, JERRY

Composer
Productions: "Star Trek - The Motion Picture"

Jerry Goldsmith was born in Los Angeles, CA, in 1930. He studied under Miklos Rosza, and began scoring both films and a great deal of television in the late

Fifties. His work for "Climax!", "Playhouse 90" and "Gunsmoke" led to a large numger of offers. He was signed to score the entire first season of ":The Man from UNCLE," but was so inundated with work he only managed the famous theme and two stories! His numerous films include "Planet Of The Apes" (1968), "Papillon" (1973), "The Omen" (1976) [Academy Award] and "The Secret Of NIMH" (1982).

GOLDSTONE, JAMES

Director
Appearancess: "Where No Man Has Gone Before"
"What Are Little Girls Made Of"

James Goldstone was born in Los Angeles, CA in 1931. At the age of 19 he became a film editor, graduatin to tv directing for a number of shows in the latre Fifties. With Stephen Kandel, he created "Iron Horse" for tv. His films include "They Only Kill Their Masters" (1972), "The Day The World Ended" (1979) and "Earth-Star Voyager" (1987). He won an Emmy in 1981 for his direction of "Kent State." He worked extensively on the first season of "Voyage To The Bottom Of The Sea," directing some of their finest episodes.

GOODWIN, JIM

Actor
Appearancess: (1) "The Enemy Within"
(2) "Mudd's Women"
(3) "Miri"
Role: Lt. John Farrell

Jim Goodwin's films include "Ten Seconds To Hell" (1959). He also appeared on shows like "Perry Mason."

GOODWIN, LAUREL

Actress
Appearancess: "The Cage"
Role: Yeoman Colt

GORSHIN, FRANK

Actor
Appearancess: "Let That Be Your Last Battlefield"
Role: Bele

GOUW, CYNTHIA

Actress
Appearances: Star Trek V
Role: Cathlin Dar

Cynthia Gouw played Cathlin Dar in Star Trek V.

GOVER, EDNA

Actress
Appearancess: "Star Trek - The Motion Picture"
Role: Vulcan Master

GOWANS, JOHN D.

Actor
Appearancess: "Star Trek - The Motion Picture"
Role: Transporter Assistant
John Gowans' films include "Lacy And The Mississippi Queen" (1978), "No Other Love" (1979) and "Anatomy Of An Illness (1984).

GRAFFEO, CHARLES M.

Set Decorator
Production: "The Wrath Of Khan"

GREEN GILBERT

Actor
Appearancess: "Patterns Of Force:
Role: SS Major

Gilbert Green's films include "God Bless The Children" (1970), "Honor Thy Father" (1973) and the pilot for "Starsky And Hutch" (1975).

GREGORY, JAMES

Actor
Appearancess: "Dagger Of The Mind"
Role: Dr. Tristan Adams

James Gregory was born in New Rochelle, NY, in 1911. He started working on Wall Street, but was hooked by acting. After several years Broadway experience, he made his first film in 1948. Among his many films are "The Naked City" (1948), "The Sons of Katie Elder" (1965) and "Beneath The Planet Of The

Apes" (1970). He was a regular on "The Lawless Years" (1959-61), "The Paul Lynde Show" (1972-73), "Barney Miller" (1975-82) and "Detective School" (1979).

GRIST, ROBERT

Director
Appearances: "The Galileo Seven"

GRUZAF, JAMES

Actor
Appearancess: "Shore Leave"
Role: Don Juan

GUEST, NICHOLAS

Actor
Appearancess: "The Wrath Of Khan"
Role: Cadet

Nicholas Guest's other films include "Trading Places" (1983) and "Cloak And Dagger" (1984).

HAIG, SID

Actor
appearances: "Return Of The Archons"
Role: First Lawgiver

Sid Haig's films include "Who Is The Black Dahlia?" (1975), "The Return Of The World's Greatest Dective" (1976), "Evening In Byzantium" (1978), "Death On The Freeway" (1979), "Chu Chu And The Philly Flash" (1981) and "Galaxy Of Terror" (1981).

HALE, DOUG

Actor
Appearancess: "Star Trek - The Motion Pictue"
Role: Computer Voice

Doug Hale's film appearances include "Charleston" (1979) again as a voice only, "Terror At Alcatraz" (1982) and "Mothers Against Drunk Drivers" (1983).

HALE, RICHARD

Actor
Appearancess: "The Paradise Syndrome"
Role: Goro

Richard Hale was born in 1893, was made a number of films, including "Julius Cesar" (1953) and "Ben Hur" (1959). On tv, however, he seemed perpetually cast as ancient Indians (as in "Star Trek"). He played the adoptive father of "Cheyenne" and roles on shows like "Iron Horse." He died in 1981.

HAMNER, ROBERT

Writer
Script: "A Taste Of Armaggedon"

Robert Hamner's tv films are "You Lie So Deep My Love" (1975), "dallas Cowboys Cheerleaders" (1979) and "The Million Dollar Face" (1981), which he also produced. He wrote for shows such as "The Man From UNCLE" and "Voyage To The Bottom Of The Sea." Lately, he produces tv films including "Fugitive Family" (1980), "Portrait Of A Showgirl" (1982) and "Malibu" (1983).

HARDER, RICHARD

Actor
Appearancess: "The Voyage Home"
Role: Joe

HARMON, DAVID P

Writer
Scripts: "The Deadly Years"
"A Piece Of The Action"
"The Eye Of The Beholder"

David Harmon has written several tv movies, includeing "Honeymoon With A Stranger" (1969), "Killer By Night" (1972), "Rescue From Gilligan's Island" (1978) and "The Harlem Globetrotters On Gilligan's Island" (1981).

HARMON, JOHN

Actor
Appearancess: (1) "The City On The Edge Of Forever"
(2) "A Piece Of The Action"

Roles: (1) Rodent
(2) Tepo

john Harmon has played bit-roles in most tv shows. His only semiregular role was in "The Rifleman."

HARRIS, LEON

Art Director
Production: "Star Trek - The Motion Picture"

Leon Harris has worked on "The Devil And Max Devlin" (1981).

HART, HARVEY

Director
Appearances: "Mudd's Women"

Harvey Hart was born in Toronto, Canada, in 1928. His work is mostly tv, though he has produced a number of low-budget films. These include "Buss Riley's Back In Town" (1965) with James Doohan, "The Pyx" (1973). "The Mad Trapper" (1979), "The High Country" (1981).

HARTLEY, MARIETTE

Actress
Appearancess: "All Our Yesterdays"
Role: Zarabeth

Mariette hartley was born in 1940, and became a familiar face on tv by the Sixties. Her numerous appearannces cover shows from "Ghost Appearances" to "Barnaby Jones." her films include "Ride The High Country" (1962), "Marooned" (1967) and "Earth II" (1972). She was a regular on "Peyton Place" (1965), "The Hero" (1966-67)" and "Goodnight, Beantown" (1983-84). She recently became a cheerful morning show hostess, and remains as charming as ever. She won an Emmy in 1978 for her performance in an episode of "The Incredible Hulk."

HAYMER, JOHNNY

Actor
Appearancess: "All Our Yesterdays"
Role: Constable

Johnny Haymer's films include "Mongo's Back In Town" (1971), "Ring Of Passion" (1978) and "The Best Place To Be" (1979). He was a regular on "M*A*S*H" (1977-79) and "Madame's Place" (1982). Guest spots include "The Girl From UNCLE."

HAYNES, LLOYD

Actor
Appearancess: "Where No Man Has Gone Before"
Role: "Communications Officer Alden"

Lloyd Haynes' films include "Assault On The Wayne" (1971), "Look What's Happened To Rosemary's Baby" (1976) and "Born To Be Sold" (1981). He was the star of "Room 222" (1969-74). He died in 1986.

HAYS, KATHRYN

Actress
Appearancess: "The Empath"
Role: Gem
Kathryn Hays' few films include "Breakout" (1970) and "Yuma" (1971). She was a regular on "The Road West" (1966-67), and guested on shows like "The Man From UNCLE" and "Circle Of Fear."

HEINEMANN, ARTHUR

Writer
Scripts: "Wink Of An Eye"
"The Way To Eden"
"The Savage Curtain"

Arthur Heinemann wrote "The Caputre Of Grizzly Adams" (1982), and scripts for "Cannon.."

HELD, CHRISTOPHER

Actor
Appearancess: "Return Of The Archons"
Role: Lindstrom

Christopher Held also appeared on "The Girl From UNCLE."

HENRIQUES, DARRYL

Actor
Appearances: Star Trek VI
Role: Nanclus

Daryl Henriques played Romulan Nanclus in Star

Trek VI.

HENTELOFF, ALEX

Actor
Appearancess: "The Voyage Home"
Role: Nichols

Alex Hentelhoff's other films include "Partners In crime" (1973), "The Invisible Man" (1975), "The Bastard" (1978), "Victims" (1982) and "The Red-Light Sting" (1984). he was a regular on "Pistols'n'Petticoats" (1966-67), "The Young Rebels" (1970-71), "Needles And Pins" (1973) and "The Betty White Comedy Show" (1977-78).

HERRON, ROBERT

Stunt Man
Appearancess: (1) "The Cage"
(2) "The Savage Curtain"
Roles: (1) Pike's Double
(2) Kahless

HICKS, CHATHERINE

Actress
Appearancess: "The Voyage Home"
Role: Gillian Taylor

Catherine Hicks was born in New York city, but grew up in Scottsdale, AR. Her first tv work was in the soap opera "Ryan's Hope" than a regular role on "The Bad News Bears" (9179-80). Her role in tv film "Marilyn: The Untold Appearances" (1980) won her an Emmy. She then starred in "Tucker's Witch" (1982-83) before concentrating on films. These include "The Razor's Edge" (1984) and her superb performance in "Peggy Sue Got Married" (1986).

HILL, MARIANNA

Actress
Appearancess: "Dagger Of The Mind"
Role: Dr. Helen Noel

Marianna Hill's films include "Death At Love House: (1976), "Rentlentless: (1977). "Blood Beach" (1981) and "Invisible Strangler" (1984). She guested on shows like "Perry Mason."

HILLYER, SHARON

Actress
Appearancess: "A Piece Of The Action"
Role: Girl

Sharon Hillyer was a regular for the third season of "The Man From UNCLE.'

HOCKRIDGE, JOHN

Firs Assistant Director
Production: :"The Search For Spock"

HOLLAND, ERIK

Actor
Appearancess: "Wink Of An Eye"

Erik Holland's films include "Friendly Persualssion" (1975), "The French Atlantic Affair" (1979), "Little House: Look Back To Yesterday" (1983) and "Table For Five: (1983). He has guested on shows such as "The Man From UNCLE" and "Voyage To The Bottom Of The Sea."

HOLMAN, REX

Actor
appearances: "Spectre Of The Gun"
Role: Morgan Earp

Rex Holman specializwes in playing shifty-eyed villains. His films include "The Bounty Man" (1972), "The Legend Of The Golden Gun" (1979) and "The Wild Women Of Chastity Gulch" (1982). Most of his film and tv appearances have been in westerns.

HOMEIER, SKIP

Actor
Appearancess: (1) "Patterns Of Force"
(2) "The Way To Eden"
Roles: (1) Melakon
(2) Dr. Sevrin

George Vincent Homeier was born in Chicago in 1930. He made his radio debu aged 6, and his first film when he was 14. Since then he has appeared on tv and in films in numerous roles His films include "The Gunfighter" (1950), "Commanche Station" (1960) and "The Greatest" (1977). He was a regular on "Dan Raven"

(1960-61) and "The Interns" (1970-71).

HOOKS, ROBERT

Actor
appearances: "The Search For Spock"
Role: Commander Morrow

Robert Hooks was born in Washington, DC in 1937. His films include "Hurry Sundown" (1967) and "Airport '77" (1977). He was a regular on "NYPD" (1967-69).

HORGAN, PATRICK

Actor
Appearancess: "Patterns Of Force"
Role: Eneg

Patrick Horgan played General Howe in the "George Washington" miniseries (1984) and was a regular on "Casablanca" (1983). Guest spots include "The Girl From UNCLE."

HORNER, JAMES

Composer
Productions: "The Wrath Of Khan"
"The Search for Spock"

James Horner made his mark with his first film score, "Battle Beyond The Stars" (1980), and "The Wrath Of Khan" cemented his reputation firmly. since this he has scored films like "Brainstorm" 91984) and "Aliens" (1986).

HOWARD, CLINT

Actor
Appearaances: "The Corbomite Maneuver"

Clint Howard was a regular on "The Bailey's Of Balboa" (1964-65), "Gentle Ben" (1967-69) and "The Cowboys" (1974). His films include "Evilspeak" (1982), "Night Shift" (1982) and "Splash!" (1984).

HOWARD, LESLIE C.

Actress
Appearancess: "Star Trek - The Motion Picture"
Role: Yeoman

HOWARD, SUSAN

Actress
Appearancess: "Day Of The Dove"
Role: Mara

Susan Howard's films include "Quarantined" (1970), "Indict and Convict" (1974) with William Shatner, "Superdome" (1978) and "The Power Within" (1979). She was a regular on "Petrocelli" (1974-76) and "Dallas" (1979-84).

HOWARD, VINCE

Actor
Appearancess: "The Man Trap"
Role: Uhura's Crewman

Vince Howard's films include "Vanished" (1971), "Love is Not Enough" (1978) and "The Red-Light Sting" (1984). He was regular on "Mr. Novak" (1963-65).

HOWDEN, MIKE

Actor
Appearancess: (1) "I, Mudd"
(2) "The Enterprise Incident"
Roles: (1) Lt. Rowe
(2) Romulan Guard

HOYT, CLEGG

Actor
appearances: "The Cage"
Role: Transporter Chief Pitcairn

Clegg Hoyt was a guest on shows like "The Rifleman" and "The Man From Uncle."

HOYT, JOHN

Actor
Appearancess: "The Cage"
Role: Dr. Philip Boyce

John Hoyt was born John Hoysradt in 1905. His long film career includes "When Worlds Collide" (1952), "Duel At Diablo" (1966) and "Flesh Gordon" (1974). He was a regular on "Tom, Dick And Mey" (1964-65) and "Gimmie A Break" (1982). His guest spots include "Planet Of The Apes," "The Man From UNCLE" and

"Voyage to The Bottom Of The Sea."

HUGHES, DAVID HILLARY

Actor
Appearancess: "Erran Of Mercy"
Role: Trefayne

HUMMEL, SAYRA

Actress
Appearancess: "Star Trek - The Motion Picture"
Role: Engine Room Technician

HUNDLEY, CRAIG

Actor
Appearancess: (1) "Operation - annihilate!"
(2) "And The Children Shall Lead"Roles: (1) Peter
(2) Tommy Stairnes

HUNTER, JEFFREY

Actor
Appearancess: "The Cage"
Role: Captain Christopher Pike

Henry Herman McKinnies was born in New Orleans, in 1925. His first film was a college production, from which he was signed under studio contract. he made many films, notably "Red Skies Of Montana" (1952), "King Of Kings" (1961) and "The Longest Day" (1962). He was a regular on "Temple Houston" (1963-64). He was filming in Spain in 1969 when he was thrown from his horse. He died following brain surgery.

HURST, DAVID

Actor
Appearancess: "The Naked Time"
"The Conscience Of The King"
Role: Kevin Riley

IMAN

Actress
Appearancess: Star Trek VI
Role: Martia

"Supermodel" Iman played shapeshifter Martia in the Rura Penthe prison in Star Trek VI. She also appeared in a Michael Jackson video and is married to rock star David Bowie.

IHNAT, STEVE

Actor
Appearancess: "Whom Gods Destroy"
Role: Garth

Steve Ihnat was born in Czecheslovakia in 1934, but grew up in the US. He made very few movies, including "The Chase" (1966) and "Fuzz" (1972). He was more noted for tv appearances, mostly in westerns such as "Iron Horse." He died in 1972.

INGALLS, DON

Writer
Script: "The Alternative Factor"

Don Ingalls has written many tv scriipts, including for the films "A Matter Of Wife...And Death" (1976), "Flood" (1976), "The Initiation Of Sarah" (1978) and "Captain America" (1979).

IRELAND, JILL

Actress
Appearancess: "This Side Of Paradise"
Role: Leila Kalomi

Jill Ireland was born in London in 1936. She trained as a ballet dancer, which led to her first film role. Prefering acting to dancing, che switched, making a name for herself in British film and tv. She married David McCallum in 1957, and the pair of them moved to the States in 1962 with him. She guested three times on his "Man Form UNCLE" series, along with other parts. Charles Bronson, then rather down on his luck, moved in with the McCallums for a short while, McCallum and Jill for divorce in 1967, and she married Bronson the following year. Since then , she has apppeared virtually exclusively in Bronson's films. Her films include "Hell Drivers" 91957). "Breakheart Pass" (1976) and "Love And Bullets" (1979). She was a regular on the short-lived "Shane" (1966).

ITZKOWITZ, HOWARD

Actor
Appearancess: "Star Trek - The Motion Picture"

Role: Cargo Deck Ensign

Howard Itzkowitz's other films include "Amateur Night At The Dixie Bar And Grill" (1979). He was a regular on the variety show "Marie" (1980-81).

JACKSON, SHERRY

Actress
Appearancess: "What Are Little Girls Made Of?"
Role: Andrea

Sherry Jackson has been much on tv since the early Fifties, when she was one of the children on "The Danny Thomas Show" (1953-58). She has appeared in shows like "Gunsmoke" and "Lost In Space." Her films include "Wild Women" (1970), "The Girl On The Late, Late Show" (1974), "Returning Home" (1975) and "Casino" (1980).

JANSON, LEN

Writer
Script: "Once Upon A Planet"

JENNINGS, JOSEPH R.

Production Designer
Production: "The Wrath Of Khan"

Joseph Jennings was the production designer on "Yellowbeard" (1983) and "Johnny Dangerously" (1984).

JENNINGS, JUNERO

Actress
Appearancess: "Star Trek - The Motion Picture"
Role: Engine Room Technician

Junero Jennings has appeared in small roles on shows like "Stone."

JENSEN, KEITH L

Stunt Man
Appearancess: "Star Trek - The Motion Picture"

JENSON, ROY

Actor
Appearancess: "The Omega Glory"
Role: Cloud William

Roy Jenson's many films include "Ride Lonesome" (1959), "Powderkeg" (1971), "Hit Lady" (1974), "Nightside" (1980), "Honkytonk Man" (1982) and "Last Of The Great Survivors" (1984). TV spots include "The Man From UNCLE" and "Voyage To The Bottom Of The Sea."

JEWELL, AUSTEN

Unit Production Manager
Production: "Star Trek - The Motion Picture"

Austen Jewell was an assistant director on films like "Gunfight At Dodge City" (1959) and "Cast A Long Shadow" (1959).

JEWELL, LOIS

Actress
Appearancess: "Bread And Circuses"
Role: Drusilla

JOCHIM, ANTHONY

Actor Appearancess: "The Cage"
Role: Survivor

Tony Jochim's films include "The Big fisherman" (1959). His tv guest spots include "One Step Beyond."

JOHNSON, GEORGE CLAYTON

Writer
Script: "The Man Trap"

SF author George Clayton Johnson's stories include "Kick The Can" (filmed twice for "The Twilight Zone") and the nove "Logan's Run" (filmed as a movie and series).

JOHNSON, JOAN

Actress
Appearancess: "Space Seed"

Role: Guard

JOHNSON, KATIE JANE

Actress
Appearances: Star Trek VI
Role: "child" Martia

Played the "child Martia" in Star Trek VI

JONES, JAY

Actor
Appearancess: (1) "The apple"
(2) "A Piece Of The Action"
Roles: (1) Mallory
(2) Mirt

Jay Jones appeared in "Man On The Outside" (1975). Guest spots include "The Man From UNCLE."

JONES JIMMY

Actor
Appearancess: "Catspaw"
Role: Jackson

JONES, MORGAN

Actor
Appearancess: "Assignment: Earth"
Role: Colonel Nesvig

Morgan Jones' films include "Doctors' Private Lives" (1978). "Advice To The Lovelorn" (1981) and "The Red-Light Sting" (1984). He was a regular on "Blue angels" (1960).

JUNG, NATHAN

Actor
Appearancess: "The Savage Curtain"
Role: Genghis Khan

JUSTMAN, ROBERT

Associate Producer
Seasons One & Two

Bob Justman worked his way up through the ranks. He served as assistant director on shows like "Stoney Burke," and then as production manager, before being associate producer on "Star Trek," He left the show to produce "Then Came Bronson" (1969). He also produced (for Herb Solow) the pilot to "The Man From Atlantis" (1977). for Gene Roddenberry, he produced "Planet Earth" (1974). He is now a supervising producer on "Star Trek - The Next Generation."

KAIL, JAMES

Make-Up Artist
Production: "The Search For Spock"

KAMAL, JON

Actor Appearancess: "Star Trek - The Motion Picture"
Role: Sonak

KANDEL, STEPHEN

Writer
Scripts: "Mudd's Women"
"I, Mudd"
"Mudd's Passion"
"The Jihad"

Stephen Kandel created the series "Iron Horse" with James Goldstone, and has written for shows like "The Green Hornet" and "Wonder Woman." His tv movies include "Deathstalk" (1975), "Dallas Cowboys Cheerleaders II" (1980), "Shocktrauma" (1982) and "Living Proof: "The Hank Williams Jr. Appearances" (1983). Theatrical movies include "Frontier Gun" (1959) and "Battle Of The Coral Sea" (1959). He is currently producer of "MacGiver."

KAPLAN, SOL

Composer
Appearancess: "The Enemy Within"
"The Doomsday Machine"
"The Deadly Years"
"Obsession"
"The Immunity Syndrome"
"The Ultimate Computer"

Sol Kaplan has composed for numerous films, including "Tales Of Manhattan" (1942) and "The Spy Who Came In From The Cold" (1965).

KARAS, GREG

Actor
Appearancess: "The Voyage Home"
Role: Intern

KAREN, ANNA

Actress
Appearancess: "All Our Yesterdays"
Role: Woman

Anna Karen appeared in "The Affair" (1973). Her tv work includes "One Step Beyond" and "Iron Horse."

KEEFER, DON

Actor
Appearancess: "Assignment: Earth"
Role: Cromwell
Don Keefer's films include "The Bait" (1973), "The Immigrants" (1978), "Marathon" (1980), "The Five Of Me" (1981) and "Creepshow" (1982). He was a regular on "Angel" (1960-61). Guest sposts include "The Guns Of Will Sonnett" and "Iron Horse."

KEHOE, PATRICK

First Assistant Director
Production: "The Voyage Home"

Pat Kehoe was assistant director on "Poltergeist" (1982), "Things Are Tough All Over" (1982), "Bad Boys" (1982), "Twilight Zone - The Movie" (1983) and "The Philadelphia Experiment" (1984).

KELEY, IRENE

Actress
Appearancess: "The Omega Glory"
Role: Sirah

KELLERMAN, SALLY

Actress
Appearancess: "Where No Man Has Gone Before"
Role: Dr. Elizabeth Dehner

Sally Kellerman was born in Long Beach, CA in 1938. She studied under Jeff Corey (see separate entry). Ghough she worked in tv and minor films for years, she only achieved success with M*A*S*H" (1970). her other films include "Reform School Girl" (1959) and "Lost Horizon" (1973).

KELLETT, PETE

Actor
Appearancess: "Mirror, Mirror"
Role: Kirk's henchman

Pete Kellett worked in many shows as a heavy, including a long stint on "Branded" and "The Man From UNCLE."

KELLEY, DEFOREST

Actor
Role: Dr. McCoy
Series regular
DeForest Kelley was born in Atlanta, Georgia in 1920. He moved to Hollywood at the age of 17. He married Carolyn Dowling and they have been married for more than 30 years. Before Star Trek, he appeared in many Westerns. On television, he appeared on Bonanza, The Lone Ranger, and Science Fiction Theatre. Today Kelley is retired from acting aside from the Star Trek films. He made a cameo as McCoy in the Next Generation pilot in 1987.

KELLICK, ROBIN

Stand-In
Appearancess: "The Search For Spock"

KENNEY, SEAN

Actor
appearances: (1) "The Menagerie"
(2) "Arena"
(3) "A Taste Of Armaggedon"
Roles: (1) The Injured Captain Pike (2) and (3) Depaul

KENT, PAUL

Actor
Appearancess: "The Wrath Of Khan"
Role: Beach

Paul Kent's films inlcude "The Astronaut" (1972),

"Pray For The Wildcats" (1974), "The Night They Took Miss Beautiful" (1977) and "If Things were Different" (1980). Guest spots include "The Man From UNCLE," "Alias Smith And Jones" and "Griff."

KENWITH, HERB

Director
Appearances: "The Lights Of Zetar"

KEPPLER, WERNER

Make-up Artist
Production: "The Wrath Of Khan"

KHAMBATTA, PERSIS

Actress
Appearancess: "Star Trek - The Motion Picture"
Role" Ilia
Persis Khambatta was born in Bombay, India in 1950. She became a model at age 13, and was Miss India at 16. After work in Indian films she moved to London as a model, and appeared in "The Wilby Conspiracy" (1975) and "Conduct Unbecoming" (1975). She then moved ot the US, and was signed to play Ilia in the projected "Star Trek II" tv series. Thopugh the series fell through, she played the same role in the film. Since then she has been in "Nighthawks" (1981) and "Megaforce" (1982) as well as guesting on "Hunter, " "MacGiver" and "The New Mike Hammer."

KINGSBRIDGE, JOHN

Writer
Script: "Return To Tomorrow"

KINO, LLOYD

Actor
Appearancess: "The Omega Glory"
Role: Wu

Lloyd Kino was in "Seizure: The Appearances Of Kathy Morris" (1980), "Hammett" (1982) and "Forced Vengeance" (1982). he appeared frequently on "The Man From UNCLE" and on "Voyage To The Bottom Of The Sea."

KLEVEN, MAX

Actor
Appeareances: "Bread And Circuses"
Role: Maximus

Max Kleven's films include "Melvin Purvis: G-Man" (1974), "Exo-Man" (1977) and "Crisis In Sun Valley" (1978). He wrote and directed "Ruckus" (1981).

KLINE, RICHARD H.

Director of Photography
Production: "Star Trek - The Motion Picture:"

Richard Kline was born in 1926. He worked for years as a camera assistant learning his trade. His many films as cinematographer incoude "The Andromeda Strain" (1971). "Battle For The Planet Of the Apes" (1973) and "King Kong" (1976).

KNIGHT, WILLIAM

Actor
Appearancess: "The Naked Time"
Role: Crewman

KNOWLAND, JOE

Actor
Appearancess: "The Voyage Home"
Role: Antique Store Owner

KOENIG, WALTER

Actor/Writer
Series Regular: Second and Third Season, Movies
Script: "The Infinite Vulcan"

Walter Koenig was born in Chicago to Lithuanian parents, though the family moved to New York soon after his birth. He majored in psychology, but prefered to become an actor. His guest spots included "The Alfred Hitchcock Hour," "I Spy" and "Jericho" before he was signed on for "Star Trek." Since then he has appeared on "The Starlost" and "Columbo." His other written works include "Chekov's Enterprise," his account of the filming of the first movie, and "Chekov's Choice," one of the DC comic adaptions of the series.

HOLMAN, REX

Actor
Appearances: Star Trek V
Role: J'Onn

Holman played J'Onn in Star Trek V.

KOMACK, JAMES

Director
Appearances: "A Piece Of The Action"

KOVACK, NANCY

Actress
Appearancess: "A Private Little War"
Role: Nona

Nancy Kovack was born in 1935, and was a popular face of the Sixties, both n tv and in films. The latter includes "Jason And The Argonauts" (1963) and "Tarzan And The Valley Of Gold" (1966).

KOWALL, JON

Actor
Appearancess: "Mudd's Women"
Role: Gossett

Jon Kowall was a guest on numerous shows of the Sixties, including "The Wackiest Ship In The Army:" and "Voyage To The Bottom Of The Sea."

KRAMER, JOEL

Actor
Appearancess: "Star Trek - The Motion Picture"
Role: Klingon

KRIKES, PETER

Writer
Script: "The Voyager Home"

LAFFERTY, MARCY

Actress
Appearancess: "Star Trek - The Motion Picutre"
Role: Chief DeFalco

Marcy Lafferty is the wife of William Shatner, and has also appeared with him in "T.J. Hooker."

LAIRD, LAMONT

Actor
Appearancess: "The Paradise Syndrome"
Role: Indian Boy

LAKSO, EDWARD J.

Writer
Script: "And The Children Shall Lead"

Edward J. Lakso wrote extensively for Aaron Spelling, notably the pilot "The Pigeon" (1969) and a number of scripts for "The Guns Of Will Sonnett." (One of which - written shortly before his "Star Trek" episode - was called "He Shall Lead The Children...") He wrote the script for "Roadracers" (1959).

LANDERS, HARRY

Actor
Appearancess: "Turnabout Intruder"
Role: Dr. Coleman

Harry Landers was in "Mad Bull (1977), and was a regular on "Ben Casey" (1961-66).

LANDO, JOE

Actor
Appearancess: "The Voyage Home"
Role: Shore Patrolman

LANE, IVA

Actress
appearances: "Star Trek - The Motion Picture"
Role: Bridge Crew

Iva Lane appeared in "10 to Midnight" (1983).

LANSING, ROBERT

Actor
Appearancess: "Assignment: Earth"
Role: Gary Seven

Robert Lansing was born Robert Brown in San Diego in 1929. His films include "The 4-D Man" (1959) and "Empire Of The Ants (1977). His tv work spans "One Step Beyond" to "Gunsmoke." He was a regular on "87th" Precinct" (1961-62), "Twelve O'Clock High" (1964-65), "The Man Who Never was" (1966-67) and "Automan" (1983-84).

LARROQUETTE, JOHN

Actor
Appearancess: "The Search For Spock"
Role: Maltz

John Laroquette is best known as a comedian. His films include "Stripes" (1981), "Cat People" (1982), "Bare Essence" (1982), "The Last Ninja" (1983) and "Meatballs II" (1984). He was a regular on "Black Sheep Squadron" (1966-68), "Doctors' Hospital" (1975-76) and "Night Court" (1984 on).

LA RUE, BARTELL

Actor
Appearancess: (1) "The City On The Edge Of Forever"
(2) "Patterns Of Force"
(3) "Bread And Circuses"
Roles: (1) Voice of the Guardian
(2) Newscaster
(3) Announcer

LEADER, TONY

Director
Appearances: "For The World Is Hollow And I Have Touched The sky"

Tony Leader has also directed for "Lost In Space."

LEE, EVERETT

Actor
Appearancess: "The Voyage Home"
Role: Cafe Owner

LE GARDE, TED & TOM

Actors
Appearancess: "I, Mudd"
Roles: Hermans

LEIGHTON, SHEILA

Actess
Appearancess: "Spock's Brain"
Role: Luma

Sheila Leighton appeared in "The Man From UNCLE."

LEMANI, TANIA

Actrss
Appearancess: "The Wolf In The Fold"
Role: Kara

Tania Lemani also appeared in "The Man From UNCLE" and "The Wackiest Ship In The Army."

LENARD, MARC

Actor
Appearancess: (1) "Balance Of Terror"
(2) "Journey To Babel"
(3) "Yesteryear"
(4) "Star Trek - The Motion Picture"
(5) "The Search For Spock"
(6) "The Voyage Home"
(7) "The Undiscovered Country"
(8) The Next Generation
Roles: (1) Romulan Commander
(2) (3) (5) (6) (7) (8) Sarek of Vulcan
(4) Klingon Commander

Star Trek was the first Hollywood role for stage actor Mark Lenard. He appeared in the episode "Balance of Terror" as the Romulan commander. He appeared on the original series a second time as his most remembered character, Sarek, Spock's father. He also appeared in Here Come the Brides (1968-1970), and Planet of the Apes (1974). He returned to Star Trek in Star Trek: The Motion Picture as the Klingon commander. He reprised his role as Sarek in the Star Trek animated series ("Yesteryear"), and in the third, fourth, and sixth Trek movies, as well as repeatedly in The Next Generation.

LESSING, ARNOLD

Actor
Appearancess: "The Changeling"
Role: Security Guard

LESTER, JEFF

Actor
Appearancess: "The Voyage Home"
Role: FBI Agent

Jeff Lester was a regular on "Walking Tall" (1981). His films include "The Little Drummer Girl" (1984).

LEAVITT, JUDY

Actress
Appearancess: "The Voyage Home"
Role: Doctor

LEWIS, SHARI

Actress/Writer
Script: "The Lights Of Zetar"
Shari Lewis is better known as the puppeteer, and operator of Lamb Chops. This was one of her infrequent forays in writer.

LINDESMITH, JOHN

Actor
Appearancess: "The Paradise Syndrome":
Role: Engineer

LINVILLE, JOANNE

Actress
Appearancess: "The Enterprise Incident"
Role: The Romulan Commander

Joanne Linville has appeared in many tv shows from the late Fifties, including "Gunsmoke" and "Dan August." Her films include "Secrets" (1977), "The Critical List" (1978), "the Users" (1978) and "The Seduction" (1982). She was a regular on "Behind The Screen" (1981-82).

LISKA, STEPHEN

Actor
Appearancess: "The Search For Spock"
Role: Torg

LIVINGSTON, HAROLD

Writer
Script: "Star Trek - The Motion Picture"

Harold Livingston has worked mostly in tv. He wrote the tv movie "Escape To Mindanao" (1968), worked with Shatner on "The Barbary Coast", and was initially signed on as a producer for the "Star Trek II" tv series that became the first film. His script "In Thy Image" eventually made the transition to the film script.

LLOYD, CHRISTOPHER

Actor
appearances: "The Search For Spock"
Role: Kruge

Christopher Lloyd was born in Connecticut, and is best known for his part as Reverend Jim on "Taxi" (1970-83). His films have recently gained him a great deal of popularity, especially "Back To The Future" (1986). His other films include "The Legend Of The Lone Ranger" (1981), "To Be Or Not To Be" (1983) and "Clue" (1986).

LOCHER, FELIX

Actor
Appearancess: "The Deadly Years"
Role: Johnson

Felix Locher's films include "Thunder In The Sun" (1959). His guest spots include "The Man From UNCLUE," "Branded" and "One Step Beyond."

LOCKWOOD, GARY

Actor
Appearancess: "Where No Man Has Gone Before"
Role: Gary Mitchell

Gary Lockwood was born John Gary Yusolfsky in Van Nuys, CA in 1937. He began his career as a stuntman and Anthony Perkins' stand-in, then graduated to his own roles. He was married for a while to Stefanie

Powers. His films include "The Magic Sword" (1962) and "2001: A Space Odyssey" (1969. He was a regular on "Follow The Sun" (1961-62) and "The Lieutenant" (1963-64), which was the first show that Gene Roddenberry produced.

LONG, ED

Actor
Appearancess: "The Cloud Minders"
Role" Midro

LOPEZ, PERRY

Actor
appearances: "Shore Leave"
Role: Esteban Rodriguez

Perry Lopez was born in New York City in 1931 and has appeared in shows like "Voyage To The Bottom Of The Sea" and "Hec Ramsay." His films include "Cry Tough" (1959).

LORMER, JON

Actor
Appearancess: (1) "The Cage"
(2) "Return Of The Archons"
(3) "For The World Is Hollow And I Have Touched The Sky"
Roles: (1) Dr. Theodore Haskins
(2) Tamar
(3) Old Man

Jon Lormer's many films include "Rally 'Round The Flag Boys!" (1959), "Frankenstein" (1973), "Conspiracy Of Terror" (1975), "The Golden Gate Murders" (1979) and "Creepshow" (1982). His tv spots include "One Step Beyond" and "Voyage To The Bottom Of The Sea." He played the autopsy surgeon in numerous episodes of "Perry Mason."

LOU, CINDY

Actress
Appearancess: "Return to Tomorrow"
Role: Nurse

LOVSKY, CELIA

Actress
Appearancess: "Amok Time"
Role: T'Pau

LUCAS, JOHN MEREDITH

Writer/Director/Producer
Scripts: "The Changeling"
"Patterns Of Force"
"Elaan Of Troyius"
"That Which Survives"
"Appearancess: "The Ultimate Computer"
"the Enterprise Incident"
"Elaan Of Troyius"
Producer: Season Two

John Meridith Lucas alternates between his various roles. He wrote and directed a segment of "Planet Of The Apes" and wrote for the series "Logan's Run" He wrote the Irwin Allen Pilot "City Beneath The Sea/One Hour To Doomsday" (1971).

LUCKINBILL, LAURENCE

Actor
Appearances: Star Trek V
Role: Sybok

Born in 1934, Laurence Luckinbill appeared on film and tv in The Boys in the Band, Winner Take All, and The Lindbergh Kidnapping Case. He played Spock's mad brother Sybok in Star Trek V.

LUKE, KEYE

Actor
Appearancess: "Whom Gods Destroy"
role: Cory

Keye Luke was born in Canton, China in 1904. While he was a child, his family moved to the US. he started his film career as an artist and poster designer, then became a consultant for movies about China. His film debut was "The Painted Veil" (1934) , then he made several "Charlie Chan" dilms as the Number One Son. He appeared in several "Dr. Kildare" movies and twice played Kato in "Green Hornet" serials. He was a regular on "Kentucky Jones" (1964-65), "Anna And the King" (1972), "Kung-Fu" (1972-75) and "Harry O" (1976). His most famous recent role is the Chinese gentleman who delivers the warning about the "Gremlins" (1984).

LUNA, BARBARA

Actress
Appearancess: "Mirror, Mirror"
Role: Marlena

Barbara Luna was born in New York city, in 1939. Her exotic looks are a result of her mixed Hungarian Philippine parentage. She made her Broadway debut at 11, and her film debut in 1958. She has been married ot Doug McClure and Alan Arkin. Her films include Five Weeks In A Balloon" (1962) and "The Gatling Gun" (1973). She also appeared in "Buck Rogers In The 25th Century" as Hawk's wife, Koori.

LUNDIN, VICTOR

Actor
Appearancess: "Errand Of Mercy"
Role: Klingon Lt.

Victor Lundin is probably most well-known from his work as the Lobster Man in the episode of the same name from "Voyage To The Bottom Of The Sea."

LUPO, TOM

Actor
Appearancess: "The Alternative Factor"
Role: Security Guard

Tom Lupo's films include "Samurai" (1979) and "Alcatraz: The Whole Shocking Appearances" (1980).

LYNCH, HAL

Actor
Appearancess: "Tomorrow Is Yesterday"
Role: Air Police Sergeant

Hal Lynch has played small roles in numerous shows, includeing "Cannon."

LYNCH, KEN

Actor
Appearancess: "Devil In The Dark"
Role: Vanderberg

Ken Lynch's films include "Anatomy Of A Murder" (1959), "Run, Simon, Run" (1970), 'Poor Devil" (1973) and "The Winds Of War" (1983). he was a regular on "The Plainclothesman" (1949-54) and "McCloud" (1972-77).

LYONS, GENE

Actor
Appearancess: "A Taste Of Armaggedon"
Role: Ambassador Fox

Gene Lyons is a familiar tv face, though his only continuing role was on "Ironside" (1967-75). He guested on shows like "One Step Beyond."

MACAULEY, CHARLES

Actor
Appearancess: (1) "The Return Of The Archons"
(2) "Wolf In The Fold"
Roles: (1) Landru
(2) Jaris
Charles MaCauley was a guest on shows like"Griff and "Shannon". His films include "A Case Of Rape" (1974), "The Return Of The World's Greatest Detective" 91976) and "The Munsters' Revenge"(1981).

MACLACHLAN, JANET

Actress
Appearances: "The Alternative Factor"
Role: Charlene Masters

Janet MacLachlan has been very active in tv work. her other credits include guest sposts in "Ghost Appearances" and "Griff". She was a regular on "Love Thy Neighbor" (1973), "Friends" (1979), and "All In The Family" (1980-81).

MADDERN, ED

Actor
Appearancess: (1) "The Cage"
(2) "The Enemy Within"
Roles: (1) Geologist
(2) Fisher

MAFFEL, BUCK

Stunt Man
Appearances: "The Galileo Seven"
Role: Creature

Robert "Big Buck" Maffei was in "Cheech And Chongs's Nice Dreams"(1981).

MAKEE, BLAISDELL

Actor
Appearancess: (1) "Space Seed"
(2) "the Changling"
Roles: (1) Spinelli
(2) Singh

Blaisdell Makee also appeared in "Iron Horse."

MANKIEWICZ, DON

Writer
Appearances: "Court Martial"

Don Mankiewicz is the son of Herman and nephew of Joseph. He was born in 1922, and his credits include films such as "I Want To Live" (1958) and numerous episodes of "One Step Beyond" and "Ironside".

MANLEY, STEPHEN

Actor
Appearances: "Star Trek III - The Search For Spock"
Role: Spock (age 17)

Stephen Manley was a regular on "Married - The First Year" (1979) and "Secret Of Midland Heights" (1980-81).

MARCELINO, MARIO

Actor
Appearances: "Star Trek III - The Search For Spock"
Role: Communications Officer, "USS Grissom"

Mario Marcelino was a regular on "Falcon Crest" (1980-81). His films include "Losin' It" (1983).

MARCUSE, THEO

Actor
Appearances: "Catspaw"
Role: Korob

Theodore Marcuse was born in 1920, and was a guest on numerous shows in the Fifties and Sixties, includeing "Voyage To The Bottom Of The Sea" and "The Man From UNCLE". His few films include "The Cincinati Kid" (1965) and "Last Of The Secret Agents" (1966). He died in 1967.

MARKO, PETER

Actor
Appearances: "The Galileo Seven"
Role: Gaetano

MARLO, STEVE

Actor
Appearances: "A Piece Of The Action"
Role: Zabo

Steve Marlo appeared in a string of low-budget westerns, like "The Young Captives" (1959) and "The Hanged Man" (1974). He also worked in tv westerns like "Branded."

MARS, BRUCE

Actor
Appearancess: (1) "Shore Leave"
(2) "Assignment: Earth"
Roles: (1) Finnegan
(2) Police officer

Bruce Mars also appeared on shows like "Voyage To The Bottom Of The Sea" and "And Then Came Bronson".

MARSHALL, DON

Actor
Appearances: "The Galileo Seven"
Role: Lt. Boma

Don Marshall was a regular on "Land Of The Giants", (1968-70) and guested in shows such as "The Bionic Woman".

MARSHALL, JOAN

Actress
Appearances: "The Deadly Years"
Role: Janet Wallace

Sarah Marshall was a regular on "Miss Winslow And Son" (1969). Her films include "Scruples" (1980), "The

Bunker" (1981) and "The Letter" (1982). Her tv work includes "Perry Mason."

MARSHALL, WILLIAM

Actor
Appearances: "The Ultimate Computer"
Role: Dr. Daystrom

William Marshall was born August 19th, 1924 in Gary, Indiana. he was educated at New York University. His best-known role is in the exploitation films of "Blacula", but other films include "The Boston Strangler" (1968) and "Twilight's Last Gleaming" (1977). He was a regular on "Rosetti And Ryan" (1977).

MARTEL, ARLENE

Actress
Appearances: "Amok Time"
Role: T'Pring

Arlene Martel was extremely active in tv in the Sixties, in series like "Iron Horse" and "The Man From UNCLE" By the Seventies, she was slowing down, appearing in less shows, including "Petrocelli". her films include "The Adventures Of Nick Carter" (1972). "Indict And Convict" (1974) and "Conspiracy Of Terror" (1975).

MARTIN, JEFFREY

Actor
Appearances: "Star Trek IV - The Voyage Home"
Role: Electronic Technician

MARTIN, MERDE

Actor
Appearances: "The Changeling"
Role: Crewman

MATHESON, RICHARD

Writer
Appearances: "The Enemy Within"

Born in 1926, Richard Matheson is a noted sf/horror writer, who has written screenplays for movies such as "The Incredible Shrinking Man" and "The Night Stalker", one of the highest-rated tv movies of all time. He also created the series "Ghost Appearances/Circle Of Fear"..

MATLOVSKY, SAMUEL

Composer
Appearances: "I,Mudd"

Now as Samuel Matlofsky, he continues to work from time to time. He composed the score to "Fish Hawk" (1981).

MAURER, RALPH

Actor
Appearancess: (1) "The Return Of The Archons"
(2) "Patterns Of Force"
Roles: (1) Bilar
(2) SS Lieutenant

MAURISHKA

Actress
Appearances: "Operation - Annihilate"
Role: Yeoman Zahra

MAXWELL, CHARLES

Actor
Appearances: "Spectre Of The Gun"
Role: Yirgil Earp

Charles Maxwell was a semi-regular on "I Led Three Lives" (1953-56). He also appeared on shows like "Branded."

MAYAMA, MIKO

Actress
Appearances: "A Tatste O Armageddon"
Role: Tarmula

Mike Mayama was a regular on "Hey Landlord" (1966-67).

MCCAULEY, DANNY

Assistant Director
Appearances: "Star Trek - The Motion Picture"

Danny McCauley was also assistant director on "Zorro - The Gay Blade" (1981), "Jinxed" (1982), "Blue Thunder" (1983).

MCCONNELL, JUDY

Actress
Appearances: "Wolf In The Fold"
Role: Yeoman Tankis

Judy McConnell was a regular on "The Beverly Hillbillies" (1969) and "green Acres" (1970-71). Her films include "Gidget Gets Married" (1972).

MCCOY, JAMES L.

Makeup Artist
Appearances: "Star Trek III - The Search For Spock"

MCCREADY, ED

Actor
Appearancess: (1) "Miri"
(2) "Dagger Of The Mind"
(3) "Patterns Of Force"
(4) "The Omega Glory"
(5) "Spectre Of The Gun"
Roles: (1) Creature
(2) Inmate
(3) SS Trooper
(4) Dr. Carter
(5) Barber

Ed McCready is still active in tv work. His other appearances include series like "Today's FBI", and films like "Partners" (1982).

MCDOUGALL, DON

Director
Appearances: "The Squire Of Gothos"

Don McDougall has also directed episodes of shows like "Ghost Appearances", "Planey Of The Apes", The Gemini Man" and "The Bionic Woman". His films include "The Aquarians" (1970), "The Heist" (1972) and "The Mark Of Zorro" (1974).

MCEVEETY, SEAN

Actor
Appearances "Miri"
Role: Red-haired Boy

MCEVEETY, VINCENT

Director
Appearancess: (1) "Miri"
(2) "Dagger Of The Mind"
(3) "Balance Of Terror"
(4) "Patterns Of Force"
(5) "The Omega Glory"
(6) "Spectre Of The Gun"

Vincent McEveety's many credits include episodes of shows like "Petrocelli". He has done much work for Disney, including "Million Dollar Duck" (1971) and "Herbie goes Bananas" (1980).

MCFADDEN, GATES

Actress
Role: Dr. Beverly Crusher
Series regular

TNG is the first television job for Gates McFadden. She grew up in Ohio, then moved to New York City. She began to work as a dancer and actress on the stage. She also worked as a director and choregrapher, including on the late Jim Henson's film Labyrinth. McFadden was away from TNG during the second season when she made a brief appearance in the film Hunt for the Read October.

MCGINNIS, SCOTT

Actor
Appearances: "Star Trek III - The Search For Spock"
Role: "Mr. Adventure"

Scott McGinnis was a regular on "Operation Petticoat" (1978-79). His films include "Survival Of Dana" (1979) and "Joysticks" (1983).

MCGOWAN, OLIVER

Actor
Appearances: "Shore Leave"
Role: Caretaker

MCNULTY, PATRICIA

Actress
Appearances: "Charlie X"
Role: Tina Lawton

Pat McNulty had been a regular on "The Tycoon" (1964-65).

MCTOSH, BILL

Actor
Appearances: "Star Trek - The Motion Picture"
Role: Klingon

MEANDER, WILLIAM

Actor
Appearances: "Court Martial"
Role: Representative Lindstrom

MEERSON, STEVE

Writer
Appearances: "Star Trek IV - The Voyage Home"

MEGNA, JOHN

Actor
Appearances: "Miri"
Role: Fat Little Boy

John Megna's films include "The Boy In The Plastic Bubble" (1976). "Skag" (1980) and "The Cannonball Run" (1981).

MEIER, JOHN

Wiliam Shatner's Stunt Double
Appearances: "Star Trek IV - The Voyage Home"

John Meier's other films inlclude "Cannery Row" (1982).

MELL, JOSEPH

Actor
Appearances: "The Cage"
Role: Orion Trader

Joe Mell's films include "City Of Fear" (1959) and "The Delphi Bureau" (1972). His tv work includes "Adventures Of Superman."

MENGES, JAMES

Actor
Appearances: "Star Trek IV - The Voyage Home"
Role: Jogger

MENVILLE, CHUCK

Writer
Appearancess: (1) "Once Upon A Planet"
(2) "The Practical Joker"

MERIWETHER, LEE

Actress
Appearances: "That Which Survives"
Role: Losira

Lee Meriwether was born in 1935, and was a regular on "The Time Tunnel" (1966-67). "The New Andy Griffith Show" (1971), and "Barnaby Jones" (1973-80). She is probably best known as one of the actresses to have played Catwoman on "Batwoman". Currently, she and her daughter are doing commercials for Uncle Ben's Rice.

MERRIFIELD, RICHARD

Actor
Appearances: "Tomorrow Is Yesterday"
Role: Technician

MEYER, NICHOLAS

Director
Star Trek II
Star Trek VI
Writer
Star Trek IV
Star Trek VI

Meyer was born in 1945. He won initial fame for his Sherlock Holmes novel, The Seven Percent Solution. He wrote and directed Time After Time. His association with Star Trek began as director of Star Trek II: The Wrath of Khan (1982). He wrote the Appearances for Star Trek IV (1984) and directed and helped write Star

Trek VI.

MICHELSON, HAROLD

Production Designer
Appearances: "Star Trek - The Motion Picture"

Harold Michelson also worked on"Mommie Dearest" (1981).

MILES, BOB

Actor
Appearances: "Miri"
Role: McCoy's Double

MILLER, ALLAN

Actor
Appearances: "Star Trek III - The Search For Spock"
Role" Alien in the Bar

Allan Miller was a regular on "AES Hudson Street" (1978), "Soap" (1980-81), "Nero Wolfe" (1981), and Knotts Landing" (1981-82). He also guested on shows like "Battlestar Galactica".

MILLKIS, EDWARD K

Assistant to Producer Season Two Assistant Producer Season Three

Edward Millkis learned his craft on "Star Trek". he later went on to produce shows like "Petrocelli", and films like "Women In Chains" (19720 and "The Devil's Daugheter" (1973). He is currently working on "Star Trek - The Next Generation."

INES, STEPHEN

Actor
Appearances: "Balance Of Terror"
Role: Tomlinson

MINOR, MICHAEL

Art Director
Appearances: "Star Trek II - The Wrath Of Khan"

Mike Minor began working on the original show, doing model effects. For the first film he was the production artist, graduating to art director for the second film. He has since worked on "The Man Who Saw Tomorrow" (1981) and "Spacehunter: Adventures In The Forbidden Zone" (1983).

MIRANDA, JOHN

Actor
Appearances: "Star Trek IV - The Voyage Home"
Role: Garbageman

John Miranda has appeared in small roles on shows like "The Paper Chase."

MITCHELL, DALLAS

Actor
Appearances: "Charlie X"
Role: Tom Nellis

Dallis Mitchell has guest-starred in shows such as "Voyage To The Bottom Of The Sea". His films include "Any Second Now": (1969), "Hijack!" (1973) and "Tail Gunner Joe" (1977).

MITCHELL, JAMES X.

Actor
Appearances: "Journey To Babel"
Role: Lt. Josephs

MONTAIGNE, LAWRENCE

Actor
Appearancess: (1) Balance Of Terror"
(2) "Amok Time"
Role: (1) Decius
(2) Stonn

Lawrence Montaigne's other guest spots include "The Man From UNCLE" "Voyage To The Bottom Of The Sea" and "The Feather And Father Gang". His films include "The Underground Man" (1974) and "Deadly Blessings" (1981).

MONTALBAN, RICARDO

Actor
Appearances (1) "Space Seed"
(2) Star Trek II - The Wrath of Khan"
Role: Khan Noonian Singh

Ricardo Montalban was born November 25th, 1920 in Mexico City. After making films in his native country, he was signed on by MGM in 1947 to play romantic leads. His films include "Neptunes Daugher" (1949), "The Singing Nun" (1966) and "Conquest Of The Planet Of The apes" (1972). More recently, he was very popular in the tv series "Fantasy Island". He was the spokesman for Chrysler cars for many years in their tv ads.

MOORDIGAN, DAVE

Actor
Appearances: "Star Trek - The Motion Picture"
Role: Klingon

Dave Moordigan was also in "48 Hrs" (1982).

MORGA, TOM

Actor
Appearancess: (1) Star Trek I, (2) Star Trek VI
Roles: (1) Klingon, (2) "the Brute"

Morga appeared as a Klingon in Star Trek: The Motion Picture and as "the Brute" in Star Trek VI: The Undiscovered Country.

MORGAN, SEAN

Actor
Appearancess: (1) "The Return of the Archons"
(2) "The Ultimate Computer"
(3) "The Tholian Web"
Roles: (1) and (3) Lt. O'Neil
(2) Ensign Harper

Sean Morgan also guested on "Voyage To The Bottom Of The Sea" He Was a regular on "The Adventures of Ozzie And Harriet" (1965-66).

MORI, JEANNE

Actress
Appearances: "Star Trek III - The Search For Spock"
Role: Helmswoman, "USS Grissom"

Jeanne Mori was also in "Night Shift" (1982).

MORRIS, PHIL

Actor
Appearances: "Star Trek III - The Search For Spock"
Role: Trainee Foster

MORROW, BYRON

Actor
Appearancess: (1) "Amok Time"
(2) :"For The World Is Hollow And I Have Touched The Sky"
Roles: (1) Komack
(2) Admiral Westervliet

Byron Morrow's other guest roles were on shows like "Lost In Space" and "The Bionic Woman". He was a regular on "The New Breed" (1961-62) and "Executive Suite" (1976-77).

MORTON, MICKEY

Actor
Appearances: "The Gamesters Of Triskelion"
Role: Kloog

Michey Morton also guest-starred on "The Bionic Woman," "The Man From UNCLE" and "Iron Horse." He provided one of the voices for "Fire And Ice" (1983).

MOSS, ARNOLD

Actor
Appearances: "The Conscience Of The Kin"
Role: Karidan

Arnold Moss was born January 28th, 1910 in Brooklyn. His films include "My Favorite Spy" (1951) and "Caper Of The Golden Bulls" (1967). His tv work includes both "The Man From UNCLE" and "The Girl From UNCLE."

MOSS, STEWART

Actor
Appearancess: (1) "The Naked Time"

(2) "By Any Other Name"
Roles: (1) Tormolen
(2) Henak

Stewart Moss was a regular on "Fay" (1975-76). His films include "Live Again, Die Again" (1974), "Conspiracy Of Terror" (18975) and "Women In White" (1979). He guest-starred on shows like "Cannon."

MUDIE, LEONARD

Actor
Appearances: "The Cage"
Role: Survivor

Leonard Mudie was born in 1894 in England, moving to Hollywood in the Thirties. He was in films like "The Mummy" (1932), "Dark Victory" (1939) and "The Magnetic Monster" (1953). He Appeared a number of times in "Adventures Of Superman" on tv. He died in 1965.

MULDAUR, DIANA

Actress
Appearancess: (1) "Return to Tomorrow", (2) "Is There in Truth No Beauty?", (3) The Next Generation second season
Roles: (1) Dr. Ann Mulhall, (2) Dr. Miranda Jones, (3) Dr. Katherine Pulaski

Diana Muldaur was born in the mid-Forties and was a regular on "The Survivors" (1969-70), "McCloud" (1970-77), "born Free" (1974), "The Tony Randall Show" (1976-78), "Hizzoner" (1979), and "Fitz And Bones" (1981). Her films include "McQ" (1973) and "The Word" (1978). She appeared as Ann Mulhall in the original series episode "Return to Tomorrow" and as Jones in "Is There in Truth No Beauty?" When Gates McFadden was absent from the second season of The Next Generation, Muldaur played the Enterprise's chief medical officer, Dr. Katherine Pulaski. She also had a recurring role on tv's L.A. Law.

MULLENDORE, JOSEPH

Composer
Appearances: The Consceience Of The King"

Joseph Mullendore also scored episodes of "Voyage To The Bottom Of The Sea" and "Lost In Space".

MURDOCK, GEORGE

Actor
Appearances: Star Trek V
Role: "God" creature

George Murdock filled the role of the "God" creature in Star Trek V.

MURDOCK, KERMIT

Actor
Appearances: "All Our Yesterdays"
Role: The Prosecutor

Kermit Murdock's films include "The Lonely Profession" (1969), "The Godchild" (1974) and "Captain And The Kings" (1976).

MUSKAT, JOYCE

Writer
Appearances: "The Empath"

MUSTIN, TOM]

Actor
Appearances: "Star Trek IV - The Voyage Home"
Role: Intern

NALDER, REGGIE

Actor
Appearances: "Journey To Babel"
Role: Shras

Reggie Nalder's films include "The Dead Don't Die" (1975), "Salem's Lot" (1979) and "The Devil And Max Devlin" (1981). His tv work includes "The Man From UNCLE."

NAPIER, CHARLES

Actor
Appearances: "The Way To Eden"
Role: Adam

Charles Napier was one of the stars of the recent "Outlaws" (1987). He had also starred in "The Oregon Trail" (1976-77). His films include "Wacko" (1982).

NARADZAY, JOSEPH

Actor
Appearances: "Star Trek IV - The Voyage Home"
Role: 1st Sgt, USMC

NARDINO, GARY

Executive Producer
Star Trek III, Star Trek VI

Nardino was Executive Producer of Star Trek III and VI.

NEEDHAM, HAL

Actor/Stuntman/Director
Appearances: "Where No Man Has Gone Before"
Role Gary Lockwood's Stunt Double

Born in 1931, Hal Needham was initially a stunt man, who turned his talents to directing action films after a huge success with "Smokey And The Bandit" (1977). He was also responsible for "The Cannonball Run" (1981) and "Megaforce" (1983).

NELSON, CAROLYN

Actress
Appearances: "The Deadly Years"
Role: Yeoman Atkins

carolyn Nelson's films include "Man On A String" (1972), "Freedom" (1981) and "Memorial Day" (1983).

NELSON, GENE

Director
Appearances: "The Gamesters Of Triskelion"

Gene Nelson was born Leander Berg in 1920. Initially an actor, he appeared in films like "Gentelman's Agreement" (1947) and "Lullaby of Broadway" (1952). In the Sixties, he moved to directing, and his films include "Kissin' Cousins" (1964) and "Washington Behind Closed Doors: (1977). He directed tv shows like "The Wackiest Ship In The Army" and "Get Christie Love!"

NEWLAND, JOHN

Director
Appearances: "Errand Of Mercy"

John Newland is an actor/director. He is most noted for hosting and directing every episode of "One Step Beyond", but he has directed many tv shows, including "The Man From UNCLE".

NEWMAR, JULIE

Actress
Appearances: "Friday's Child"
Role: Eleen

Julie Newmar was born Julie Newmeyer on August 16th, 19035 in Los Angeles. She is best known as having played the Catwoman on "Batman". Her other guest spots include "The Twilight Zone" and "The Bionic Woman". She was "My Living Doll" (1964-65). Her films include "Seven Brides For Seven Brothers" (1954) and "McKenna's Gold" (1969).

NICHOLS, NICHELLE

Actress
Regular
Role: Uhura

Nichelle Nichols was born in Robbins, IL. After studying balley, she switched to music and acting. In her teens, she was discovered by Duke Ellingotn and spent a while as a singer for his band. This led to her first film, "Porgy And Bess" (1959), though most of her role wound up on the cutting room floor! Since then she has sung and danced across the world. A small role in "The Lieutenant" for Gene Roddenberry led to her casting as Uhura. A strong advocate of real spaceflight, she has also done promotional work for NASA to encourage minorities to apply for work on the space shuttle program.

NIMOY, LEONARD

Actor/Director/Writer
Actor:
Regular Role:
Spock
Director:
Appearances: (1) "Star Trek III - The Search For Spock"
(2) "Star Trek IV - The Voyage Home"
Writer:

Appearances:
"Star Trek IV - The Voyage Home"

Leonard Nimoy was born March 26th, 1931 in Boston, MA. Moving to Hollywood in 1954, he married actress Sandi Zober. The couple have two children, Julie and Adam. He began with small roles in films like "Zombies Of The Stratosphere" (1952) and tv shows such as "Gunsmoke" and "Dragnet" before a spot on Roddenberry's "The Lieutenant" led to his casting as Spock. Since then, he has become famous. He has done much stage work, written poetry, made records and continued to act. He directed Star Trek III and IV, and the feature Three Men and a Baby. He also helped script Star Trek IV. He served as executive producer on Star Trek VI. He made a guest appearance as Spock on The Next Generation. He and Zober divorced.

NIMS, SHARI

Actress
Appearances: "The Apple:"
Role: Sayana

NIVEN, LARRY

Writer
Appearances: "The Slaver Weapon"

Larry Niven is a noted sf author. Among his works are "Ringworld". "Oath Of Fealty" and "Footfall".

NOLAND, VALORA

Actress
Appearances: "Patterns Of Force"
Role" Daras

Valora Noland also appeared on "The Man From UNCLE".

HORNSTEIN, MARTY

Unit Production Manager
Star Trek VI

NORWICK, NATALIE

Actress
Appearances: "The Conscience Of The King"
Role: Martha Leighton

NOWELL, DAVID

Camera Operator
Appearances: "Star Trek III - The Search For Spock"

NUYEN, FRANCE

Actress
Appearances: "Elaan Of Troyius"
Role: Elaan

France Nuyen was born France Nguyen Vannga on July 31st, 1939. She moved to the US to star in occassional films and tv shows, and married Robert Culp. Her films include "South Pacific" (1958), "A Girl Named Tamiko" (1963) and "Battle For The Planet Of The Apes" (1973). She currently appears as a regular on "St. Elsewhere."

O'CONNELL WILLIAM

Actor
Appearances: "Journey To Babel"
Role: Thelev

William O'Connell's films include "The Dead Don't Die" (1972).

O'CONNOR, TERRANCE

Actor
Appearances: "Star Trek - The Motion Picture"
Role" Chief Ross

Terrance O'Connell has had small roles in shows like "Barnaby Jones."

O'HERLIHY, MICHAEL

Director
Appearances: "Tommorrow Is Yesterday"

Michael O'Herlihy was born in Ireland in 1929. He worked for Disney on and off on films such as "The Fighting Prince of Donegal" (1966) and "The One And Only Genuine Original Family Band" (1968). He has also directed episodes of "The Guns Of Will Sonnett" and "Today's FBI".

OLIVER, SUSAN

Actress
Appearances: "The Cage"
Role: Vina

Susan Oliver was born in 1937. She was a regular on "Peyton Place" (1966). Her other guest spots include "The Man From UNCLE," "Alias Smith And Jones" and "Circle Of Fear." Her few films include "Green Eyed Blonde" (1957) and "Looking For Love" (1964).

OPATASHU, DAVID

Actor
Appearances: "A Taste Of Armageddon"
Role: Anan VII
David Opatashu was born January 30th, 1918 in New York City. He Began his career in the Yiddish theatre. He has guest-starred on shows like "The Man from UNCLE", "Voyage To The Bottom Of The Sea" and "The Bionic Woman". He was a regular on "Bonino" (1953) and "The Secret Empire" (1979). His films include "Exodus" (1960) and "Tarzan And The Valley Of Gold" (1966).

ORANGE, DAVID

Actor
Appearances: Star Trek VI
Role: Sleepy Klingon

OSWALD, GERD

Director
Appearancess: (1) "The Conscience Of The King" (2) "The Alternative Factor"

Gerd Oswald was born June 9th, 1916 in Berlin. He was a child actor, son of Producer/director Richard Oswald. He fled Germany when the Nazis came to power in 1938, and he and his father moved to Hollywood. His career there began as an assistant director, then on to B-movies. His many other tv credits include "The Outer Limits", "Bonanza" and "Voyage To The Bottom Of The Sea". His films include "A Kiss Before Dying" (1956) and "Agent for harm" (1956).

OVERTON, FRANK

Actor
Appearances: "This Side Of Paradise"
Role: Elias Sandoval

Frank Overton was a regular on "Twelve O'Clock High" (1964-67). His films include "The Las Mile" (1959). He guested in series like "One Step Beyond" and "Perry Mason."

PALMER, CHARLES

Actor
Appearances: "Amok Time"
Role: Vulcan Litterbearer

Charles Palmer was also in "Little Gloria...Happy At Last" (1982)

PALMER, GREGG

Actor
Appearances: "Spectre Of The Gun"
Role: Rancher

Gregg Palmer was born Palmer Lee on January 25th, 1927, in San Francisco. He began his career as a disc jockey before switching to acting. He also guested on shows like "Alias Smith And Jones". He was a regular on "Run Buddy Run" (1966-67). His films include "The Creature Walks Among Us" (1956), "The Rare Breed" (1966) and "The Shootist" (1976).

PARRISH, JULIE

Actress
Appearances: "The Menagerie"
Role: Miss Piper

Julie Parrish was a regular on "Good Morning, World" (1967)-68. Her films include "The Time Machine" (1978), "When She Was Bad..." (1970), and "The Devil And Max Devlin" (1981)

PARRISH, LESLIE

Actress
Appearances: "Who Mourns For Adonais?"
Role: Lt. Caroline Palmas

Leslie Parrish's films include "Li'l Abner" (1959) and the pilot for "Banyon": (1971). She has guest-starred on shows like "Perry Mason" and "
The Man From UNCLE."

PARSONS, Jr. LINDSLEY

Executive in Charge of Production
Appearances: "Star Trek - The Motion Picture"

Lindsley Parsons Jr. began his career as assistant director on films like "Al Capone" (1959) and "The Purple Gang" (1959) (this latter being produced by his father).

PARTRIDGE, DEREK

Actor
Appearances: "Plato's Stepchildren"
Role: Dionyo

Derek Partridge's films include "The Ivory Ape" (1980) and "Savage Harvest" (1981)

PASKEY, EDDIE

Actor
Appearancess: (1) "Where No Man Has Gone Before"
(2) "The Conscience Of The Kind"
(3) "The Return Of the Archons"
(4) "A Taste Of Armageddon"
(5) "This Side Of Paradise"
(6) "The Alternative Factor"
(7) "The Omega Glory"
Roles: (2), (3), (5), (6), (7) Lt. Leslie
(1) Security Guard
(4) Eminian Technician

PATAKI, MICHAEL

Actor
Appearances: "The Trouble With Tribbles"
Role: Korax

Michael Pataki was a regular on "Paul Sand In Friends And Lovers" (1974-75), "Get Christie Love!" (1975), "The Amazing Spiderman" (1978), and "Phyl And Micky" (1980). He guested on series like "Voyage To The Bottom Of The Sea". His films include "Dead And Buried" (1981) and "Sweet Sixteen" (1983).

PATRICK, CHRISTIAN

Actor
Appearances: "The Alternative Factor"
Role: Transporter Technician

PAZ, JOE

Actor
Appearances: "Amok Time"
Role: Vulcan Litterbearer

Joe Paz's films include "Never Steal Anything Small" (1959).

PECK, ED

Actor
Appearances: "Tommorrow Is Yesterday"
Role: Colonel Fellini

Ed Peck was Officer Kirk on "Happy Days". He was a regular on "Major Dell Conway Of The Flying Tigers" (1951), "The Super" (1972) and "Semi-Tough" (1980). His films include "Zoot Suit" (1982).

PEEK, RUSS

Actor
Appearances: "Amok Time"
Role: Vulcan Executioner

PEEPLES, SAMUEL A.

Writer
Appearancess: (1) "Where No Man Has Gone Before"
(2) " Beyond The Farthest Star"

Samuel Peeples also wrote for shows like "Rawhide" and "The Girl From UNCLE". He also wrote the script for Roddenberry's "Spectre" (1977) and "A Real American Hero" (1978), which he produced himself.

PENN, LEO

Director
Appearances: "The Enemy Within"

Leo Penn's many other directing credits include episodes of "Voyage To The Bottom Of The Sea", "Lost In Space", "The Bionic Woman" and "Remington Steele".

PERKINS, JACK

Actor
Appearances: "Bread And Circuses"

Role: Master of the Games

Jack Perkins was a guest on shows like "The Young Rebels" and "Hart To Hart". His films include "Killer Bees" (1974), and "Night Shift" (1982).

PERNA, VIC

Actor
Appearancess: (1) "The Corbomite Maneuver"
(2) Arena"
(3) "The Changeling"
(4) Mirror, Mirror"
Roles: (1) Balok's Voice
(2)Metron's Voice
(3)Nomad's Voice
(4) Tharn

Vic Perrin's films include "Dragnet" (1969), "The Abduction Of Saint Anne" (1975) and "The UFO Incident" (1975). His tv roles include appearances on "Perry Mason."

PERRY, JOYCE

Writer
Appearances: "The Time Trap"

PERRY, ROD

Actor
Appearances: "Star Trek - The Motion Picture"
Role: Security Officer

Rod Perry was a regular on "SWAT" (1975-76). His other films include, "The Autobiography of Miss Jane Pittman" (1974) and "Trapped Beneath The Sea" (1974).

PERRY, ROGER

Actor
Appearances: "Tommorrow Is Yesterday"
Role: Major Christopher

Among Roger Perry's other guest roles are Barnaby Jones" and "The Bionic Woman". He was a regular on "Harrigan And Son" (1960-61), "Arrest And Trial" (1963-64), "The Facts Of Life" (1981-83), and "Falcon Crest" (1982-84).

PETERMAN, DONALD

Director of Photography
Appearances: "Star Trek IV - The Voyage Home"

Donald Peterman also worked on "King Of The Mountain" (1981), "Rich And Famous" (1981), "Kiss Me Goodbye" (1982), "Flashdance" (1983).

PETERMAN, KEITH

Camera Operator
Appearances: "Star Trek IV - The Voyage Home"

PETERS, BROCK

Actor
Appearances: "Star Trek IV - The Voyage Home", "The Undiscovered Country"
Role: Admiral Cartwright

Brock Peters was born on July 2nd, 1927 in New York City. His films include "Porgy And Bess" (1959), "To Kill A Mockingbird" (1962) and "Soylent Green" (1973). His tv work includes spots on "The Girl From UNCLE" and "The Bionic Woman."

PETERS, GREGG

Assistant Producer
Season Three

PETTIJOHN, ANGELIQUE

Actress
Appearances: "The Gamesters Of Triskelion"
Role: Shahna

Angelique Petijohn also worked on shows such as "The Man From UNCLE" and "Batman." She recently issued a pair of posters of herself as Shahna, one of which was topless...

PEVNEY, JOSEPH

Director
Appearancess: (1) "Arena"
(2) "Return Of The Archons"
(3) "A Taste Of Armageddon"
(4) "Devil In The Dark"

(5) "The City On The Edge Of Forever"
(6) "Amok Time"
(7) "The Apple"
(8) "Catspaw"
(9) "Journey To Babel"
(10) "Friday's Child"
(11) "The Deadly Years"
(12) "Wolf In The Fold"
(13) "The Trouble With Tribbles"
(14) "The Immunity Syndrome"

Joseph Pevney was born in New York City in 1920, and started in vaudeville in 1920. In the forties, he moved to Hollywood as an actor, then became a director. His films as director include "Air Cadet" (1951), "Away All Boats" (1956) and "The Night Of The Grizzly" (1966). He has also directed episodes of shows like "Petrocelli".

PHILLIPS, FRED B.

Makeup Artist
Seasons One - Three
Star Trek - The Motion Picture.

Fred Phillips also worked on shows like "Stoney Burke."

PHILLIPS, JANNA

Makeup Artist
Appearances: "Star Trek - The Motion Picture"

Janna Phillips is the daughter of Fred, and is following in her father's footsteps.

PHILLIPS, ROBERT

Actor
Appearances: "The Cage"
Role: Orion Space Officer

Robert Phillips also guest starred on shows like "Planet Of The Apes". His films include "Yuma" (1971), "The Gun And The Pulpit" (1974) and "The Ultimate Imposter" (1979).

PHILLIPS, WILLIAM F.

Associate Producer
Appearances: "Star Trek II - The Wrath Of Khan"

William Phillips produced the "Richie Brockelman" series, as well as tv films like "The Night Rider" (1979) and "Listen To Your Heart" (1983).

PIKE, DONALD

Stunt Coordinator
Star Trek VI

PILLAR, GARY

Actor
Appearances: "A Private Little War"
Role: Yutan

PILLER, MICHAEL

Executive Producer
The Next Generation

Michael Piller began his career at CBS News. He went on in television news at stations in Chicago and Charlotte, NC. He attended the Julliard School of Music. He was a writer/producer for the series Simon and Simon, Cagney & Lacey, Probe, and Miami Vice. He will create Deep Space Nine with Rick Berman.

PILLSBURY, GARTH

Actor
Appearancess: (1) "Mirror, Mirror"
(2) "The Cloud Minders"
Roles: (1) Wilson
(2) Prisoner

PINE, PHILIP

Actor
Appearances: "The Savage Curtain"
Role: Colonel Green

Philip Pine was born in Hanford, CA on July 16th, 1925. He also guest-starred on "Voyage To The Bottom Of The Sea" and "Barnaby Jones". He was a regular on "The Blue Knight" (1975-76). His films include "The Big Fisherman" (1959).

PISTONE, MARTIN

Actor
Appearances: "Star Trek IV - The Voyage Home"
Role: Starfleet Controller

PLUMMER, CHRISTOPHER

Actor
Appearances: Star Trek VI
Role: Gen. Chang

Christopher Plummer appeared as Klingon Gen. Chang in Star Trek VI. Plummer was born in Montreal, Canada in 1927. In his long and distinguished career he has appeared on tv, film, and the stage. He has been featured in The Sound of Music, International Velvet, The Return of the Pink Panther, and Dragnet.

POLITE, CHARLENE

Actress
Appearances: "The Cloud Minders"
Role: Vanna

Charlene Polite also appeared in "Love Hate Love" (1971).

POLLACK, NAOMI

Actress
Appearancess: (1) "The Paradise Syndrome"
(2) "That Which Survives"
Roles: (1) Indian Woman
(2) Rahda

POLLARD, MICHAEL J.

Actor
Appearances: "Miri"
Role: Jahn

Michael Pollard was born Michael Pollack on May 30th, 1939 in Pacific, NJ. He also guested on "Lost In Space". It was his role in "Bonny And Clyde" (1967) that brought him to fame, since which he has made films like "Dirty Little Billy" (1972) and "Melvin And Howard".

PORTER, BRETT

Actor
Appearances: Star Trek VI
Role: Gen. Stex

POTENZA, VADIA

Actor
Appearances: "Star Trek III - The Search For Spock"
Role: Spock (age 13)

POVILL, JOHN

Associate Producer
Appearances: "Star Trek - The Motion Picture"

PROHASKA, JANOS

Monster actor
Appearancess: (1) "Devil In The Dark"
(2) "A Private Little War"
Roles: (1) Horta
(2) Mugato

Janos Prohaska also played monsters in "The Outer Limits" (for which he originally made the Horta costume), "Lost In Space" and "Voyage To The Bottom Of The Sea". He was a regular on "The Andy Williams Show" (1969-71) as a bear...

PROKOP, PAUL

Actor
Appearances: "Mirror, Mirror"
Role: Guard

PULFORD, DON

Star Trek V
Stunt Double for William Shatner

PYNE, FRANCIN

Actress
Appearances: "The Man Trap"
Role: Fake "Nancy Crater"

RALSTON, GILBERT A.

Writer
Appearances: "Who Mourns For Adonais?"

RALSTON, KEN

Visual Effects Supervisor
Appearances: "Star Trek IV - The Voyage Home"

RAMSAY, LOGAN

Actor
Appearances: "Break And Circuses"
Role: Claudius

Logan Ramsay was born in Long Beach, CA on March 21st, 1921. He also guested on "Petrocelli," "The Man From UNCLE" and "Alias Smith And Jones." He was a regular in "On The Rocks" (1975-76).

RAMSAY, TODD

Film Editor
Appearances: "Star Trek - The Motion Picture"

Todd Ramsay also edited "Escape From New York" (1981) and "The Thing" (1982).

RAMUS, NICK

Actor
Appearances: "Star Trek IV - The Voyage Home"
Role: Helmsman, "USS Saratoga"

Nick Ramus was a regular on "The Chisholms" (1980) and "Falcon Crest" (1981-1982). His films include "Windwalker" (1981).

RAWLINGS, ALICE

Actress
Appearances: "Court Martial"
Role: Jame Finney

RAWLINS, PHIL

Unit Production Manager
Appearances: "Star Trek - The Motion Picture"

Phil Rawlins also worked as an assistant director on films such as "Al Capone" (1959).

RAYMOND, GUY

Actor
Appearances: "The Trouble With Tribbles"
Role: Trader

Guy Raymond was a regular on "Ichabod And Me" (1961-62) and "90 Bristol Court" (1964-65). His films include "Queen Of The Stardust Ballroom" (1975) and "4D Man" (1959).

RAYMONE, KIRK

Actor
Appearancess: (1) "Friday's Child"
(2) "The Cloud Minders"
Roles: (1) Duur
(2) Cloud Guide

REASON, RHODES

Actor
Appearances: "Bread And Circuses"
Role: Flavius

Rhodes Reason was born in Berlin, November 30th, 1928, twin brother of Rex. He was a regular on "White Hunter" (1958) and "Bus Stop" (1961-62). His few films include "Jungle Heat" (1957) and "King Kong Escapes!" (1968).

REDDIN, JAN

Actress
Appearances: "Space Seed"
Role: Crewmember

REIMERS, ED

Actor
Appearances: "The Trouble With Tribbles"
Role: Admiral Fitzpatrick

Ed Reimers was the announcer of the quiz show "Do You Trust Your Wife?" (1956-57).

RESCHER, GAYNE

Director of Photography
Appearances: "Star TRek II - The Wrath Of Khan"

Gayne Rescher's other films include "Rachel Rachel" (1968) and "Claudine" (1974).

RHUE, MADLYN

Actress
Appearances: "Space Seed"
Role: Marla McGivers

Madlyn Rhue was born in 1934, and was very visible on tv in the Sixties. Her other guest roles were on shows like "The Guns Of Will Sonnett", "The Man From UNCLE" and "Ghost Appearances". She was a regular on "Bracken's World" (1969070) and "Executive Suite" (1976-77) and a semi-regular on both "Fame" and "Days Of Our Lives". Recently, she was struck with multiple sclerosis, which has severely curtailed her acting appearances. Her films include "Operation Petticoat" (1959) and "It's A Mad, Mad, Mad Mad World" (1963).

RICHARDS, CHET

Writer
Appearances: "The Tholian Web"

RICHARDS, MICHAEL

Writer
Appearancess:
(1) "That Which Survives"
(2) "The way To Eden"

RICHMOND, BRANSCOMBE

Actor
Appearances: "Star Trek III - The Search For Spock"
Role: Klingon Gunner

Branscombe Richmond was a regular on the short-lived "Hawaian Heat" (1984). His films include "Death Moon" (1978), "Damien: The Leper Priest" (1980) and "The Mystic Warrior" (1984)

ROARKE, ADAM

Actor
Appearances: "The Cage"
Role: CPO Garrison

Adam Roarke was a regular on "The Keegans" (1976), and guested on shows like "The Man From UNCLE".

ROBERTS, DAVIS

Actor
Appearances: "The Empath"
Role: Dr. Ozaba

David Roberts also guest-starred on "The Feather And Father Gang", "Branded" and "The Man From UNCLE," and appeared in films like "The Challenge" (1970), "Return To Earth" (1976) and "The Winds Of War" (1983).

ROBERTS, JEREMY

Actor
Appearances: Star Trek VI
Role: Excelsior officer

ROBINSON, JAY

Actor
Appearances: "Elaan Of Troyius"
Role: Petri

Jay Robinson was born in New York City, April 14th, 1930, and has guested in a vast number of tv shows, including "Planet Of The Apes" and "Voyagers!". His films include "The Robe" (1953) and "Shampoo" (1975).

ROCCO, TONY

Actor
Appearances: "Star Trek - The Motion Picture"
Role: Klingon

RODDENBERRY, GENE

Creator/Producer/Writer
Writer
Appearancess: (1) "The Cage"

(2) "Charlie X"
(3) "Mudd's Women"
(4) "The Menagerie"
(5) "The Return Of The Acrhons"
(6) "A Private Little War"
(7) "The Omega Glory"
(8) "Bread And Circuses"
(9) "Assignment: Earth"
(10) "The Savage Curtain"
(11) "Turnabout Intruder"

Gene Roddenberry is an ex-WWII pilot, and worked as a policeman whilst trying to sell scripts in Hollywood after the war. He was a regular contributor to shows like "Have Gun, Will Travel" and "Highway Patrol", before getting his first shot at production with "The Lieutenant" (1953-54) for Norman Felton. He made several pilots during this period, and finally his second one for "Star Trek" was accepted. Since the cancellation of the show, he has made numerous other pilots, all of which have failed to be picked up. These include "Genesis II" (1973), "The Questor Tapes" (1974) and "Spectre" (1977). He was creator and executive producer for The Next Generation. He died in October, 1991 of a heart attack.

RODRIGUEZ, PERCY

Actor
Appearances: "Court Martial"
Role: Portmaster Stone

Percy Rodriguez was born in 1924, and has appeared in numerous shows, including "Tarzan" and "Planet Of The Apes". He was a regular on "Peyton Place" (1968-69), "The Silent Force" (1970-71), "Executive Suite" (1967) and Roddenberry's "GenesisII".

ROGERS, ELIZABETH

Actress
Appearancess: (1) "The Doomsday Machine"
(2) "The Way To Eden"
Role: Lt. Palmer

Elizabeth Rogers was also in films like "Something Evil" (1972) and "An Officer And A Gentleman" (1982).

ROMERO, NED

Actor
Appearances: "A Private Little War"
Role: Krell

Ned Romero was a regular on "Dan August" (1970-75) and "The DA" (1971-72). His films include "Winchester 73" (1967), "I Will Fight No More Forever" (1975) and the miniseries
George Washington" (1984).

RONDELL, R.A.

Stunt Coordinator
Appearances: "Star Trek IV - The Voyage Home"

ROPELYE, MARY-LINDA

Actress
Appearances: "The Way To Eden"
Role: Irina

ROSENMAN, LEONARD

Composer
Appearances: "Star Trek IV - The Voyage Home"

Leonard Rosenman was born September 7th, 1924 in Brooklyn. After service with the Air Force in World War Ii, he took up musical composition. His works include a one-act opera and various pieces of chamber music. His other films include "Rebel Without A Cause" (1955), "Beneath The Planet Of The Apes" (1970) and "Lord Of The Rings" (1978).

ROSS, DAVID L.

Extra
Appearancess: (1) "Miri"
(2) "The Galileo Seven"
(3) "The Return Of The Archons"
(4) "A Taste Of Armageddon"
(5) "The City On The Edge Of Forever"
(6) "The Trouble With Tribbles"
(7) "The Omega Glory"
(8) "The Day Of The Dove"
(9) "Turnabout Intruder"
Roles: (4), (5), (7) and (9) Galloway
(1), (3) and (6) Security Guard
(8) Lt. Johnson

ROSS, STEVEN

Star Trek V
Producer

ROSSILLI, PAUL

Actor
Appearances: Star Trek VI
Role: Kerla

Played Klingon Kerla in Star Trek VI.

ROYGAS, MICHAEL

Actor
Appearances: "Star Trek - The Motion Picture"
Role: Lieutenant Cleary

RUBENSTEIN, PHIL

Actor
Appearances: "Star Trek IV - The Voyage Home"
Role: Garbageman

Phil Rubenstein was a regular on the short-lived "Working Stiffs" (1979). His films include "Contract On Cherry Street" (1977), "The Last American Virgin" (1982) and "Getting Physical" (1984).

RUBIN, RICHARD

Property Master
Appearances: "Star Trek - The Motion Picture"

RUGG, JIM

Special Effects
Seasons One - Three

RUSKIN, JOSEPH

Actor
Appearances: "The Gamesters Of Triskelion"
Role: Galt

Joseph Ruskin is almost invariable cast as villains in shows like "Voyage To The Bottom Of The Sea", "Planet Of The Apes" and "The Bionic Woman". His films include "Panache" (1976), "Captain America" (1979) and "The Munsters' Revenge" (1981).

RUSS, JANE

Actress
Appearances: "The Gamesters Of Triskellion"
Role: Tamoon

RUSSELL, MARK

Actor
Appearances: "Amok Time
Role: Vulcan Litterbearer

RUSSELL, MAURI

Actor
Appearances: "Amok Time"
Role: Vulcan

RUSSO, BARRY

Actor
Appearancess: (1) "The Devil In The Dark"
Roles: (1) Giotto
(2) Commodore Wesley

RUTTER, GEORGE A.

Script Supervisor
Seasons One - Three

RYDER, ALFRED

Actor
Appearances: "The Man Trap"
Role: Professor Robert Crater

Alfred Ryder is invariably cast as a rather gullible type, believing too much in the wrong types. His other appearances include "One Step Beyond" and "Voyage To The Bottom Of The Sea".

RYUSAKI, KIMBERLY L.

Stand-in
Appearances: " Star Trek III - The Search For Spock"

SABAROFF, ROBERT

Writer
Appearances: "The Immunity Syndrome"

SACKETT, SUSAN

Gene Roddenberry's Assistant
Appearances: "Star Trek - The Motion Picture"

Susan Sackett was initially Gene Roddenberry's secretary. She penned "Letters To Star Trek" as a result. During the making of the first film, she authored a book on the making of the movie, nominally with Roddenberry but actually alone. She now works as Roddenberry's assistant on "Star Trek - The Next Generation."

SAGE, WILLARD

Actor
Appearances: "The Empath"
Role: Thann

Willard Sage has appeared in shows like "Voyage To The Bottom Of The Sea", "The Man From UNCLE," Perry Mason" and "The Young Rebels," and films like "Timbuktoo" (1959) and "A Step Out Of Line" (1971).

SALLIN, ROBERT

Producer
Appearances: "Star Trek II - The Wrath Of Khan"

SAMPSON, ROBERT

Actor
Appearances: "A Taste Of Armageddon"
Role: Sar VI

Robert Sampson has also appeared in "Voyage To The Bottom Of The Sea". He was a regular on "Bridet Loves Bernie" (1971-72) and "Falcon Crest" (1981-82). His films include "Fear No Evil" (1969), "Shell Game" (1975) and "The Jerk Too"(1984).

SAND, SERENA

Actress
Appearances: "The Cage"
Role: Talosian

SANDOR, STEVE

Actor
Appearances: "The Gamesters Of Triskelion"
Role: Lars

Steve Sandor was a regular on "Amy Prentiss" (1974-75). His films include "The Young Country" (1970), "Stryker" (1983) and "Fire And Ice". His TV roles include shows like "Alias Smith and Jones."

SARGENT, JOSEPH

Director
Appearances: "The Corbomite Maneuver"

Joseph Sargent was born in Jersey City, NJ in 1925. After years of TV work (including notable "The Man From UNCLE"), he moved on to films. These include "Colossus - The Forbin Project" (1970) and "MacArthur" (1977). He won an Emmy in 1973 for "The Marcus-Nelson Murders," the first "Kojak" Appearances.

SARGENT, WILLIAM

Actor
Appearances: "The Conscience Of The King"
Role: Dr. Leighton

William Sargent's other guest spots include "Voyage To The Bottom Of The Sea," "The Immortal" and "Barnaby Jones".

SARLATTE, BOB

Actor
Appearances: "Star Trek IV - The Voyage Home"
Role: Waiter

SAWAYA, GEORGE

Actor
Appearancess: (1) "The Menagerie"

(2) "Errand Of Mercy"
Roles: (1) Chief Humbolt
(2) Klingon Soldier

George Sawaya's films include "Moon Of The Wolf" (1972), "The Red Badge of Courage" (1974) and "Dead Men Don't Wear Plaid" (1982). His tv guest spots include "The Man From UNCLE," "Perry Mason," "Branded" and "Barnaby Jones."

SCHAFFER, SHARON

Stunt Woman
Appearances: "Star Trek IV - The Vogage Home"

SCHALLERT, WILLIAM

Actor
Appearances: "The Paradise Syndrome"
Role: Miramanee

Sabrina Scharg guested on many Sixties shows, including "The Man From UNCLE" and "Hunter".

SCHMERER, JAMES

Writer
Appearances: "The Survivor"

James Schmerer produced and wrote for the short-lived series "Chase" (1973-74).

SCHMIDT, GEORGIA

Actress
Appearances: "The Cage"
Role: Talosian

Georgia Schmidt's films include "A Killing Affair" (1977) and "Terror At Alcatraz" (1982).

SCHNEIDER, PAUL

Writer
Appearancess: (1) "Balance of Terror"
(2) "The Squire of Gothos"
(3) "The Terratin Incident"

SCHOENBRUN, MICHAEL P.

Unit Production Manager
Appearances: "Star Trek III - The Search for Spock"

SCHUCK, JOHN

Actor
Appearances: Star Trek IV, Star Trek VI
Role: Klingon Ambassador

John Schuck was born in 1944 and was a regular on "McMillan and Wife (1971-77), "Holmes and Yoyo" (1976), "Turnabout" (1979) and "The Odd Couple" (1982-83). His films include "M*A*S*H" (1970) and "Earthbound" (1981). He played a Klingon ambassador in the fourth and sixth Star Trek films.

SCHULTZ, JOEL

Actor
Appearances: "Star Trek - The Motion Picture"
Role: Klingon

SCOTT, JUDSON

Actor
Appearances: "Star Trek II - The Wrath of Khan", The Next Generation
Role: Joachim

Judson Scott was the star of the ultra short-lived series "The Phoenix" (1982). His films include "I, the Jury" (1982).

SCOTT, TED

Actor
Appearances: "Plato's Stepchildren"
Role: Eraclitus

SCOTTER, DICK

Actor
Appearances: "This Side of Paradise"
Role: Pinter

SEALES, FRANKLYN

Actor
Appearances: "Star Trek - The Motion Picture"
Role: Bridge Crewman

Franklyn Seales was a semi-regular on "Silver Spoon" (1982-85). His films include "Beulah Land" (1980) and "Southern Comfort" (1981).

SEEL, CHARLES

Actor
Appearances: "Spectre of the Gun"
Role: Ed

Charles Seel has also appeared in "One Step Beyond", "The Guns of Will Sonnett" and "Griff". He was Barney, a semi-regular on "Gunsmoke" and was a regular on "The Road West" (1966-67). His films include "Duel" (1983).

SELSBY, HARVE

Actor
Appearances: "The Cloud Minders"
Role: Guard

Harve Selsby was also in "Sergeant Matlovich vs. The US Air Force" (1978).

SENENSKY, RALPH

Director
Appearancess: (1) "This Side of Paradise"
(2) "Metamorphosis"
(3) "Obsession"
(4) "Return to Tomorrow"
(5) "Bread and Circuses"
(6) Is There in Truth No Beauty?"

Ralph Senensky has also directed episodes of "Planet of the Apes". His tv films include "A Dream for Christmas" (1973), "Death Cruise" (1974) and "The New Adventures of Heidi" (1978).

SEURAT, PILAR

Actress
Appearances: "Wolf in the Fold"
Role: Sybo

Pilar Seurat has also appeared in "Voyage to the Bottom of the Sea" and "The Man From UNCLE".

SHANKLIN, DOUGLAS ALAN

Actor
Appearances: "Star Trek III - The Search for Spock"
Role: Prison Guard

SHATNER, WILLIAM

Actor
Series Regular
Writer
Star Trek V
Director
Star Trek V

William Shatner was born on March 22, 1931, in Montreal, Canada. After studying commerce in college, he switched to acting. In 1956, he moved to New York where he attracted the attention of live tv producers. He appeared in his firm silm, "The Brothers Karamazov," in 1958. In 1965, he starred in his first series, "For The People." Since "Star Trek," he has appeared in "The Barbary Coast" (1975-76) and "T.J. Hooker" (1982-86). His films include "Kingdom of the Spiders" (1977) and "White Comanche" (1968). He directed and assisted in the writing of Star Trek V. He hosts Rescue 911 on CBS.

SHATNER, MELANIE

Actress
Appearances: Star Trek V
Role: Starfleet officer

William Shatner's daughter Melanie made a cameo appearance in Star Trek V.

SHEGOG, CLIFFORD

Actor
Appearances: Star Trek VI
Role: Klingon officer

SHELYNE, CAROLE

Actress
Appearances: "Arena"
Role: Metron

Carole Chelyne has also been on on "The Man From UNCLE".

SHEPARD, DODIE

Costume Designer
Star Trek V, Star Trek VI

SHERVEN, JUDI

Actress
Appearances: "Wolf in the Fold"
Role: Nurse

SHIRRIFF, CATHIE

Actress
Appearances: "Star Trek III - The Search for Spock"
Role: Valkris
Cathie Shirriff has appeared in series like "Today's FBI". She co-hosted "Ripley's Believe It Or Not" (1982-83). Her films include "Friendships, Secrets and Lies" (1979), "She's Dressed to Kill" (1979) and "One Shoes Makes it Murder" (1982).

SHUGRUE, ROBERT F.

Editor
Appearances: "Star Trek III - The Search for Spock"

Robert Shugrue had worked with Harve Bennett in the past on series like "The Gemini Man" as a film editor.

SHUTAN, JAN

Actress
Appearances: "The Lights of Zetar"
Role: Lt. Mira Romaine

Jan Shutan was a regular on "Sons and Daughters" (1974). Her films include "Message To My Daughter" (1973), "Senior Year" (1974) and "This House Possessed" (1981).

SIKKING, JAMES B.

Actor
Appearances: "Star Rek III - The Wrath of Khan"
Role: Captain Styles

James Sikking was Hunter on "Hill Street Blues", and was a regular in "Turnabout" (1979). His films include "The Star Chamber" (1983). His tv guest spots include "Perry Mason", "The Bionic Woman", and "Cannon".

SILVER SPIKE

Stunt Man
Appearances: "Star Trek IV - The Voyage Home"

SIMPSON, JONATHAN

Actor
Appearances: Star Trek V
Role: young Sarek

Jonathan Simpson was the young Sarek in Star Trek V.

SINGER, ARTHUR H.

Appearances Consultant
Series Three
Writer
Appearances: "Turnabout Intruder"

SINGER, RAYMOND

Actor
Appearances: "Star Trek IV - The Voyage Home"
Role: Young Doctor

Raymond Singer's other guest spots include "The Feather and Father Gang" and "Remington Steele". He was a regular on "Operation Petticoat" (1977-78) and "Mama Mallone" (1984). His films include "The Entity" (1983).

SINGH, REGINALD LAL

Actor
Appearances: "Court Martial"
Role: Board Officer Chandra

SIRTIS, MARINA

Actress
Role: Deanna Troi
Series regular

Born of Greek parents, Marina Sirtis was raised in England, where she attempted to work as an actress. Her first professional job was as Ophelia in Hamlet. After some success, she moved to the States, where she won the role of Counselor Deanna Troi after only two months in the country. She originally tried out for the Tasha Yar character. Sirtis also appeared in the films Deathwish III and The Wicked Lady.

SLAVIN, GEORGE F.

Writer
Appearances: "The Mark of Gideon"

George Slavin also wrote "Son of Robin Hood" (1959).

SLATER, CHRISTIAN

Actor
Appearances: Star Trek VI
Role: Starfleet officer

Christian Slater is a young actor known for his resemblance to Jack Nicholson. He starred in Pump Up the Volume and Heathers. His role in Star Trek VI was in a brief walk-on as a Starfleet officer.

SMITH, EVE

Actress
Appearances: "Star Trek IV - The Voyage Home"
Role: Elderly Patient

SMITH, K.L.

Actor
Appearances: "Elaan of Troyius"
Role: Klingon

K.L. Smith's films include "Battle of the Coral Sea" (1959), "Incident in San Francisco" (1971) and "The Delphi Bureau" (1972).

SMITH KEITH

Director of Photography
Appearances: "By Any Other Name"

SMITH, KURTWOOD

Actor
Appearances: Star Trek VI
Role: Federation president

Federation president in Star Trek VI.

SMITH, SANDRA

Actress
Appearances: "Turnabout Intruder"
Role: Dr. Janice Lester

Sandra Smith also guest-starred on shows like "Iron Horse". She was a regular on "The Interns" (1970-71).

SMITHERS, WILLIAM

Actor
Appearances: "Bread and Circuses"
Role: Merik

William Smithers also appeared in "Voyage to the Bottom of the Sea" and "Barnaby Jones". He was a regular on "The Witness" (1960-61), "Peyton Place" (1965-66), "Executive Suite" (1976-77), and "Dallas" (1981).

SNYDER, MICHAEL

Actor
Appearances: "Star Trek IV - The Voyage Home"
Role: Starfleet Communications Officer

SOBELMAN, BORIS

Writer
Appearances: "The Return of the Archons"

Boris Sobelman also wrote for "The Girl From UNCLE".

SOBLE, RON

Actor
Spisode: "Spectre of the Gun"
Role: Wyatt Earp

Ron Soble was a regular on "The Monroes" (1966-

67). His films include "The Daughters of Joshua Cabe" (1972), "The Beast Within" (1982) and "The Mystic Warrior" (1984).

SOFAER, ABRAHAM

Actor
Appearancess: (1) "Charlie X"
(2) "Spectre of the Gun"
Roles: (1) Thasian
(2) Melkotain Voice

Abraham Sofaer was born October 1, 1896, in Rangoon, Burma. He moved to England in the Twenties, then the US in the Fifties. He appeared in many plays, films and tv shows. His films include "Quo Vadis" (1951), "Captain Sinbad" (1963) and "Journey to the Center of Time" (1967).

SOHL, JERRY

Writer
Appearancess: (1) "The Corbomite Maneuver"
(2) "This Side of Paradise"
(3) "Whom Gods Destroy"
Jerry Sohl is a writer of sf. His novels "The Time Dissolvers" and "The Odious Ones" are his most well-known works.

SOLARI, RUDY

Actor
Appearances: "The Paradise Syndrome"
Role: Salish

Rudy Solari has also been seen in "Voyage to the Bottom of the Sea" and "The Bionic Woman". He was a regular on "Redigo" (1963), "The Wackiest Ship in the Army" (1965-66) and "Garrison's Gorillas" (1967-68). His films include "The Boss' Son" (1982).

SOLOW, HERBERT F.

Executive in Charge of Production
Seasons One and Two

Herbert Solow now produces films like "Heatwave!" (1974) and "Get Crazy" (1983). He worked with Bob Justman on "Man From Atlantis".

SOREL, LOUISE

Actress
Appearances: "Requiem for Methuselah"
Role: Rayna

Louise Sorel also guest-starred in shows like "Iron Horse". She was a regular on "The Survivors" (1969-70), "The Don Rickles Show" (1972) "The Curse of Dracula" (1979), and "Ladies Man" (1980-81). Her films include "Airplane II - The Sequel" (1982),

SORENSEN, PAUL

Actor
Appearances: "Star Trek III - The Search for Spock"
Role: Merchantship Captain

Paul Sorensen's other guest roles include shows like "Iron Horse", "The guns of Will Sonnett" and "Barnaby Jones".

SOUL, DAVID

Actor
Appearances: "The Apple"
Role: Makora

David Soul was born on August 28, 1943, and starred in "Her Come the Brides" (1968-70), "Owen Marshall, Counselor at Law" (1974), "Starsky and Hutch" (1975-79), "Casablanca" (1983) and "The Yellow Rose" (1983-84). He also made a few hit singles during his days on "Starsky and Hutch", but the singing career collapsed after the show was cancelled.

SOWARDS, JACK B.

Writer
Appearances: "Star Trek II - The Wrath of Khan"

Jack B. Sowards also wrote "Deliver Us From Evil" (1973), "Cry Panic" (1974), "Death Cruise" (1974) and "Desperate Women" (1978). He was written for shows like "Barnaby Jones".

SPARR, ROBERT

Director
Appearances: "Shore Leave"

Robert Sparr also directed episodes of "Voyage to the

Bottom of the Sea".

SPENCER, JIM

Actor
Appearances: "Tomorrow is Yesterday"
Role: Air Policeman

SPIES, ADRIAN

Writer
Appearances: "Miri"

Adrian Spies also wrote for shows like "The Man From UNCLE". His films include "Hauser's Memroy" (1970), "The Family Kovack" (1974) and "Hanging By a Thread" (1979).

SPINER, BRENT

Actor
Role: Lt. Cmdr Data
Series regular

Spiner was born and raised in Houston, Texas. He says he did a lot of "gritty, ugly plays" off-Broadway after college. He appeared in the Woody Allen film Stardust Memories. On television, he appeared on Cheers, Night Court, and Hill Street Blues. On TNG, Spiner also played the parts of Lore and Dr. Noonian Soong.

SPINRAD, NORMAN

Writer
Appearances: "The Doomsday Machine"

Norman Spinrad is one of the "new wave" sf authors, probably best known for novels like "The Iron Dream" and "The Void Captain's Tale".

STEELE, KAREN

Actress
Appearances: "Mudd's Woman"
Role: Eve McHuron

Karen Steele also appeared in shows like "Voyage to the Bottom of the Sea", "Branded" and "The Wackiest Ship in the Army". Her films include "Ride Lonesome" (1959).

STEINER, FRED

Composer
Appearancess: (1) "Charlie X"
(2) "Mudd's Women"
(3) "What Are Little Girls Made Of?"
(4) "The Corbomite Maneuver"
(5) "Balance of Terror"
(6) "Who Mourns for Adonais?"
(7) "The Changeling"
(8) "Mirror, Mirror"
(9) "The Deadly Years"
(10) "The Immunity Syndrome"
(11) "By Any Other Name"
(12) "The Ultimate Computer"
(13) "Spock's Brain"
(14) "The Day of the Dove"
(15) "The Tholian Web"
(16) "Elaan of Troyius"
(17) "Whom Gods Destroy"
(18) "Let That Be Your Last Battlefield"
(19) "The Mark of Gideon"
(20) "That Which Survives"
(21) "Requiem for Methuselah"
(22) "The Way to Eden"
(23) "The Cloud Minders"
(24) "The Savage Curtain"
(25) "Turnabout Intruder"

Fred Steiner also composed extensively for "Lost in Space". He wrote the well known theme for "Perry Mason".

STEVEN, CARL

Actor
Appearances: "Star Trek III - The Search for Spock"
Role: Spock (age 9)

Carl Steven was in "Rosie: The Rosemary Clooney Appearances" (1982) and "Wait Till Your Mother Gets Home!" (1983).

STEVENS, WARREN

Actor
Appearances: "By Any Other Name"
Role: Rojan

Warren Stevens was born in 1919 and appeared in the classic "Forbidden Plant" (1956). His other tv guest spots include "Voyage to the Bottom of the Sea", "I Spy" and "Griff". He was a regular on "Tales of the

77th Bengal Lancers" (1956-57), "The Richard Boone Show" (1963-64), "Bracken's World" (1969-70) and "Behind the Screen" (1981-82).

STEWART, CHARLES J.

Actor
Appearances: "Charlie X"
Role: Captain Ramart

STEWART, PATRICK

Actor
Role: Captain Jean-Luc Picard
Series regular

Patrick Stewart hails from the English town of Mirfield. He worked as a newspaper reporter there before going on to acting. He sold furniture while trying to make it as an actor. He landed roles in the BBC productions I, Claudius, Smiley's People, and Tinker, Tailor, Soldier, Spy. Most notably, he is a member of the Royal Shakespeare Company, performing in the roles of Shylock, King John, and Henry IV. He is a winner of the London Fringe Best Actor Award. He was spotted for the role of Picard when a producer saw him on stage at UCLA.

STIMSON, VIOLA

Actress
Appearances: "Star Trek IV - The Voyage Home"
Role: Lady in Tour

STRINGER, KEN

Second Assistant Director
Appearances: "Star Trek III - The Search for Spock"

STRONG, MICHAEL

Actor
Appearances: "What Are Little Girls Made Of?"
Role: Dr. Roger Korby

Michael Strong also appeared in the tv shows "Plant of the Apes", "The Man From UNCLE", "Cannon" and "Barnaby Jones". His films include "Vanished" (1971), "Queen of the Stardust Ballroom" (1975) and "This Year's Blonde" (1980).

STUART, NORMAN

Actor
Appearances: "Star Trek - The Motion Picture"
Role: Vulcan Master

Norman Stuart was in "79 Park Avenue" (1977).

STURGEON, THEODORE

Writer
Appearancess: (1) "Shore Leave"
(2) "Amok Time"

Theodore Sturgeon was born February 16, 1918 on Staten Island. His works included numerous novels and short stories in the sf and western fields. Among his best-known works are "Alien Cargo" and "The Dreaming Jewels". He died on May 8, 1987.

SULLIVAN, KEVIN

Actor
Appearances: "Star Trek II - The Wrath of Khan"
Role: March

SULLIVAN, LIAM

Actor
Appearances: "Plato's Stepchildren"
Role: Parmen

Liam Sullivan was seen in "Voyage to the Bottom of the Sea" and "Lost in Space". He was a regular on "The Monroes" (1966-67). His films include "The Best Place To Be" (1979) and "Ernie Kovaks: Between the Laughter" (1984).

SULLIVAN, SUSAN J.

Actress
Appearances: "Star Trek - The Motion Picture"
Role: Woman in Transporter

SWIFT, JOAN

Actress
Appearances: "Operation - Annihilate"
Role: Aurelan

TAKAKI, RUSSELL

Actor
Appearances: "Star Trek II - The Wrath of Kan"
Role: Madison

TAKEI, GEORGE

Actor
Series Regular

George Takei was born in Los Angeles and studied drama at UCLA before taking a course at the Desilu Workshop. Small parts in shows like "Playhouse 90", "Hawaiian Eye" and "I Spy" followed. After "Star Trek", he became extremely active in politics, and served for a while on the board of the Southern California Rapid Transit District. He is an active jogger. Recently, he has returned to acting in earnest, with guest roles on shows like "Trapper John, MD" :MacGuyver", "Miami Vice", and "Adderley".

TAKO, RICHARD

Actor
Appearances: "I, Mudd"
Role: Norman

TARCH, JEREMY

Writer
Appearances: "The Lights of Zetar"

TARRANT, NEWELL

Actor
Appearances: "Star Trek IV - The Voyage Home"
Role: CDO

Newel Tarrant appeared in shows like "Hawaii Five-O".

TAYBACK, VIC

Actor
Appearances: "A Piece of the Action"
Role: Jojo Krako

Vic Tayback was a regular on "Griff" (1973-74), "Khan" (1975) and "Alice" (1976-85). His films include "Bullitt" (1968) and "The Choirboys" (1977).

TAYLOR, JUD

Director
Appearancess: (1) "The Paradise Syndrome"
(2) "Wink of an Eye"
(3) "Let That Be Your Last Battlefield"
(4) "The Mark of Gideon"
(5) "The Cloud Minders"

Jud Taylor also directed episodes of "The Guns of Will Sonnett" and "The Man From UNCLE". His many tv films include "Future Cop" (1976) and "Return to Earth" (1976).

TAYLOR, KEITH

Actor
Appearances: "Miri"
Role: Jahn's friend

Keith Taylor also appeared in "Lost In Space". He was a regular on "McKeever and the Colonel" (1962-63).

THATCHER, KIRK

Actor/Musician/Associate Producer
Appearances: "Star Trek IV - The Voyage Home"
Role: Punk

Kirk Thatcher is the son of English Prime Minister Margaret Thatcher.

THATCHER, TORIN

Actor
Appearances: "The Return of the Archons"
Role: Marplan

Torin Thatcher was born January 15, 1905 in Bombay. He was a teacher who then trained at RADA before taking to the stage and films in Englad. In the Fifties he moved to the US, mostly playing villainous roles. He died in 1981. His films include "Great Expectations" 91946), "The Seventh Voyage of Sinbad" (1958) and "Mutiny on the Bounty" (1962). Among his many tv roles are spots on "Voyage to the Bottom of the Sea", "Lost in Space", "One Step Beyond", and "The Guns of Will Sonnett". He died March 4, 1981.

THEISS, WILLIAM WARE

Costume Designer
Seasons One to Three

William Ware Theiss also designed costumes for "Heart Like a Wheel" (1983). He is also the costume supervisor for the new "Star Trek - The Next Generation" series.

THOMAS, CRAIG

Actor
Appearances: "Star Trek - The Motion Picture"
Role: Klingon

Craig Thomas' other films include "Spring Fever" (1983).

THOMAS, SHARON

Actress
Appearances: "Star Trek III - The Search for Spock"
Role: Waitress

Sharon Thomas' films include "Portrait of a Showgirl" (1982).

THOMPSON, GARLAND

Actor
Appearancess: (1) "Charlie X"
(2) "The Enemy Within"
Roles: (1) Crewman
(2) Wilson

THORNE, DYANNE

Actress
Appearances: "A Piece of the Action"
Role: Girl

THORNTON, COLLEEN & MAUREEN

Actresses
Appearances: "I, Mudd"
Role: Barbara

THRETT, MAGGIE

Actress
Appearances: "Mudd's Women"
Role: Ruth Bonaventure

THRONE, MALACHI

Actor
Appearances: "The Menagerie"
Role: Commodore Mendez

Malachi Throne was a guest on shows like "Iron Horse", "Voyage to the Bottom of the Sea" and "Lost in Space". He was a regular on "It Takes A Thief" (1968-69). His films include "The Doomsday Flight" (1966), "Assault on the Wayne" (1971) and "The Sex Symbol" (1974).

TIFFE, ANGELO

Actor
Appearances: Star Trek VI
Role: Excelsior Navigator

TIMONEY, MIKE

Actor
Appearances: "Star Trek IV - The Voyage Home
Role: Electronic Technician

Mike Timoney was also in "The Dollmaker" (1984).

TOBIN, MARC

Actor
Appearancess: (1) "Space Seed"
(2) "Day of the Dove"
Roles (1) Joaquim
(2) Klingon

TOCHI, BRIAN

Actor
Appearances: "And The Children Shall Lead"
Role: Ray

Brian Tochi was a regular on "Anna and the King" (1972) and "Renegades" (1983). His films include "We're Fighting Back" (1981).

TOM, SEBASTIAN

Actor
Appearances: "Shore Leave"
Role: Samurai

TOWNES, HARRY

Actor
Appearances: "The Return of the Archons"
Role: Reger

Harry Townes has appeared in many tv shows, including "Rawhide", "Planet of the Apes" and "Voyagers!". His films include "Cry Tough" (1959) and "Agent of HEAT" (1983).

TOWNSEND, SHERRI

Actress
Appearances: "Tomorrow is Yesterday"
Role: Crew woman

TRIVERS, BARRY

Writer
Appearances: "The Conscience of the King"

TROUPE, TOM

Actor
Appearances: "Arena"
Role: Lt. Harold

Tom Troupe also guested on "The Young Rebels" and "Griff". His films include "The Big Fisherman" (1959) and "The Alpha Caper" (1973).

TROY, DAVID

Actor
Appearances: "The Conscience of the King"
Role: Lt. Matson

TRUMBLE, DOUG

Special Photographic Effects
Appearances: "Star Trek - The Motion Picture"

Doug Trumble was the special effects man who worked on "2001) and "Close Encounters". He attempts to turn director occasionally, but his films ("Silent Running" and "Brainstorm") have never been too successful.

TUMEN, MARION

Script Supervisor
Appearances: Star Trek V

VALLONE, JOHN

Art Director
Appearances: "Star Trek - The Motion Picture"

John Vallone's other films include "Southern Comfort" (1981), "48 Hours" (1982), "Brainstorm" (1983).

VAN ZANDT, BILLY

Actor
Appearances: "Star Trek - The MOtion Picture"
Role: Alien Ensign

billy Van Zandt was also in "Taps" (1981).

VARGAS, JOHN

Actor
Appearances: "Star Trek II - The Wrath of Khan"
Role: Jedda

John Vargas was a regular on "At Ease" (1983). His other films include "Only When I Laugh" (1981), "Emergency Room" (1983) and "My Tutor" (1984).

VAUGHN, REESE

Actor
Appearances: "The Galileo Seven"
Role: Latimer

Reese Vaughn also guested in series like "Dan August".

VETO, RON

Actor
Appearancess: (1) "A Taste Of Armageddon"

(2) "The Alternative Factor"
Roles: (1) Eminian Technician
(2) Security Guard

VICTOR, TERESA E.

Actress
Appearances: "Star Trek IV - The Voyage Home"
Role: Usher

VINCI, FRANK

Stunt Man
Appearancess: (1) "The Galileo Seven"
(2) "A Taste of Armageddon"
(3) "Amok Time"
Roles: (1) Stunt Double
(2) Eminian Technician
(3) Vulcan

VIRGO, PETER

Actor
Epsiode: "The Paradise Syndrome"
Role: Warrior

VOLLAERTS, RIK

Writer
Appearances: "For the World is Hoow and I have Touched the Sky"

Rik Vollaerts also wrote for "Voyage to the Bottom of the Sea".

VON PUTTKAMER, JESCO

Advisor
Appearances: "Star Trek - The Motion Picture"

Jesco von Puttkamer works for NASA, and he had written a Appearances for the collection "Star Trek - The New Voyages", establishing his credentials as a fan of the show. He was asked to act as advisor for the first film, and for a while was dating Nichele Nichols.

WALBERG, GARY

Actor
Appearances: "Balance of Terror"
Role: Hansen

Gary Walberg was Speed on "The Odd Couple" (1970-74) and was a regular on "Quincy (1976-83). His films include "The Challenge" (1970), "Man on the Outside" (1975) and "Rage" (1980).

WALKER, ROBERT JR.

Actor
Appearances: "Charlie X"
Role: Charlie Evans

Robert Walker, Jr., was born April 15, 1940, in New York City. He is the son of Robert Walker and actress Jennifer Jones. Among his many films are "Ensign Pulver" (1964), "Easy Rider" (1969), and "The Passover Plot" (1976).

WALLACE, ART

Writer
Appearancess: (1) "Obsession"
(2) "Assignment: Eart"

Art Wallace also wrote for "Dark Shadows" and "Planet of the Apes". His tv movies include "Dr. Cook's Garden" (1971), "She Waits" (1972), and "Charlie and the Great Balloon Race" (1981).

WALLERSTEIN, HERB

Director
Appearancess: (1) "The Tholian Web"
(2) "Whom Gods Destroy"
(3) "That Which Survives"
(4) "Turnabout Intruder"

Herb Wallerstein moved up through the ranks. He worked as an assistant director on shows like "Father Knows Best". He was the unit production manager for "Iron Horse". "Star Trek" marked the beginnning of his directing career, and he has since worked on shows like "Petrocelli". He was assistant director on "The Tingler" (1959) and direct the tv movie "Snowbeast" (1977).

WARBURTON, JOHN

Actor
Appearances: "Balance of Terror"
Role: Centurian

John Warburton was born in Ireland in 1903. His film career began in 1932, and included "A Study in Scarlet", "Tarzan and the Huntress", and "City Beneath the Sea". He guested in numerous tv shows, including "Perry Mason". He died October 27, 1981.

WARNER, DAVID

Actor
Appearances: (1) Star Trek V, (2) Star Trek VI
Roles: (1) St. John Talbot, (2) Chancellor Gorkon

British actor David Warner played Federation ambassador St. John Talbot in Star Trek V and Klingon Chancellor Gorkon in Star Trek VI. He has also appeared in The French Lieutenant's Woman, Holocaust, and Time Bandits.

WASHBURN, BEVERLY

Actress
Appearances: "The Deadly Years"
Role: Arlene Galway

Beverly Washburn was a regular on "Professional Father" (1955) and "The New Loretta Young Show" (1962-63). She guested on "Adventures of Superman".

WASHINGTON, KENNETH

Actor
Appearances: "That Which Survives"
Role: Watkins

Kenneth Washington was a regular on "Hogan's Heroes" (1969-70). His tv films include "Climb an Angry Mountain" (1972), "Cry Rape!" (1973) and "Money on the Side" (1982).

WASSON, SUZANNE

Actress
Appearances: "Dagger of the Mind"
Role: Lethe

WATSON, BRUCE

Actor
Appearances: "The Man Trap"
Role: Crewman Green

Bruce Watson's films include "Dragnet" 9169), "Judge Horton and the Scottsboro Boys" (1976), and "Billy: Portrait of a Street Kid" (1977).

WEBB, RICHARD

Actor
Appearances: "Court Martial"
Role: Benjamin Finney

Richard Webb also appeared in "Voyage to the Bottom of the Sea" and "The Guns of Will Sonnett". His films include "On the Beach" (1959). He is best known, however, for playing the title role in the Fifties tv show "Captain Midnight".

WEBBER, BARBARA

Actress
Appearances: "The Return of the Archons"
Role: Young Woman

WEBER, PAUL

Actor
Appearances: "Star Trek - The Motion Picture"
Role: Vulcan Master

WEBSTER, JOAN

Actress
Appearances: "Seed in Space"
Role: Nurse

WEINSTEIN, HOWARD

Writer
Appearances: "The Pirates of Orion"

Howard Weinstein was born in 1954, and lives in New York City. His sale to the animated show was his first professional piece of writing. He has since written two "Star Trek" novels, three "V" novels and many articles for sf magazines.

WELLMAN, JAMES

Actor
Appearances: "And the Children Shall Lead"
Role: Professor Starnes

WESTON, BRAD

Actor
Appearances: "The Devil in the Dark"
Role: Appel

WEYLAND, PHIL

Stand In
Appearances: "Star Trek III - The Search for Spock"

WHEELER, JOHN

Actor
Appearances: "Journey to Babel"
Role: Gav

John Wheeler's films include "Kate Bliss and the Ticker Tape Kid: (1978), "Rescue From Gilligan's Island" (1978), and "The Wild, Wild West Revisited" (1979).

WHITING ARCH

Actor
Appearances: "The Alternative Factor:
Role: Engineering Assistant

Arch Whiting is best known for his semi-regular role as Sparks in "Voyage to the Bottom of the Sea" (1964-68). He has also appeared on shows like "Cannon" and "Barnaby Jones"

WHITNEY, GRACE LEE

Actress
Season One
Star Trek: The Motion Picture
Star Trek III - The Search for Spock
Star Treck IV - The Voyagle Home
Star Trek VI: The Undiscovered Country
Role: Yeoman Janice Rand/Transporter Chief Janice Rand/Commander Rand

Grace Lee Whitney was born in Detroit, MI, on april 1, 1930. She began as a singer at the age of 17, and made her move to Hollywood at the end of the Fifties. She was cast as a mermaid in the "Chicken of the Sea" tuna commercials, then began getting film roles, such as "Some Like It Hot" (1959). Her tv guest spots include roles on "The Twilight Zone", "Batman" and "The Next Step Beyond." She appeared as Yeoman Janice Rand in the first season of the original series. She came back as Transporter Chief Rand in Star Trek: The Motion Picture, and Commander Rand in Star Trek IV. She was the Excelsior communications officer in Star Trek VI.

WHITNEY, MICHAEL

Actor
Appearances: "A Private Little War"
Role: Tyree

Michael Whitney has also appeared in shows like "Iron Horse" and "Cannon".

WIEDLIN, JANE

Actress
Appearances: "Star Trek IV - The Voyage Home"
Role: Alien Communications Officer

WILBER, CAREY

Writer
Appearances: "Space Seed"

Cary Wilber also wrote for "Lost in Space", "Bonanza", and "The Wackiest Ship in the Army".

WILDER, GLENN R.

Stunt Coordinator
Star Trek V

WILLIAMSON, FRED

Actor
Eqpisode: "The Cloud Minders"
Role: Roka

WILSON, STARR & TAMARA

Actresses
Appearances: "I, Mudd"
Role: Maisie

WINCELBERG, SHIMON

Writer
Appearancess: (1) "Dagger of the Mind"
(2) "The Galileo Seven"

Shimon Wincelberg also writes as S. Bar-David. He crafted the pilot Appearances for "Lost in Space", and also wrote for series like "Voyage to the Bottom of the Sea" and "Planet of the Apes".

WINDOM, WILLIAM

Actor
Appearances: "The Doomsday Machine"
Role: Commodore Matt Decker

William Windom was born in New York City on September 28, 1923. Among his many guest roles, he appeared in "Iron Horse", "The Feather and Father Gang", and "The Bionic Woman". He was a regular on "The Farmer's Daughter" (1963-66), "My World and Welcome To It" (1969-72), for which he won an Emmy in 1970, "The Girl With Something Extra" (1973-74), and "Brothers and Sisters" (1979). His films include "To Kill A Mockingbird" 91962) and "Mean Dog Blues" (1978).

WINFIELD, PAUL

Actor
Appearances: "Star Trek II - The Wrath of Khan"
Role: Captain Terrell

Paul Winfield was born in Los Angeles in 1940, and trained at UCLA. His films include "Damnation Alley" (1977) and "The Terminator" (1984).

WINGREEN, JASON

Actor
Appearances: "The Empath"
Role: Dr. Linke

Jason Wingreen appeared frequently on tv in the Sixties, including on "The Man From UNCLE", "Voyage to the Bottom of the Sea" and "The Guns of Will Sonnett". He was a regular on "The Rounders" (1966-67) and "All in the Family" (1977-83).

WINSTON, JOHN

Actor
Appearancess: (1) "Tomorrow is Yesterday"
(2) "Space Seed"
(3) "The City on the Edge of Forever"
(4) "Who Mourns for Adonais?"
(5) "Mirror, Mirror"
(6) "The Apple"
(7) "The Doomsday Machine"
(8) "Catspaw"
(9) "Wolf in the Fold:
(10) "The Immunity Syndrome"
(11) "The Lights of Zetar"
(12) "Star Trek II - The Wrath of Khan"
Role: Transporter Chief Styles

John Winston also appeared in "The Young Rebels" and "The Man From UNCLE".

WINTER, RALPH

Associate Producer
Appearances: "Star Trek III - The Search for Spock"
Executive Producer
Appearances: "Star Trek IV - The Voyage Home"

WINTERSOLE, WILLIAM

Actor
Appearances: "Patterns of Force"
Role: Abrom

William Wintersole also guested on "The Young Rebels." He was a regular on "Sara" (1976). His films include "Pray for the Wildcats" (1974), "Son Rise: A Miracle of Love" (1979) and "The Day the Bubble Burst" (1982).

WISE, DONALD

Writer
Appearances: "How Sharper Than a Serpent's Tooth"

WISE, DOUG

Second Assistant Director
Appearances: "Star Trek - The Motion Picture"
First Assistant Director
Appearances: "Star Trek IV - The Voyage Home"

Doug Wise was also the assistant director of "The Private Eyes" (1981).

WISE, DOUGLAS E.

First Assistant Director
Star Trek V, Star Trek VI

WISE, ROBERT

Director
Appearances: "Star Trek - The Motion Picture"

Robert Wise was born September 10, 1914, in Winchester, IN. He began in films as a cutter in 1933, then edited films like "Citizen Kane" and "The Magnificent Ambersons" for Orson Welles. When "Curse of the Cat People" (1944) was having director problems, he was given the chance to direct, and never looked back. Other firlms include "The Day the Earth Stood Still" 91951), "West Side Appearances" (1961), "The Haunting" (1963), "The Sound of Music" (1965), and "The Andromeda Strain" (1971).

WOLF, VENITA

Actress
Appearances: "The Squire of Gothos"
Role: Teresa Ross

WOLFE, IAN

Actor
Eqpisodes: (1) "Bread and Circuses"
(2) "All Our Yesterdays"
Roles: (1) Septimus
(2) Mr. Atoz

Ian Wolfe was born in 1896 in Canton, IL, entering films in the 1930s. These include "The Scarlet Claw" (1944), "The Lost World" (1960), and "The Terminal Man" (1974). HIs long career also included guest spots in shows such as "The Feather and Father Gang". He was Wizard Tranquil on "Wizards and Warriors" (1983).

WOLFE, LAWRENCE N.

Writer
Appearances: "The Ultimate Computer"

WONG, NANCY

Actress
Appearances: "Court Martial"
Role: Personnel Officer

WOOD, LAURA

Actress
Appearancess: (1) "Charlie X"
(2) "The Deadly Years"
Roles: (1) Old Lady
(2) Mrs. Johnson

WOODS, GRANT

Actor
Appearancess: (1) "The Galileo Seven"
(2) "Arena"
(3) "This Side of Paradise"
Role: Lt. Commander Kelowitz

Grant Woods was a regular on "Custer" (1967). He has guested on shows like "The Man From UNCLE" and "The Wackiest Ship in the Army".

WOODVILLE, KATE

Actress
Appearances: "For the World is Hollow and I have Touched the Sky"
Role: Natira

Kate Woodville was once married to Patrick Macnee, and appeared in an episode of "The Avengers" with him. Since moving to the US, her films have included "Fear No Evil" (1969), "Widow" (1976) and "Keefer" (1978). She also guest-starred on shows like "Kolchak - The Night Stalker."

WOODWARD, MORGAN

Actor
Appearancess: (1) "Dagger of the Mind"
(2) "The OMage Glory"

Roles: (1) Dr. Simon van Gelder
(2) Captain Ronald Tracy

Morgan Woodward was a regular on "The Life and Legend of Wyatt Earp" and "Dallas" and guest starred in shows such as "Iron Horse" and "Planet of the Apes". His films include "Yuma" (1971), "The Last Day" (1975) and "A Last Cry for Help" (1979).

WRIGHT, GARY

Actor
Appearances: "Amok Time"
Role: Vulcan Litterbearer

WYATT, JANE

Actress
Appearances: (1) "Amok Time"
(2) Star Trek IV - The Voyage Home"
Role: Amanda
Jane Wyatt was born August 12, 1911, in Campgaw, NJ. She was signed up for Universal in 1934, making films like "Lost Horizon" (1937) and "Gentleman's Agreement" (1947). When she switched to tv, she became famous for her long-running role in "Father Knows Best", for which she won Emmy Awards three years running.

WYLLIE, MEG

Actress
Appearances: "The Cage"
Role: The Keeper

Meg Wyllie was a regular on "Hennesey" (1959-62) and "The Travels of Jaime McPheeters" (1963-64). Her films for tv include "Death Sentence" (1974), "Elvis" (1979) and "The Thorn Birds" (1983). She has guested on many shows, including "Perry Mason", "The Man From UNCLE" and "Alias Smith and Jones".

YARNELL, CELESTE

Actress
Appearances: "The Apple"
Role: Yeoman Martha Landon

Celeste Yarnell's films include "In Name Only" (1969), "Ransom for a Dead Man" (1971) and "The Judge and Jake Wyler" (1972). She also guested on "The Man From UNCLE". Disillusioned with the lack of progress in her career, she went into real estate instead.

YASHIMA, MOMO

Actress
Appearances: "Star Trek - The Motion Picture"
Role: Bridge Crewwoman

Momo Yashima was a regular on "Behind The Screen" (1981-82). Her films include "Charlie Chan and the Curse of the Dragon Queen" (1981), the original "V" (1983), and "The Return of Marcus Welby, MD" (1984).

YOUNG, TONY

Actor
Appearances: "Elaan of Troyius"
Role: Kryton

Tony Young also appeared in shows like "Iron Horse," "Get Christie Love!" and "Barnaby Jones". He was a regular in "Gunslinger (1960-61). His films include "He Rides Tall" (1963) and "Charro" (1969).

YURICICH, RICHARD

Special Photographic Effects Producer
Appearances: "Star Trek - The Motion Picture"

Richard Yuricich also worked on "Brainstorm" (1983).

ZASLOW, MICHAEL

Actor
Appearancess: (1) "The Man Trap"
(2) "I, Mudd"
Roles: (1) Darnell
(2) Jordan

ZAUTCKE, DONALD W.

Actor
Appearances: "Star Trek IV - The Voyage Home"
Role: 1st Lt., USMC

ALONDRA

Story: "One of our Planets is Missing"

This is the planet that is missing. The entire world was engulfed by a cosmic cloud and turned into rubble. There is no point in trying to get a visa to visit here, therefore.

ALPHA 177

Story: "The Enemy Within"

Alpha 177 is a desert world, with little but sand and rocks in evidence anywhere on its surface. Water seems almost non-existent, sucked into the dry sands. The planet has minor forms of life there. At night, the place gets extremely cold, down to lethal temperatures if there is no protection available. Since the planet is uniformly sand and rock, any protection must be brought by the tourist foolhardy enough to venture to this wasteland.

If all of that were not unappetizing enough, there is a yellowish ore on the surface that interferes with transporter signals. One party from the "Enterprise" was stranded on the surface for a good portion of one night due to the problems the ore caused. The group almost perished of cold before they could be finally rescued.

If alternating massive sunburns and frost-bite are your thing, this is the world for you. Otherwise, choose somewhere a little nicer to vacation.

ALTAIR VI

Story: "Amok Time"

Altair VI is a problem planet with a history of unrest. Every now and again (or again and again), the natives seem to have a revolution or two to break the monotony. The Federation is constantly trying to encourage them to calm down, but without much noticeable effect on matters. Unless you like the sound of guns going off all day, and the possibility of becoming a statistic in the next overthrow of a government, don't bother stopping here.

ANDOR (EPSILON INDII VIII)

Story: "Journey to Babel"

Andor is one of the nicer planets in the Federation. The natives are a warrior race, so the general culture is a trifle spartan, but they are shaping up nicely. The planet is full of fascinating things to do and see, especially if you like museums of warfare, or taking part in mock combats.

ANDROID PLANET

Story: "I, Mudd"

This is actually more of a planetoid, but who's quibbling? The place is filled with androids, who are very courtly and helpful. They'll do anything for you, which is most gratifying. Good help is so hard to find. They were builty by long-dead beings from Andromeda to be helpers.

They weren't always quite so benevolent; originally, they had latched onto Harry Mudd (remember him?) and decided quite rightly that if he was an example of humanity, it was time to lock the race up for their own good. Fortunately, Captain Kirk and his resourceful crew soon put paid to that idea, and reprogrammed the androids into the nice folk that they are today.

ANTOS IV

Story: "Whom Gods Destroy"

Antos IV is a fairly pleasant world, whose natives have the disconcerting ability to change their physical appearance. This can be quite unsettling for anyone not used to such matters. They are also known for being the race that Garth of Izar wanted to lead in Galactic conquest. Whey they -sensibly- refused his offer, he wanted to wipe them out. His own men arrested him, and he is now locked up on Elba II, where modern medical techniques are leading to some signs of improvement in his condition.

ARCADIA III (Motherlode)

Story: "Mudd's Passion"

Motherlod is what its name implies - a mining planet. The Federation has trading agreements with it, but it isn't actually a member of the UFP. Accordingly, it isn'g easy to get a visa to go there. On the other hand, it's a fairly primitive place, with few facilities, and just a whole lot of mines, so who wants to visit it anyhow?

ARCTURUS

Story: "The Conscience of the King"

Arcturus and its system of planets is one of the oldest and finest of the human colony worlds. The planets are all well domesticated, and boast spacious cities, fine food and wines — Arcturan brandy, of course, being famous throught the Empires also — and gracious natives. There's literally something for everyone on at least one of the Arcturan worlds. If you've never been there, the arts and culture of the plants are as excellent as their reputation claims, with especially high standards for classical drama.

All major currencies are accepted, and Galactic Express is especially beloved. The worlds have strong tourish industries, and much to offer. One of the best places to get away from it all without actually giving up anything worthwhile.

ARDANA

Story: "The Cloud Minders"

Ardana is both a great place to visit, and a lovely place to avoid — it all depends on where you go. The surface of the planet is pretty dreary, and below ground are the mines that make the planet wealthy. It was also the home, until recently, of the Trogs - nasty, brutish, dumb types. Then Captain Kirk discovered that the mines gave off a gas making the Trogs this way, and Dr. McCoy fitted them with masks. Now their IZ has risen - and so has production.

None of the mines are worth seeing, though. What is definitely (if you'll pardon the expression) a high is the cloud city of Stratos. Built on hugh anti-gravity discs, the city literally floats in the clouds. Provided that you don't suffer from a fear of heights, it's a terrific place to visit. The city is filled with dignified people, who love science and arts equally. The buildings are filled with masterpieces, and the people eager to chat. Their prejudice against the Trogs is vanishing, and there's a lot to recommend them.

Highlight (sorry about that) of the city is the view. Looking at the inside of clouds sounds kind of dull, but isn't. And the views straight down (assuming you can take them) are spectacular. The place is definitely a great place to visit.

ARGELIAS II

Story: "Wolf in the Fold"

Argelia II is definitely one of the best places in the Galaxy to visit. It's one of those professional pleasure planets where you can find any kind of entertainment you might desire. If you're alone, you can also find some friendly native to share the places with you. The natives are a nice bunch, totally without crime or violence of any kind. Before you get nasty, larcenous ideas into your heads, however, they do have a police force, solely to keep the tourists in line.

Some of the natives have psychic powers also, which is not a fact made too common. They don't want to scare off tourists who think that their minds are being rad. Anyone who might think that the Argelians would want to read their minds probably doesn't have much of a mind to read in the first place, however.

There was a little trouble with a hack'n'slash murder spate on the planet a few years back, but Captain Kirk and the "Enterprise" sorted it out, finally tracking down the immortal killer known as Jack the Ripper.

ARGO

Story: "The Ambergris Element"

Argo is a world with unstable geology, and land masses periodically rise and sink into their voluminous seas. The native race exists in two forms, one purely aquatic, the other purely terrestrial. Though there were some problems with them a while back, Captain Kirk managed to calm them down, and they are now very peaceful. In the seas, however, there are occasional monsters lurking, so be careful if you go fishing here - if you don't hook a native, you may hook a monster... That aside, the planet is a lovely place to stop off and soak your feet.

ARIANIS

Story: "Let That Be Your Last Battlefield"

Arianis is not a great place to visit. They've recently had rather a virulent plague, and severe decontamination of the entire planet was called for.

ARRET

Story: "Return to Tomorrow"

Arret is a dead, sterile world. There's no atmosphere - literally, not just a lack of interesting things to do. The civilization as a whole died out millennia ago, though

three disembodied surivors hung on until the "Enterprise" discovered them. They tried to restart their race, but came to the conclusion that they had already had their day, and quit.

ARRET

Story: "The Counter-Clock Incident"

There's no way to get to this planet, since it's simply Earth in another dimension, where times flows backwards. No one notices, since they are in with the the flow. On the other hand, why would anyone want to visit the place. Oh, it bears no relationship to the Arret mentioned above.

BENACEA COLONY

Story: "Conscience of the King"

Benacea Colony is one of the many colony worlds established early in the human expansion period. A gracious world, well-planned and laid out, it cultivates the arts and sciences. The place has some fine scenic views, and lots to do for the average tourist.

BETA III

Story: "The Return of the Archons"

Beta III is now rather a pleasant world, whose inhabitants are learning to stand on their own fett. They had been ruled for several thousand years by a computer name Landru. Landru had felt that all humans needed a very strict supervisor to behave, and kept the whole planet more or less in line. It also stifled freedom and creativity, so Captain Kirk managed to talk it to death, thus giving back to the Betans freedom, dignity, and the problems of running a planet. They are making an admirable attempt, and have just managed to invent the internal combustion engine. Now would be a find time to visit before they also invent the concept of expressways and cross-country highways.

BETA VI

Story: "The Squire of Gothos"

Beta VI is a nice colony world (not in the same system as Beta III mentioned in the above entry), with the general amenities available. On the other hand, it simports a lot of its medical supplies and other ncessities, so prices are pretty steep yet. When it gets on better footing, it should be a find place to visit. Until then, it's a trifle too pricey for what you get.

BETA LYRAE

Story: "The Slaver Weapon"

Beta Lyrae is a wasteland with nothing to recommend it unless one wishes to get away from it all. There's certainly nothing else here.

BETA PORTALIN

Story: "Operation - Annihilate!"

Beta Portalin is a historian's paradise, but has little else to recommend it. The sentient race there was wiped out millennia ago by the mind parasites that later attacked Deneva. There are lots of ruins, but nothing much more recent other than a few study bases from various Glactic Universities.

CAMUS II

Story: "Turnabout Intruder"

Remember all those dead worlds? Well, here's another. The natives were an advanced race, but finally died out, presumably by being too darned smart for their own good. Carelessly, they left around some of their old inventions, which have been of great interest to archaeologists and less scrupulous folks. One such maching was a device to transfer a person's mind into another's body. What it was used by the natives for is open to conjecture — punishment? fun? kinky sex? — but Dr. Janice Lester used it to get control of Captain Kirk's body and to take over the "Enterprise". Her own unstable personality finally wiped out her chances of success, but as a result of this, Camus was placed off-limits until the Federation has discovered what other problem devices that race may have forgotten to destroy.

CAPELLA IV

Story: "Friday's Child"

Capella IV is a hands-off world. If you land here, the natives chop your hands off. Seriously, the effects are not pleasant - you are likely to find yourself vacationing

at Federation expense on Tantalus if you do try and land on Capella. They have a few internal problems that have to be sorted out before the place is opened up for tourists.

The native race, frankly, leaves a lot to be desired. They have plenty of odd customs, most of which end up in the demise of anyone who breakes them. They also tend to be nomadic warriors, and fight quite frequently for power, women and anything else that they want badly enought. It's most depressing, really. They are an inventive bunch, but their inventiveness is most limited to inventing new weapons and new ways to kill people with them.

CATULLA

Story: "The Way to Eden"

Catulla is, of course, one of the Federation planets. It's pretty dull are for the most part.

CESTUS III

Cestus III is currently undergoing dispute between the Federation and the Gorns. A small colony there - once noted for the fine meals - was wiped out by the Gorns, who believed it an invasion foce. After a certain amount of arbitration under the Metrons, the Gorns agreed to discuss matters. Since this is now in diplomatic channels, the chances of the place being opened up again in the near future are pretty small. Pity. They had some fine restaurants, too.

CETI ALPHA V/VI

Stories: "Space Seed" "Star Trek II - The Wrath of Khan"

Ceti Alpha V was the planet where Captain Kirk left the made superman Khan Noonian Singh to start up his colony. It was a hard world but possible to transform. Back at the time, you didn't object to having lunch with a mmegalomaniac, it might have been a nice place to visit. However, six months later, problems arose when the original twin-world to Ceti Alpha V blew up. This caused severe changes to V, and real problems to the colonists. The spin of the world was changed, and the whole place became one vast desert, with howling winds and generally unlivable conditions. Khan and his few followers survived only at the expenditure of much effort and ingenuity. That was when their problems really started.

There are these really nasty little lifeforms native to the planet, Ceti eels. The adults have nasty jaws and perforce eat anything they come across. If you're lucky, they'll get you and devour you. Two or three adults can strip a sentient being to nothing (they eat the bones, too) in about a minute and a half. If you're unlucky, the babies get you. Baby Ceti eels are about as cute as their parents (resembline a cockroach hit with a brick) and have a habit of crawling into the ears of people and boring into the brain. There they feed on whatever brains a visitor to this world might have left and grow till they explode your skull. Not exactly the sort of souvenir you'd bring home for anyone you liked. (On the other hand, maybe your boss deserves one?)

In short, anyone who visits this planet needs their head examined. The Ceti eels will provide this service, free of charge, from the inside.

CHERON

Story: "Let That Be Your Last Battlefield"

Another top rated place on the "not to visit" list. The entire planet is dead - with the exception of a few minor nuclear burns that are smouldering still. The population of this planet were even more crazy than most. There were two races here, with black and white faces. One was black and white, the other white and black. For some reason, both groups felt that the difference was highly important - important enough to kill one another over. The final members of each race were Lokai and Bele. They managed to chase one another across half the Galaxy before returning home to do one another in. If you ask me, the Galaxy won't miss two races that were that dumb.

CORIDAN

Story: "Journey to Babel"

The Coridan planets are relatively recent additions to the Federation, and as such haven't been opened up to tourists yet. They're pretty close to the Orion system, which has caused trouble in the past by raiding Coridan. They have mostly been stopped, but every now and then they get itchy trigger fingers and head in looking for trouble. Maybe in a few years the whole place will be nicer.

DARREN IV

Story:
"For the World is Hollow, and I have Touched the Sky"

Darren IV is one of those vastly overcrowded worlds that tourists flee from. Be wise and do the same.

DELTA THETA III

Story: "BEM"

Delta Theta III is a forbidden world. The natives there are rather savage still, and inclined to attack anyone that they don't know. There's also a very spooky disembodied intelligence that's trying to help them to evolve. Lord knows they need to. the intelligence is concentrating hard on its job, and doesn't want any strangers butting into either mess things up or to offer unwanted advice. So say clear, and be nice to the poor thing.

DELTA VEGA

Story: "Where No Man has Gone Before"

Delta Vega is a very dull world near the Galactic rim. If a tourist really wants to visit the place, there are two points of interest. The first is a lithium cracking station. Since this is totally automoated (the world is so dull that no one wants to work there), there are not even guided tours. They second site is out in the bleak, rocky wilderness a short way from the station. It is twin graves, for Gary Mitchell and Dr. Elizabeth Dehner. Both were given enhanced psi abilities at the galactic edge, and both perished as a result. This site is for students of the morbid only.

Galactic Express is not accepted here, but that's no real problem. There's nothing to spend it on anyway, outside of cracked lithium, and that's hardly the souvenir that your friends and relatives would like brought back for them.

DENEVA

Story: "operation: Annihilate!"

Deneva is now recovered from the rather nasty invasion of mind parasites that almost destroyed the entire population a few years back. Thanks to Captain Kirk having wiped the whole mess of the creatures out, the planet was finally freed (and the inhabitants received a nice sun tain in the process, but that's another story).

The planet is a very pleasant colony world, with temperate weather and fine walks. Large, spacious cities and a cheerful population (well, you'd be cheerful if you were saved from impending and extremely painful deaths at the last second, wouldn't you?) make the place a pure delight to visit.

DRAMIA

Story: "Albatross"

Dramia is a pleasant world, with cheery natives. They've had long contacts with the Federation, and apart from a minor misunderstanding with Dr. McCoy over whether he was a mass-murderer or not, they have been very friendly. A colony world, Dramia II, was wiped out by a rather virulent disease, but one McCoy managed to find a cure for. It's terrific having a doctor like him who makes planet calls.

829-IV

Story: "Bread and Circuses"

892-IV is a world controlled by the Prime Directive. A good thing, really, considering the fact that its natives are in their version of the Earth 20th Century and Rome is still active. Their idea of fun things for tourists to do is to pit them against one another in the arena, and bet on who survives. Unless you are into blood sports (with the shedding of your blood being the sport), there's not a lot here for you.

EARTH

Stories: "Tomorrow is Yesterday"
"The City on the Edge of Forever" "Assignment: Earth"

Earth is a nice place to visit, but you wouldn't want to live there. Well, perhaps you would, but it would very much depend upon the time period (for those who can time travel, naturally). At the present time, it's definitely a beautiful planet, with a great deal to recommend it. One the other hand, there are several periods it is definitely better to give a miss.

The 1930's. They called this ear the Depression and

it's an accurate term. The place is very depressing. Dirty towns, poor food, lousy accommodation (called "flop houses" — they're flops, all right), aggressive population. They were getting ready for another war, too, so tensions were rife. This is the place to send the kids, so that they won't complain about not having his year's model sports car, or more than three hundred dinners to choose from in the freezer.

The 1960's. Totally a paranoid time. Alternately, the population disbelieved in life on other worlds, or spent their time looking for "flying saucers". If they knew you were from another planet, the chances are that they'd capture you, exhibit you, mock you, or buy you a drink. It's not worth taking chances on the latter. On the positive side, they had some great tv shows in this era.

The 1980's. In some ways, the worst of them all. The people back then were into all kinds of weird things, in a schizoid sort of way. Some wanted to save the whales, others to murder the lot. some wanted to nike the planet, and others to ban the bomb. A very confusing period, and it's a wonder that anyone lived through it.

Nowadays — well, that's more like it. There's a bit of overcrowding in some places, but there's no place like home, as they say. Urban renewal has improved virtually everywhere, and there are still plent of things to see from the past. Natural wonders abound, and on the whole the Earth turned out okay, despite the efforts of everyone in the Bad Old Days to tally mess up the planet.

Technologically, it's hard to find a planet anywhere that is so well adapted to human comfort. With the growth of the Federation, just about anything can be obtained — even Romulan ale, if you have the right contacts. Many people feel that it's the best of all possible worlds, and it's hard to disagree with that view.

EDEN

Story: "The Way to Eden"

Everyone has their own idea about paradise, and this isn't it for anyone. The planet looks very nice - grass, trees, lakes, waterfalls and so forth. The problem is that everything is simply loaded with acid. The fruit, the tress, the grass, the water... Put simply, most people prefer to die and go to heaven. In this place, you go to heaven first, then you die. Not a very good trade-off, in anyone's book.

EKOS

Story: "Patterns of Force"

Ekos is one of twin worlds, the other being Zeos. The Ekosians are a pretty primitive lot, just in their early atomic age, and rather short-tempered. Needless to say, they are still under the Prime Directive, so you're warned to stay away. Considering the last Federation observer there started up the Nazi Party again, I think staying away is a fine idea. Captain Kirk seems to have weaned the world off that philosophy, and gotten them cooperating with their neighbors again, but if you gave them a few hundred years, it would probably be safer.

ELAS

Story: "Elaan of Troyius"

Elas is one of those places that is so refined and cultured that you feel like screaming. They have art galleries, concerts, theatre and so forth - plus loads of shops with elegant wares and clothing. The problem is that the natives think that everyone else is barbaric, and tend to look down their noses at off-worlders. They take your money, but never offer friendship. Stuck up little snobs is what they are.

ELBA II

Story: "Whom Gods Destroy"

You literally have to be crazy to go to Elba II — it's the final mental asylum left in Federation space. That should be enough to put you off, but in case it isn't then there was actually a revolt there a while back, led by Garth of Izar. Then the patients controlled the doctors, which was not a nice situation to be in. Thankfully, Captain Kirk settled the problem, and even brought in a new drug to try and help treat the last patients there. Soon, the Galaxy may be perfectly sane — a debatable good according to a number of sentient beings.

EMINIAR VII

Story: "A Taste of Armageddon"

Now is a good time to visit this world. It's a high-tich society, with nice, friendly natives. A few years back, the chances were you would have ended up in a disintegration chamber, as the result of a computer attack from their ex-colony Vendikar. Captain Kirk managed

to sort that lot out, and opened the planet up for safe tourism. The Eminians had gotten far too used to their odd form of bloodless warfare (sort of like the stock exchange, with disintegrator cannons), and were reluctant to give it up. Equally, Kirk was just as reluctant to roll over and play dead when they ordered it, and promptly destroyed their compute network. Kirk has this thing about computers; they simple don't interface.

Rather than destroy a sophisticated civilization, the Eminians agreed finally to negotiate for peace. A good thing, too, because the place is wonderful for the tourists. There are plenty of facilities, and the natives are quite accomplished with their art and sciences. They are experiencing post-war euphoria, so it's a great place to go.

EPSILON CANARIS III

Story: "Metamorphosis"

Epsilon Canaris is a nice, pleasant little world, apart from one small problem: wars. The natives seem to have distinct problems in getting along with one another. Countless minor skirmishes are always under way and a seaside resort one day may become a battle zone the next. Not unnaturally, this has reduced tourism to the planet to a dead halt. Though the wars are generally soon resolved, they tend to break out afresh every three or four weeks. Who needs that sort of trouble when you're catching some rays?

EXCALBIA

Story: "The Savage Curtain"

This is definitely a place to get away from it all - especially living. The atmosphere is poisonous to all known forms of life. The surface temperature is enough to melt down starships. Living conditions are non-existent - unless you happen to be animated silica-based rocks. That's what the inhabitants are like, but they are also terribly curious creatures who spend most of their time debating issues. Considering the surface of their world, there's probably not a whole lot more that they can do.

Their problem is that they tend to get into arguments on matters of which they haven't the baguest practical knowledge. One such discussion was about good and evil. Faced with a total lack of experience, they simply kidnapped Captain Kirk and Spock and set up an experiment for those two to demonstrate the difference. It didn't work too well, but what do you expect of a race with a head full of rocks? In any event, the world is now off-limits to all other races, and it's a small loss to the tourist business, believe you me.

EXO-III

Story: "What Are Little Girls Made Of?"

If you're into winter sports, this is the planet for you! Vast mountains, deep rifts and snow as far as the eyes can see. In fact, the entire planet is a frozing paradise for the skiing enthusiast. The place is totally lifeless, so there aren't too many amenities if you don't bring them with you.

The planet was once inhabited, but the local population got rather lazy and built androids to do all of the work for them. The androids promptly decided that they were better than their creators, whom they massacred rather nastily. They then spent the next few millennia discovering that they lacked any imagination. Having claimed the world for their own, there was nothing for them to actually do with it.

By the most recent past, only one such adoid survived - a rather homicial maniac named Ruk. He rescued one survivor from a crash there (it's not the easiest planet to negotiate), a Dr. Roger Korby. Korby was converted into an android and provided the spart of imagination that Ruk and his kind had lacked. He aimed to take over the Galaxy and convert everyone into androids. The day was saved by the usual intervention from Captain Kirk, who disposed of the final adroid population, making Exo-III the haven for winter sports enthusiasts that it now is.

Korby's laboratories are now open to the public for a small fee. Tourists are warned not to touch the equipment, since much of it isn't well understood, and since it was built by homicidal androids, it probably isn't designed to dispense Romulan ale.

FIRST FEDERATION

Story: "The Corbomite Maneuver"

Not a lot is known about the First Federation. It's an area of space goverened very loosely by the tiny, child-like inhabitants of vast starships. These folks are friendly and cheerful, if a little inclined to play rough. One of their favorite games is to grab passing spaceships and threaten the inhabitants with death. They then allow the captives to get the upper hand, apparently their idea of figuring out whether passing travelers are worth knowing. Obviously what the First Federation needs is a good guide book to Known Species, written by a reliable reporter...

GALACTIC EDGE

Stories: "Where No Man Has Gone Before" "By Any Other Name" "Beyond The Farthest Star"

There are always those travelers who wish to take their vacations off the beaten track, but it is recommended that they do not consider leaving the Galaxy for intergalactic space. For one thing, there is not a great deal out there to see (it is, after all, mostly just open space). There is also a slight problem with exit visas. Surrounding our Galaxy appears to be an energy field of unknown composition and tremendous strength. All ships attempting to pass through find their control systems inoperative, their sensors uesless and many of the crew brain-dead.

It is possible to survive the experience, but it is debatable if this is even worth it. Some survivors find their mental abilities increased, and become almost god-like in power. Since this transformation generally knocks the recipients of these powers well and truly off the deep end, it isn't a very good trade-off. Such super-powered beings are inevitably killed off as soon as praticable by the nearest normal survivors. To be truthful, these murders are actually doing the human race a big favor - allowing it to survive.

The Kelvans have managed to build a device to allow penetration of the energy field, but they aren't overly keen on sharing their ideas. Considering the vast number of worlds that can be visited in this Galaxy alone, it's not likely to be needed in a hurry. A small colony of Kelvans has settled on a planet near the Galactic rim. Its name and location are not general information, as the Federation feels that they need time to themselves.

GAMMA 7-A

Story: "The Immunity Syndrome"

The Gamma 7-A system is now totally devoid of life. A huge, space-faring amoeba drained the energy from the system, killing everyone. Until the planets are repopulated, it's too depressing to visit anywhere in the area.

GAMMA CANARIS

Story: "Metamorphosis"

Gamma Canaris is a small asteroid just off the beaten path. It is currently the home of Zefram Cochrane and Nancy Hedford - well, sort of. Nancy is actually now a double being, having conjoined with a creature called the Companion. The Companion had saved Cochrane's life a couple of hundred years ago - yes, that Zefram Cochrane - fallen in love with him. since she was dependant on the planetoid for her life-force, she couldn't leave, and she kept Cochrane there. When she finally merged with Nancy Hedford to become human, he agreed to stay with her.

The planetoid is very pleasant and the couple (or rio) have a fine house and gardens. They do ask to be left alone, and don't encourage visitors. If you do drop in, please don't tell them I sent you, okay? Thanks.

GAMME HYDRA IV

Story: "The Deadly Years"

Gamma Hydra IV is not a cheerful place to visit. For one thing, it's rather close to the Romulan Neutral Zone, and even a few light years off, you can almost feel the Romulans staring at the back of your neck. For another, everyone who does visit the planet dies of old age. That wouldn't be so bad if it wasn't accelerated old age. You can age a few decades in your sleep, which doesn't give much faith in the old truism about "beauty sleep". It's possible, as Captain Kirk and his crew discovered, to stave off the aging disease by taking shots of adrenaline, but the planet isn't exciting enough to warrant that.

GAMMA TRIANGULAE VI

Story: "The Apple"

This is another good place to avoid. The natives are quite friendly sorts, but the planet itself isn't. It has improved slightly since Captain Kirk destroyed the computer known as Vaal. Vaal had kep the natives - the Feeders of Vaal - eternally young, but also eternally the same. Vaal had even forbidden sex. If that wasn't bad enough, Vaal also discouraged tourists, tending to hit them with lightning bolts and other such off-putting activities. For once, you can't blame Kirk for having destroyed the thing.

On the other hand, this doesn't mean the planet is all sunshine and roses. There are rocks that have a rather nasty habit of exploding like landmines. If they don't get you, there are also dart-throwing plants that kill their victims and wait for them to decay and provide compost. Cheerful world, no? These are not the sort of attractions the average tourist really wants to see. Skip this place and go elsewhere.

GENESIS PLANET

Stories: "Star Trek II - The Wrath of Khan"
"Star Trek III - The Search for Spock"

Despite the fact that this appeared to be a lovely green world, with lots of grass, trees, and flowers and so forth, it was inherently unstable. Dr. David Marcus had utilized proto-matter in making the world, and this was Not A Good Thing. Protomatter is banned by all respectable scientists, because it has a tendency to come apart at the seams - which is roughly what happened to Genesis. This means that there is nothing there now to see but rubble.

GHOST PLANET

Story: "That Which Survives"

This world has never been officially named, because it's not really that interesting. The Kalandans tried to colonize the place, but accidentally created a mutant virus here that decimated both the colony and the home world. As a result, it's about as cheerful a place to spend a few weeks as camping out on an iceberg in winter. There was a rather lethal computer here that drove off all visitors, which was pretty much a waste of time, since there weren't very many at the best of times. Captain Kirk, following his usual inclinations, destroyed the computer.

GIDEON

Story: "The Mark of Gideon"

Another wonderful winner of a planet. There's absolutely no point in visitng this place, because there's nowhere - quite literally - for you to stay. The whole planet is overpopulated, and under-interesting. If you like looking at people, then you'll be find, because that's all this entire planet has to offer. In fact, they're stacked six or seven deep. It seems that they don't like birth control, but they do like sex. That's a tough combination. It naturally resulted in a whole planet full of people, everyone standing on everyone else's toes.

Captain Kirk reported that they are trying to do something about the whole situation. It appears to hinge upon giving everyone Vegan minigitis, and hoping that will decimate the excess population. Personally, I think they should adopt Russian roulette as the national sport if they're that desperate. Talk about the cure that kills....

In short, another great place to wave to as you head to greener pasture.

GOTHOS

Story: "The Squire of Gothos"

Gothos is a small world in Quadrant 904 which has a poisonous atmosphere, high winds and a life expectancy for visitors of about as long as you can hold your breath and keep your orifices closed - provided you can stand up in the gale-force blasts that scour the planet. As you may gather, it's not exactly high on most people's lists of places to spend their summer vacations.

On the other hand, it did for a short while sport a small area that was made habitable by a being called Trelayne. This maniac was actually the child of some odd alien race that let him play by creating his own world and having fun. It takes all sorts to make a galaxy, of course. Anyhow, he made himself a castle and cultivated manners patterned on Napoleonic Era England. He then compelled Captain Kirk and the crew of the "Enterprise" to play with him. It might have had tragic overtones had his parents not called him in for dinner at the crucial point.

It is entirely possible that the castle and all his souvenirs are still there. On the other hand, since the small bit of breathable atmosphere isn't no one is really that keen on finding out.

HALCON

Halcon is a warm, friendly world. The people are delightful, and very peaceful. There may not be a lot to actually do on this world, but you can do it in a relaxed style. The only real problem with the planet is the plethora of magnetic storms that ravage the place now and again. Just like on trips to England, if you visit Halcon, be sure to pack a good umbrella.

INGRAHAM B

Story: "Operation - Annihilate!"

Ingraham B was the final world whose population was wiped out by the mind parasites that were destroyed by the Enterprise on Deneva. Having perished so recently, the native cities are very intact. It's like visiting a ghost world, however, and far too depressing for most tourists. There's talk of resettling the planet, so maybe soon it's be worth taking a look again. Till then, you'd probably have more fun camping out a week in a mausoleum.

JANOS VI

Story: "Devil in the Dark"

There's not a lot to see on Janos VI. Actually, there's nothing at all on the surface, unless you like collecting rocks wearing vacuum suits (you, not the rocks, in the suits). Below the surface is a pergium mine that extends for miles, but if you've seen one pergium mine, you've seen them all. If you haven't seen one, then you're lucky. On the other hand, this planet has a very unusual native life-form, the Horta.

When it was first discovered, the Horta proved to be something of a leghal beastie. It looks like a collection of rocks lumped together, since it's made from silicon, and secretes acid to burrow through the rocks and eat. The only live Horta at that point was guarding its eggs pretty strongly, and the humands, not kowing they were eggs, were collecting or smashing them. The Horta promptly retaliated by jumping on humans, leaving a smoking stain on the ground and little else. Captain Kirk settled the whole problem, establishing intelligent contact with the Horta. Now there are thousands of little hatchlings burrowing away in the planet. They're not great conversationalists, limited to pig Standard, but they are kind of cute in an off-beat way.

Janos is thus a great place for the amateur naturalist to visit, provided you remember not to stroke the Horta - they're covered in acid, if you recall.

KALANDA

Story: "That Which Survives"

Remember all of those dead worlds we've been discussing? Well, this is another of them. The Kalandan race were all wiped out by a mutant disease that one of their colony worlds accidentally created. The disease appears to be dead, but why take chances?

KELVA

Story: "By Any Other Name"

This is included just to annoy the readers. It's in the Adromeda Galaxy, so you can't get there anyway. Not only that, its natives are shape-changers with a low toleration of other species. Unless you happen to be a shape changer also, there's not a lot of chance of poppig in for quick sightseeing tour. On the other hand, considering it would take over three hundred years at top speed to get there, you'd have to be a very long-lived shape changer, also.

KHITTOMER

Story: Star Trek VI: The Undiscovered Country

Khittomer is located near the mutual Federation/Klingon/Romulan border. It was the sight of the first peace conference between the UFP and the Klingons. Conspirators from both sides attempted to sabotage the proceedings and assassinate the Federation president. The attempt failed and the peace process continued. Many years later, the Romulans attacked Khittomer. One of the survivors of the raid was Lt. Worf.

KZIN

Story: "The Salver Weapon"

Actually, no one has ever visited the homeworld of the Kzinti and returned to talk about it. The natives are very nasty meateaters and anything still alive is food for more than thought. Only visitors who fancy being basted and served in marnay sauce need try visiting the Kzinti.

L-370 to L-374

Story: "The Doomsday Machine"

These five systems are not there anymore, though a few older books still list them. They were taken apart into dust and rubble by a rampaging planet wrecker from some other galaxy. Captain Kirk managed to destroy the wrecker before it disposed of any more interesting places to visit.

LACTRA VII

Story: "The Eye of the Beholder"

Lactra VII is a lovely planet, with natives that look like huge slugs with tentacles. They are, in fact, far more intelligent than you are, and thinking down to our level hurts their brains. They are so advanced that at first contact, they didn't even realize that human beings are intelligent at all. (Some races still maintain that human beings, in fact, are not terrifically intelligent, and the Lactrans were right). They began collecting humans as specimens for their zoo. Now, however, they know their mistake and instead are willing to give guided tours of their zoo. Since they have a vast number of specimens from hundreds of worlds, this is a terrific stopover to make.

LAZARUS' WORLD

Story: "The Alternative Factor"

This is a very dull, boring and pretty pointless place to visit. It's most desrt and scrub rock, with no really run places to be, and no inhabitants. It was named after the one (or two) person found there, Lazarus. He was a traveler across time from another plane of reality, chasing himself. Despite the fact that he caught himself, both of him are now stuck in limbo. If they had taken this planet with them, no one would have missed it.

LEVINIUS V

Story: "Operation - Annihilate!"

Levinius V is another world whose population was completely wiped out by the mind parasites that were destroyed on Deneva. Another world of crumbling stones and ruins. There are plenty of others, so why visit this one?

M113

Story: "The Man Trap"

M113 is a fine place for an archaeologist, and an exercise in total boredom for everyone else. The whole planet is now dead, and scattered ruins are just about the only surface features worth seeing. The native race died out some long time in the past, leaving the ruins. The final survivor of the planet proved to be a salt vampire, who had the power to assume the form of anyone it could read in a victim's mind. It made the mistake of picking on Captain Kirk's crew for a meal, and was promptly dispatched to join the race of its race in oblivion.

The surface of the planet is mostly rock and sand, with scattered clumps of Borgia plants. Vegetarian travelers should note that Borgia plants are not edible, and should never be tried without competent medical help close at hand, since the taste of a portion of the plant is lethal in three to five seconds.

MAD PLANET

Story: "The Jihad"

There's a very good reason that this is called the Mad Planet - it refuses to recognize and obey most natural laws of the Universe. It's like a spoiled brat, flinging rocks about in tantrums, belching out volcanoes, or tossing snowstorms at you. You can stop off here, but don't expect a rest. It's more like a very lethal video game.

MALURIAN SYSTEM

Story: "The Changeling"

This is another of those very depressing lifeless places. The inhabitants of four planets, over four billion people, were wiped out some years back by a probe called Nomad. The thing had originally been one of those space probes sent out from 20th Century Earth that travelers still moan about nowadays cluttering up the space lanes. It had collided with an alien probe, and the two had gotten their wires crossed on what their mission was. The new Nomad decided it should sterilize imperfect planets, and the Malurian system failed to meet its grades.

The four worlds are completely intact, but with no inhabitants now. Once they are resettled, they should be nice worlds again. Right now, they are empty and serve only to make visitors feel very down.

MANTILLES

Story: "One of our Planets is Missing"

Mantilles is a very pleasant, advanced Earth colony, currently run by Governor Bob Wesley. It's a fun place to stop off and relax for a few days. If you're lucky enough to get invited in by the Governor, you'll find him an excellent host. Even if you aren't, this world is worth stopping off to see. Nice landscapes, pleasant folks and all the comforts of home are a strong allure.

MARKUS III

Story: "The Galileo Seven"

Markus III is a colony world, getting along at just over subsistence level. A recent plague wiped out a large minority of the population, before it was brought under control. As a result, manpower is pretty scarce on the world, and there are few facilities to cater for tourists. On the other hand, if you've had your shots and like backpacking through unspoiled wilderness, this is the place for you.

MEDUSA

Story: "Is There in Truth No Beauty?"

Unless you're a Vulcan, blind or insane, stay away from this place. Far away. The natives are likable sorts, but it's definitely not a wise move to look on them. They have this sort of four dimensional geometry about them that the eye tries to follow and can't. That way lies madness, and few people want to travel there. I can't say I blame them.

As a result of all this, Medusans all travel round in boxes, which is smart of them. No one knows what Medusa itself looks like, since there's no way to visit the place without going crazy — a planetful of creatures that give you the screaming heebie-jeebies is not a place most folks want to go. Vulcans have never been allowed on the planet, so even they can't tell us. The Medsans themselves see things very differently than us, so even if they tried they couldn't tell us what their world looks like to us — only to them, and that's no help at all.

MEGAS-TU

Story: "The Magicks of Megas-Tu"

If you can find your way here, you can have a great time. The problem is that the planet is mobile, and doesn't always want to be found. The natives are a very odd lot, all having what amounts to be magical powers. They once visited the Earth and were condemned as witches. Now, however, they are happy that humans have matured a little, and are willing to accept them for what they are — nioce people. If you want a magical holiday that isn't Disneyworld, try this place. If you can find it.

MELKOTIA

Story: "Spectre of the Gun"

No one has actually been to Melkotia, since the natives are pretty secretive about themselves. They're rather like wispy balls of light, and do generally like to be left alone. After something of a bad start, Captain Kirk managted to get along with them. At first they just thought he and the crew of the "Enterprise" were crude barbarians, and tried to get them to kill themselves off in a mock-up version of Dodge City. (You wouldn't like the real place any better, believe me). Thanks to Spock and his mental disciplines, Kirk and his fellows survived the test, and the Melkotians agreed to pow-wow.

As a result, they are now far less prejudiced, but still pretty quiet about themselves. They aren't keen on having tourists flood in, so won't tell us their home world, or allow more than an occasional visit from Starfleet.

MEMORY ALPHA

Story: "The Lights of Zetar"

This isn't technically a place to spend a vacation, but it's a terrific place, and this is my book, so I'm including it. It's one of a number of repositories for all unclassified Federation knowledge. The place is a vast, hollowed-out asteroid, and is loaded to the lid with books, videos, discs and so forth. You could browse here for a lifetime or two and not see a tenth of what they have. For those of you with intellectual leanings, this is the next best thing to paradise.

For those who are worried, yes, everyone here a few years back died off. The problem was with a cloud of sentient survivors from Zetar, and won't happen again. Captain Kirk blew out the lights.

MERAK IV

Story: "The Cloud Minders"

Merak IV is a nice place, if you like denuded landscapes. A recent biological plague killed off a large portion of the plant life there, inducing a minor famine. The matter has been settled now, one gathers, but frankly all of the nice views have been spoiled. Maybe in a couple

of years, the place will be back to looking as good as new. Till then, forget it.

MINARA II

Story: "The Empath"

Forget it. The star went nova, and all of the remaining planets in this system are so much burnt-out rubble.

MIRI'S WORLD

Story: "Miri"

Miri's world is named for the leader of the small group of survivors discovered there by Captain Kirk and his crew. It orbits the star 70 Ophiucus, and is virtually a second Earth. There are few natives left, since a coupld of hundred years ago (in their version of the 20th Century), a rather nasty biological plague got loose. It was supposed to confer immortality on the population, but worked in a somewhat different manner. It was only effective inpeople who had not reached puberty - everyone else is drove insane and then killed. What happened was that society totally degenerated, with all of the adults killed off, and only the very slowly aging children left.

Naturally, the whole palce went to ruin. The kids couldn't look after themselves too well, and so formed gangs. They raided stores for food, clothing and entertainment with the older children looking after the younger. The older children, however, began to enter puberty, catch the maia and die. As a result, the planet was slowly decaying as stores vanished, and the population was heading towards extinction. The "Enterprise" arrived in answer to an automated distress beacon and managed to cure the plague. Currently, the planet is under Starfleet control, as the natives are being helped back to self-sufficiency. No tourism is hus allowed. On the other hand, since packs of screaming kids have been tearing the place apart for two hundred years, it's not exactly likely that there will be a lot left there in a state worth visiting.

MURASAKI 312

Story: "The Galileo Seven"

Not a planet, but a very bizarre stary, Murasaki 312 is a quasar-like star, with very odd properties. There's a scientific station close to the really weird edge of things here. If you idea of fun is exploring strange new phenomena, this place can guarantee them. There's no guarantee of safety attached to trip here, however.

NEURAL

Story: "A Private Little War"

Not a nice place to take the family. For one thing, the Federation and the Klingons are supplying two sides of the population with arms, and there is constant fighting going on. The Hill People and the Towns People are fighting a war to see who will control the planet. As a result, tourism is not waht you'd term an active industry.

Secondly, there are witch-women who live on this planet who have a deep knowledge of the local flora and its effects on people. As a result, if they take a dislike to you, you can soon wind up dead. On the other hand, if they take a liking to you, you can end up as their love-slave. then when they get bored, you end up dead.

Thirdly, there's a rather unpleasant large white creature called a Mugato that runs around the place. It's a big, vicious brute with a poisonous horn. It attacks without provocation, warning or cure, so it's best to avoid them by avoiding the whole planet.

NEUTRAL ZONE

Stories: "Balance of Terror"

Make a very careful note: avoid like the plagues.

Apart from the fact that if you accidentally entered the Neutral Zone with Romuland space you'd probably set off a war between the Federation and the Romuland Empire (which would not make you terribly welcome anywhere in the Galaxy), you'd probably get blown to bits by the Romulans, who are not noted for their tolerance of idiots, or anyone, for that matter. Your only chance of survival is if you're a Vulcan — then they'd save you for rape, humiliation and finally, suicide.

Even if you were insane enough to want to risk all this, there is actually nothing much to see there. There are a few Outposts watching the Neutral Zone from the Federation side, and lots of warships watching it from the Romulan side. You could have lots more fun beaming down into a minor nuclear way somewhere if the Neutral Zone is your idea of a vacation spot.

NIMBUS III

Story: Star Trek V: The Final Frontier

Nimbus III was named the "Planet of Galactic Peace", and was to be an effort of cooperation between the Federation, Klingons, and Romulans. In reality, the planet is desolate almost beyond compare and nothing grows. Inhabitants, many of them criminals, dig for water in the sand. Each of the three governments have installed ambasadors, but they are all washed-up bureaucrats. Sybok goes there and takes hostages luring the Enterprise there for his adventure to ShaKaRee.

OMEGA

Story: "Requiem for Methuselah"

A small world in the Omega system, Omega is host to a very strange castle, built by an immortal human, Flint. Well, simi-immortal, because he's not agin normally. Flint's castle is a veritable wonderland for the culture lovers among you because he was, in his time, people like Brahms, Da Vinci and Methuselah. As a result, he's got a collection of antiques and fresh material from the pens of all those folks. If he weren't such a hermit, forever trying to build a better android, he'd be a wonderful dinner guest, one imagines. As it is, he just wants to be left alone.

OMEGA IV

Story: "The Omega Glory"

Omega IV is another one of those worlds that somehow paralleled the Earth's development. It is stuck in roughly late 29th Century time. Despite a recent war between the Yangs and the Kohms there, matters have settled down somewhat. The planet is under the Prime Directive, though, and you're to stay clear. Captain Ronald Tracy lost the entire cress of the USS Exeter to a deadly virus in the atmosphere there, if you need further encouragement to steer clear.

the natives are very long-lived, but not immortal. The viruses flating about the place are the result of a dirty little war fought there a century or two back. The effects of the virus wear off in time - provided you stay on the planet, where other bacteriological agents can immunize you.

OMICRON CETI III

Story: "This Side of Paradise"

This is definitely off the intinerary for the travelers. Oh, it's a lovely world, with lots of nice plants, trees, cool brooks and the like. a regular haven for the weary traveler. The problem is that the planet is flooded with Berthold radiation from a nearby star, and this disintegrates flesh in about a week. It's not even the sort of place you'd go to lose a few pounds, since they'd probably be from your head..

There is a way to survive this, however, as the Sandoval colony discovered. There's a native plant that produces spores which enable the body to regenerate itself with wonder efficiency. The problem is that the spores are sporific, and make you so laid back folk will think you're from California. You lose all initiative, all drive, and all enthusiasm for anything but the good life. On the other hand, if you happen to be from California, this probably sounds like heaven to you. The rest of us like a little more entertainment, thank you very much.

OMICRON DELTA

Stores: "Shore Leave" "Once Upon A Planet"

Now, this is more like it! Talk about the world of your dreams...quite literally. In fact, Omicron Delta was constructed by a strange alient race purely for the purpose of having fun. The whole world is artificial, but bearin gnan excellent simulacra of the real thing. Under the planet's surface are vast factories, and the plant is webbed by devices to minor thoughts and produce whatever you might want — quite literally. It's a great idea to be careful what you might wish for, because it will literally come true.

Since this world was specifically constructed for the purposes of pleasure, there's no way it can be beaten. On the other hand, the whole place is monitored extremely carefully by Starfleet, who don't like the idea of lots of tourists trampling about on the planet and getting whatever they want to play with. It's not easy to get a permit to visit the place — but if you can beg, steal or borrow one, do it. This is definitely the place to have fun!

There was a slight problem with the place for a short while, following the death of the Caretaker. THe computer system got a little revolted with humans (and who doesn't at times?) and tried to dispose of the "Enterprise". Captain Kirk and his crew convinced it of the

error of its ways, and it's now back to being friendly and cheerful again.

OPHIUCUS III

Story: "Mudd's Women"

Ophiucus II is a barely marginal colony world. It is settled by ex-natives of Earth, and the colony seems to be prospering. There is a noted shortage of women there, however. Due to the rural atmosphere of the planet, it is quite a pleasant place to visit by those wishing to get away from the pains and problems of civilization. Native and Terran animal rides are available through pleasnat scenery. Certainly one of the nicer worlds for those who do not mind a little roughing it.

ORGANIA

Story: "Errand of Mercy"

an odd place. The natives are balls of light, but they are fond of posing as regular style hman beings so as not to upset visitors. They are amiable enough, as long as you don't disturb them, but since they have incredible mental abilities, they give most visitors a decided inferiority complex. They never really flaunt the fact that they're superior, but it isn't too easy to put up with it.

these are, of course, the folks responsible for the current cold war between the Federation and the Klingon Empire. On the other hand, a cold war is far better than a hot one, which tends to wreck plants and ruin matters for the average tourist, so we should be grateful for that. The Organians are keeping an eye (or whatever balls of light use in the place of an eye) on both sides, making sure that war never again erupts between the two sides. Most kind of them.

In short, Organia is a great place to develop a strong feeling of ineriority. Send your boss there for his vacation, but go somewhere a little nicer yourself.

ORION

Stories: "The Cage" "Journey to Babel"
"The Pirates of Orion"

The worlds of Orion are a strange mixture of types. Some of them have inhabitants who could easily pass for human, save for their green-hued skin. Others resemble the andorians more. The society behind the linked worlds is one based on free enterprise - any enterprise you can get away with is legal. This means that there is a great deal of slave-trading, smuggling and other illicit activities undertaken. Tourists are advised that they run serious risks of being kidnapped, either for slavery, prostitution or just plan ransom.

On the other hand, there are some advantages to visiting the system. The slave girls of Orion are widely and accurately reputed to be the most lascivious dancers alive. Male tourists frequently enjoy discovering this for themselves. Many fail to return from such trips; some because they are kidnapped, others because the slave girls are reputedly just as aggressive in bed, which can be fatal for those with weak hearts or jealous wives.

All of the worlds of Orion will take Galactic Express - along with luggage, money and anything else not nailed down. Recreational facilities are everywhere, tending to range from drug heavens to bordellos to hunting galleries (careless tourists may end up in one of these arcades as the moving target). Few reputable travel agents will even consider trips to the system for clients that they actually like.

PANDRO

Story: "BEM"

Pandro is the home of some very odd creatures that can split themselves into three separate beings and carry out independent actions. If the sight of an apparently normal being splitting into three parts doesn't make you toss your cookies, then try this world. The natives are so egotistical, they can soon induce either an inferiority complex or an overshelming desire in a visitor to split them into three million pieces.

PHYLOS

Story: "The Infinite Vulcan"

Phylos is a nice place, if you're into botany, because there's no animal life on the whole place. It's filled instead with many and varied kinds of plants. It's a horticultural wonderland, though some - like ambulatory poisoners - are dangerous. There are even flying plants, and an intelligent race of plant being who run the world. Bring along your Culpepper's Herbal, and have fun.

PLATONIA

Story: "Plato's Stepchildren"

Platonia is another nice place to avoid. It's quite a nice little place, but the inhabitants have definite personality problems. They liked to consider themselves followers of the simple philosophies of the ancient Greek, Plat. They were actually much more in line with the ancient French philosopher, the Marquis de Sade. With vast mental powers, they spent their time in sex and violence - sex with each other, and violence with everyone else.

Captain Kirk and his crew fell foul of their bad temper. Kirk made friends with the only nice fellow in the bunch, Alexander, and finally managed to gain mental powers of his own greater than those of the Platonians. How? Kironide injections, it seems. This would work nicely elsewhere also if there were only more kironide around. anyhow, Kirk then proceeded to smack the Platonians around until they promised to behave. If you feel like risking their having reformed, try visiting them. If you'd sooner be cautious (like the rest of us), go somewhere nicer, where the natives are more accommodating.

POLLUX IV

Story: "Who Mourns for Adonis?

Pollux IV is the only nice planet in the Beta Geminorum system - unless you're into breathing methane for a hobby. Pollux is a nice, garden planet, with little native life, and none that's harmful. It's very definitely a place to go to get away from the pressures of everyday life. Take a walk in the gardens, a swim in the lakes, or just while the time away in the sun.

It's also the last place wehre the Greek gods lived. They all gave up and dissipated into the ether, or some place, so the planet's up for grabs now. The last inhabitant was Apollo, who had a rather naive expectation that humans wold come along and burn a few fatted calves for him. The Enterprise ran across him, but they had - surprise! - forgotten to stock up on fatted calves. Apollo was a trifle peeved that they weren't inclined to worship him any longer, and left in a huff to join his old friends. He didn't leave much when he went, so the planet is still unspoiled.

PRAXIS

Story: Star Trek VI: The Undiscovered Country

The moon Praxis was the Klingon Empire's primary energy source. It self-destructed, leaving the Empire sustainable for only six months. The Klingons immediately began peace proceedings with the Federation to save the Empire.

PRESERVERS' WORLD

Story: "The Paradise Syndrome"

Actually, there are most likely more than one Preservers' World, but we've only run across one so far. The Preservers are some vast, ancient civilization that kidnapped a bunch of folks from a culture somewhere and transplanted them to a fresh planet, allowing their society to grow unfettered and unconquered by nastier types. The one example we know of is a world full of American Indian types. It's strictly keep-out, however, so you can't go there.

But if you could? Well, it;s lovely. There are vast lakes, deep forests, abundant game. You can sit and fish all day, or trek into the mountains. the natives are a cheerful, uncomplicated bunch of folks. They simply enjoy their lives and live it from day to day as they wish. No wonder they call this place paradise. No wonder they won't let a bunch of tourists in to spoil the place.

PSI 2000

Story: "The Naked Time"

Psi 2000 doesn't exist any longer, since it has been ripped apart by tidal stresses from its star. For the average tourist, therefore, there is literaally nothing to see, unless you are strongly into rock collecting.

For those with time travel capabilities, Psi 2000 is still not worth seeing. It was a craggy lump of rock and frozen gases, spinning about its star. There was for a short whole a research station on the place, but the entire group had a wild party one evening and cracked the airlocks,killing themselves off. It was, for once, not the alcohol imbibed that caused the problems, but a mutated water molecule. The samd molecule infected the starship "Enterprise," but the redoubtable Dr. McCoy worked out a fast and efficient cure.

RIGEL II

Story: "Shore Leave"

Rigel II is a pleasure world. If you like your entertainment prepackaged, this is the place for you. There are night-spots, cabarets, casinos, bars, videodromes, games, races... The natives have cheerfully turned the place into a huge tourist trap. With no local taxes, you're encouraged to spend, spend, spedn. If that's your idea of a vacation, build up your bank account and pay Rigel II a visit. You'll undoubtedly spend a small fortune, but most piople recon it's worth it.

RIGEL IV

Story: "The Wolf In The Fold"

Rigel IV is a pleasant enough world, whose main exports are efficeiency experts, policement and other such organizational minded types. As a result, Rigel IV is run extremely methodically and tidily. It's the sort of place tourists come from, not go to.

RIGEL VII

Story: "The Cage"

Rigel VII is a world still in its medieval stage. Castles abound, with roaming bands of warriors raiding and pillaging the population. Life there is frequently short and sharp. There is little medical care, and no major cities. The natives dwell in the shadows of the huge castles, owing fealty to the lords of the manor.

This is not a world recommended for tourists, unless they are heavily into "Dungeons And Dragons" or the Society for Creative Anachronisms. The food is terrible, the people insular and the life-expectancy low.l They do not take Galactic Express preferring chunks of gold, jewls, or the heads of local notables as methods of exchange.

RIGEL XII

Story: "Mudd's Women"

Farther out from the same star is Rigel XII. This is an even less appealing planet to visit, since the whole planet is wracked with terrible storms - mostly of driven sand and dust that can blind and kill in less than an hour. Once you've lost your way on this planet, you're as good as dead. The only sights to see on the place are the dillithium mines and the small homes of the miners. though mining can be more than rewarding financially, the small collection of miners huts is like a sum in a sleazy world off Orion somewhere. There are virtually no amenities, no welcome and not even a local bar. Unless touring primitive mining facilities turns you on, turn this place off your list of selections.

ROMULAN EMPIRE

Stories: "Balance Of Terror"

There really isn't a lot of point putting this entry in, since Romulans don't like tourists at all. You are not allowed into Romulan space, period.

SARPEDON

Story: "All Our Yesterdays"

Sarpedon lies in the orbit of Beta Niobe, which has now gone nova. The planet is now a molten slag-heap, and not attractive to visitors. the native race, however, excaped the destruction through time-traveling into their own past to escaped the destruction through time-traveling into their own past to escape. Smart folks without a doubt. So, visitors with time machines might have a little fun. There's the usual stages of evolution, passing into vast wastelands of their ice ages - which contain scattered humans, left to live out their lives in exile. Then, thereafter, the rise to a rather fine technological society before the big bang swept the surface clean.

SCALOS

Story: "Wink Of An Eye"

One of the obvious reasons to go on vacation is to unwind. This is therefore a fine place to avoid, since the natives here wind you up, and not the reverse. The planet looks nice, but rather badly polluted. In fact, one of the waste products affects humanoid life-forms and speeds up their bodily metabolisms to a break neck (very literally) pace. If you're into pollution and dropping dead at a fast pace, the Scalos is for you. Since noone sane, is, very few people ever want to go within a parsec of the planet. Starfleet is supposedly helping the last few natives to clean up their act, but don't hold your breath waiting.

Actually, this area of space is now a lot safer for travlers thanks (as I'm sure you guessed) to Captain Kirk. The Scalosians used to lure in passing ships and accelerate their crews for their own pleasures. Since in that state even a tiny cut could prove fatal, this was not appreciated. Kirk and his crew managed to stop this from happening, and isolated the Scalosians to wait for help.

SHERMAN'S PLANET

Story: "The Trouble With Tribbles"

Sherman's Planet is a recently opened agricultural world. If your idea of a good time is watching quadrotriticale waving in the wind, then this is the place for you. If you prefer something a little livelier, go elsewhere.

In orbit in the same system is Deep Space, Station K-7. This is one of those Starfleet outposts that has minimal recreational facilities for passing ships. If want to buy tribbles cheap (and you need your head examined if you do), then stop off here. They have them on permanent mark-down.

SIGMA DRACONIS VI

Story: "Spock's Brain"

If you're one of those folks that likes your menfolk to act like cavemen, or your women to be pure, unadulterated dumb blondes - then this is heaven for you. The planet is admittedly rather cold, but the people here are certainly as described. It seems that centuries back, the women got control of the underground cities and expessed their men to the surface. there they kept the men in primitive conditions, taking them below only when they wanted a little romp in the high-tech hay. As a result of all this, the women's brains turned to jello. Captain Kirk happened by, and managed to stop their two-party system, forcing the women to join their menfolk on the surface.

Not surprisingly, civilization is taking its time about growing up here. The men aren't used to anything more innovative than fire, and the women seem content to snuggle down next to one in their bear skins with a man. Well, some people do think civilization is vastly overrated, anyhow.

SIGMA IOTIA II

Story: "A Piece Of The Action"

Another of those wolds under the control of the Primej Directive. Theer's good reason for it, since the Iotians are extremely good mics, and can adapt their whole planetary lifestile to whatever takes their fancy. After the visit of the "USS-Horizon" the Iotians discovered about Chicago gangs of the 1930's. A hundred years later, when the "Enterprise" stopped by, the whole planet was organized as Chicago had been. Talk about imitation being the sincerest form of flatter - Captain Kirk and his crew were almost imitated to dath. Though they escaped, and tried to set up up a better system, there's no telling what the Iotians may be up to now.

SIGNIA MINOR

Story: "The Conscience Of The King"

An Earth colony close to Arcuturus, Signia Minor has periodic bouts with famine. It's a pleasant place otherwise, so if you want to visit, check the status of the food situation first.

SKORR

Story: "The Jihad"

Skorr is the home of a race of birdmen. Pardon the expression, but they are rather flighty beings. They were once a race of terrifying warriors, but were thankfully talked into hanging up their ray-guns and adopting the ways of peace. Still, the Skorr are rather excitable, and seem like they're looking for any excuse to take up the guns again and start blasting. If you visit their world, be prepared ot have the natives get very annoyed very with you. Since they can fly, and you probably can't, they do have a rather dirty advantage in a flight.

SHAKAREE

Story: Star Trek V: The Final Frontier

ShaKaRee is the place where "God" is said to exist. Sybok, Spock's brother, believes it and is on a holy mission to reach it. To that end, he takes hostages on Nimbus III, and comandeers the Enterprise. The ship reaches ShaKaRee and a "God-like" being does exist there. While powerful, this being is selfish and evil, not the

God Sybok envisioned. Sybok uses his mind-control in an attempt to kill the evil God creature and dies. The creature is killed by a Klingon ship. Outside of the creature, ShaKaRee is barren and rocky.

STARBASES

Stories: "The Menagerie"
Starbase 11 (Commodore Menzies commanding)
"Court Martial"
Starbase 11 (Postmaster Stone commanding)
"The Deadly Years"
Starbase 10 (Commodore Stocker commanding)
"The Immunity Syndrome"
Starbase 6

Starbases are fine places to stop if there's nowhere better about. Though primarily set up for the Starfleet ships, they also take visitors and treat them pretty well. Facilities are rather limited, but you can generally get good repairs, food and a pretty nice selection of shops. The best place to stop off on the way home for those gifts you forgot to buy whilst on the planet of your choice.

All Starbases have areas off-limits to civilian personnel, like shuttle bays, weapons rooms, computer sections and so forth. Unless you'd like an extended vacation on Tantalus (see separate entry), it is best to obey all restrictions posted. Starfleet is not overly tolerant of tourists in the wrong sectors.

In the area of Starbase 11, periodic ion storms are observed. Keep tuned ot ht esub-space radio channels in that area for updated weather reports.

TALOS IV

Stories: "the Cage" "The Menagerie"

Visiting Talos IV is not advised, since trepassing there is one of the few capital offenses still on the books at Starfleet. The world is pleasant enough, though apparently barren. The Talosians all live underground, in their warren-like cities. They resemble humanoids, with vastly oversized craniums to hold their extremely active brains. Talosians can project all kinds of illusions that are totally realistic. Their mental abilities can thus force any vistors into doing whatever the Talosians want.

Due to this incredible mental control, Talos IV was placed off-limits. More recently, the Talosians have shown indications that they may not be quiet as implacably hostile as first it seemed. Starfleet is not, however, considering opening the world up to the tourist trade.

TANTALUS

Story: "Dagger Of The Mind"

Anyone who wants to visit Tantalus probably deserves to be there; the only thing on the entire planet is one of the very last penal colonies in the Federation space. It's got most of the incurables inside, and specializes in a variety of treatments. One that is luckily no longer applied is the neural neutralizer, an invention utilized by the crazed Dr. Tristan Adams. It could blank a person's mind, leaving them extremely susceptible to suggestion. Still, it's no fun being even in a model penal colony. Anyone wishing to visit the place can probably have a small sentence applied ot facilitate matters.

TARSUS IV

Story: "The Conscience Of The King"

A very pleasant little colony world. The population is friendly, the facilities admirable and the planet most attractive. It is noted as being the planet where the famed Captain James Kirk grew up. Various sites are clearly marked, and tours of the old farm where he lived are conducted daily.

On a less cheerful note, it is also known as the world where Kodos the Executioner came to infamy. In order to stave off what he felt was a food shortage, Kodos had half the population of the planet butchered. Then a relief ship came, and the turth was revealed. Kodos skipped the planet, and was later discovered to have been making his living as an actor. Numerous relics of the Executions are preserved on the planet and are open for tours.

TAURUS II

Story: "The Galileo Seven"

Taurus II comes under the heading of "a must to avoid." It's a nasty, cold, inhospitable planet. Sights to see are rocks, rocks and more rocks. Even mountain climbing fanatics should avoid this place, though. There's a native race that grows over ten feet tall, throws spears and generally gets its fun from killing they're just as inclined to eat visitors as to behead them.

TAURUS II

Story: "The Lorelei Signal"

Not the same planet as in the previous entry, but just as good a place to avoid. Just a few years bsck, the women of thsi all-female planet were kidnapping men every 27 years to give themselves a recharge. This recharge invariably proved fatal to the men. They bit off rather more than they could chew when they picked on "Enterprise," however. The gals of that ship soon stopped the nasty shenanigans of the natives. They were then transported to another world, leaving this one free and open...

You wouldn't want to claim it, howver. There's something in the soil that drains the life-energies of all humanoid beings who live here. Hardly appealing, and certainly not the spot for a vacation.

TELLAR (61 CYNGI V)

Story: "Journey To Babel"

Tellarites are notorious for being rude, snippy and argumentative. Alone or in small groups, they are pretty insufferable. Why anyone would want to visit a place that is simply overflowing with the little so-and sos is beyond me.

TERRATIN

Story: "The Terratin Incident"

Terratin was actually a corruption of the form "Terra Ten", being a lost Earth colony. The problem was that the planet managed somehow to shrink in size all of the colonists by natural radiation. They are just a sixteenth of an inch high. The same shrinkage would affect all visitors, so unless you're grossly over-tall, stay clear of the place. The inhabitants were transferred to Verdanis, a xalmer world, because Terratin is subject to planet - widce quakes of great frequency. With both of these problems to take into consideration, the wise traveler will visit some quieter, safer world.

THASUS

Story: "Charlie X"

Thasus is a strange world, of which virtually nothing but legend is known. Even its exact location is somethingj of a mystery. Tourists do not have to be warned to avoid the place, since it is virtually impossible to find anyhow. There is a native race, about whom almost nothing is known, save that many worlds credit the Thasians with being magicians, gods, devils or just plain weird. At any event, the consensus of opinion is that you're better off for never having met them.

there is one documented story of a young man who did, onej Charles Evans. Charile had been stranded on Thasus as a child, and seized his first opportunity to excape as soon as he could. He maintained that the inhabitants were not merely dull, but incorporeal (neither of which serves as a strong inducement for visitors). They had, however, given him amazing mental abilities that caused considerable problems for Captain Kirk and the "Enterprise." It seems that the Thasians had felt it necessary to give Charlie the powers so that he could survive on their planet. This does not suggest that the world is a very pleasant place to stay unless the visitor has equally strong psionic abilities. The gift of those powers mad Charlie rather bad company, since he had been brought up rather poorly, the Thasians having no previous experience with corporeal life-forms. In the end, they were forced to take Charlie back home with them, as he would have proven rather a nasty delinquent anywhere else in the Galaxy.

None of this implies that visiting Thasus should be a priority trip on the itinery. Local currency is apparently non-existent, and given the native race's total lack of familiarity with visitors, it must be said that there are a lot of nicer places to see.

THETA VII

Story: "Obsession"

The recent terrible medical problems of this planet have just about cleared up by now, thanks to the vaccines delivered by the "Enterprise." If your shots are up to date, it should be safe for your to visit.

THETA CYGNII XII

Story: "Operation - Annihilate!"

Another world whose natives were killed by the mind parasites that Captain Kirk destroyed on Deneva. There are lots of interesting ruins, if you happen to be into that sort of thing, but nothing much else to see.

THOLIA

Story: "The Tholian Web"

Nobody visits Tholia for a few very good reasons. First, the natives look like an accidental mating of a microwaved steak with an interferometer readout. Second, the Tholians have the geniality and grace of a Klingon with a toothache. They're very jealous of their personal living space, and are inclined to execute trespassers. This does not make them the best sort of people to spend a week with, since the chaces are you'd not last that long. It is speculated that the reason they are so nasty is everyone with nicer worlds, and aren';t letting anyone see their home planet, for fear that they'll be laughed at. Well, it's as good an explanation as any.

TIBURAN

Story: "The Savage Curtain"

Tiburan is another of those worlds to avoid. The people are savage little monsters, with the ethics of jackals. They'll welcome visitors with relish - as a side dish. Not nice people. To be frank, with a world like theirs, they don't have a lot to be cheery about. It's mostly thick forests and jungles, and nasty animals. It wouldn't put anyone into a good mood.

TRANSMUTER"S WORLD

Story: "Catspaw"

Another dead ball of rock, the Transmuter's World was named after the off-beat couple that visited it. Captain Kirk ran across them, and they were two would-be invaders of our Galaxy. By all accounts, the world was fare more interesting while they were there than it is now. They did populate it with haunted castles, talking corpses, witches and lots of things spending the nights bumping away. Now, as mentioned, it's a dead ball of rock. Admitted, Kirk was justified in killing off the Transmuters, but it's a shame he couldn;'t have figured out some way of keeping the hauntedk house. It would have been a terrific tourist attraction.

TRIACUS

Story: "And The Children Shall Lead"

Triacus is a world of Epsilon Indae. Now you know that, you needn't worry about visititng it. It was once the home of a very despicable civilization that fought anyone else they came across. Naturally, this annoyed the heck out of all of those other worlds, and their inhabitants bunched together and beat the stuffing out of the Triascans. It served them right, and they were wiped out, save for a single survivor, who cunningly hid himself away. The Federation sent in an archaelolgical team a few centureis or so later, and they accidentally made contact wiht that sneaky survivor, Gorgan. He managed to take over the minds of the children and wipe out th eadults. An attempt to take over the "Enterprise" failed, however, and Captain Kirk managed to destroy Gorgan. Triacus has since been left alone, and no-one really feels bad about that.

TRISKELION

Story: "The Gamesters Of Triskelion"

This is still not a terribly fun place to visit, since there is only a small population trying to tame the whole planet, but it's better than it used to be. Until a few years back, any passing travelers were likely to be kidnapped and trained for the arena. The last three survivors of the original inhabitants of the planet were giant brains in nutrient tanks, and they had been pretty bored. To relieve their montony , they had taken to kidnapping likely-looking candidates for fights to the death that they would then wager on. They were unlucky enough to pick Captain Kirk and a couple of his crew for this end, and he managed to convince them that their system was inefficient. He got them to switch to starting civilization up again. That's definetely a more wholesome aim, but a slower task.

TROYIUS

Story: "Elaan Of Troyius"

This is another macho world, where men are men and women are available - if you fight for them. Whatever turns you on, but they're pretty savage here. On top of that, the women's tears secrete a strange substance that literally can enthrall a man. some people think Troyian women are worth it, though. The planet itself is pretty nice, from all accounts, but there's not much leisure time or peace, since the natives are either practising or fighting for real.

TYCHUS IV

Story: "Obsession"

A small, insignificant little ball of dirt, this planet was homej to the vampire cloud that attacked and killed half of the crew of the "USS Farragut." It later attacked the "Enterprise, " before Captain Kirk destroyed it. There probably aren't any more of these things on Tychus, but do you really want to take the chance, just to visit a cosmic waste?

VEDELA ASTEROID

Story: "The Jihad"

Forget it. The Vedela like to be left alone, and since no-one can find their home without their help, you may as well think of somewhere else to spend the summer holidays.

VENDIKAR

Story: "A Taste Of Armageddon"

Vendikar is an ex-colony of Eminiar VII (see separate entry). After a disagreement over the importing of tea or something, the two worlds declared war, and waged it entirely on computer. Well, if you must have a war, at least that way you don't clutter up the planet with lots of radiation, bomb craters and mess. On the other hand, warfare of any kind is not the sort of thing that the average tourst likes to pass through. It's a trifle too terminal. Thankfully, Captain Kirk sorted the whole matter out, and forced the two sides to talk peace. the only warfare between the worlds now is economic, both vying for tourist dollars.

VENDOR

Story: "The Survivor"

Vendor is off-limits, and for excellent reasons. The natives - looking like refugees from a Greek salad - are all shaechangers, and remarkably easily influenced. They tend to try and take on the identities of other beings. Who can blame them? Who wants to look like a Greek salad all their life? On the other hand, it would be very dangerous to allow a species like this to get off its homej world and loose in the Galaxy, so no-one is allowed to drop in and visit.

VERDANIS

Story: "The Terratin Incident"

As its name implies, Verdanis is a pleasant, green world. It's not advisable to visit here, though, because all of the inhabitants are a mere one sixteenth of an inch tall. An incautious step could make a visitor a mass-murderer. The inhabitants were once colonists of Terratin.

VULCAN

Stories: "Amok Time", "Yesteryear", "Star Trek III - The Search For Spock, "Star Trek IV - The Voyage Home"

Visiting Vulcan can be a great pleasure or a real pain in the rear, depending on what you go for. The place is very advanced, and the civilization is naturally highly cultured. If you're the quiet, studious type, then Vulcan is heaven - provided you drink lots of water and stay indoors when there's air conditioning. The normal temperatures are very high, and even walking about can be exhausting. As for taking trips into the desert - don't.

Apart from the cities, or occasional wildlife safaris, there isn't much to see. The Vulcan people don't allow even the killingk of an animal, so take cameras, not elephant guns with you. The animals aren't so careful about observing the "no-killing" rule, so make sure you don't give them a good look at you.

As for night life - forget it. The Vulcans are vegetarians, so restaruants are very limited. They do not drink, so the planet is driver than the desert. They don't believe in frivolity, so there' no night life. Culturally, this is a great planet; for whooping it up, it's hell. So if you're into the arts, make this a must. If you're into the bottle, skip it entirely.

The natives are a nice lot, if infuriating to chat with. They are calm, unemotional and precise - their good points. They are also insufferably accurate, uninvolved and don't worry about anything. It can get on your nerves extremely quickly.

YOLANDA

Story: "For The World Is Hollow, And I Have Touched The Sky"

Okay, technically this isn't really a world - it's a hollowed out asteroid. Then again, it's got as much interior surface as a small world, so who cares? On the other hand, there isn't a lot to see here, since the "sky" is metal, there are no seasons and everything is grown artificially. Adde to all of that, it's due to go into orbit about a regular planet any day now. Then all of the inhabitants are gooing to disembark and presumably sell of Yolanda for scrap.

Dr. McCoy almost stayed here once, and was briefly married to Natira, the priestess of the People on Yonada. Then he was vured from his xnopolycythemia and left again. As you may have gathered, these folks have terrific hospitals.

ZEOS

Story: "Patterns Of Force"

Zeos is one of twin planets, the other being Ekos. Zeos is slightly more advanced, and the natives are friendly and helpful. Their level of technology is just about up to space travel between the worlds, so they aren't open yet for visitors. Small loss, since they probably don't even have indoor bathrooms yet.

ZETAR

Story: "The Lights Of Zetar"

Another dead world. The Galaxy is full of them, it seems. All humanoid life here died out, leaving the planet full rubble and ruins. The final hundred, however, managed to band together into a strange life-force like perambulating lights, seeking new bodies to take over. They made the mistake of picking on a member of the "Enterprise" crew, and Captain Kirk finally despatched the lights to join the rest of their dead race.

APPENDIX

The Enterprise

The most apparent permanent device in the series is that of the "Enterprise" herself. "Star Trek" (in the original series) never attempted to show the Earth of the future. Instead, all of the action was begun aboard the "USS Enterprise," one of a line of special ships commissioned by Starfleet Command to patrol, map and explore. The credibility of the entire show rested upon the viewers being able to accept the "Enterprise" as a "real" starship.

Thanks to a beautifully designed model, the physical appearance of the ship was elegant, not merely acceptable. The simple lines hold a promise of power, and its unusual shaping is both eye-catching and esthetically pleasing. However, as in any show, looks aren't everything unless there is a substance behind this appearance. With the "Enterprise," there was plenty of substance.

The ship was apparently capable of long interstellar voyages. Its means of propulsion was never clearly explained, but it had something to do with the mutual annihilation of matter and anti-matter. This is a perfectly sound scientific principle, in that if equal amounts of matter and anti-matter were to meet, they would destroy one another and liberate energy according to Einstein's well-known E = MC squared. Because the size of the speed of light is so large, even destroying minute amounts of matter creates huge amounts of energy.

On this solid foundation, the rest of the propulsion rests. We do know that in the engineering bay, the reaction was controlled. The long pods that stuck out of the back of the ship housed the matter and anti-matter, along with the converters that housed them and harnessed their power. This power was then fed through the dilithium crystals, which acted as some sort of buffer and controller of the power.

Quite what dilithium crystals are, we are never really told. They are not too common, because the ship can carry no spares. On the other hand, on some worlds (such as those of "Elaan Of Troyius") they are so common they are used as semi-precious stones. Dilithium (in the second pilot, "Where No Man Has Gone Before" it is called simply lithium) are crystalline. In "The Terratin Incident" episode of the animated series, we are told that dilithium is the only naturally-occuring crystal with a helix-shaped molecular pattern. Obviously, the crystals are pretty sensitive, because they frequently burned out in the series when pushed over their limits.

The energy-controlling capacity of the dilithium is the basis for almost all of the devices used by the Federation. Small chips of the crystals are used to power tricorders, phasers and communicators. Clearly, they are highly adaptable, and completely essential to the economy of the Federation. It is of little wonder that the Federation likes to secure as many sources for the crystals as possible.

With the energy produced on the "Enterprise" funnelled through the crystals, the ship is somehow able to warp space. Instead of travelling along at normal rocket speeds, or even higher, the "Enterprise" is somehow about to travel faster than light. If it couldn't, then its voyages would take impossibly long periods of time. Instead, they can make distances in very reasonable time. Various levels of warp speed are available, though the higher the warp factor (and thus the speed), the higher the risk of burning out either the dilithium crystals or the engines themselves (a constant source of near-panic from Scotty). Generally, the ship will proceed at anything from warp two to warp six. Higher speeds to warp eight or nine are available, but never for extended periods.

The concept of warping space somehow is an interesting one. Back to Einstein again, he showed in his theory of relativity that the speed of light was the limiting speed factor according to the laws of physics. It would take an infinite amount of energy to exceed this speed by any known method. According to Einstein, then, the "Enterprise" is impossible. On the other hand, Einstein was using only what he knew or could deduce. There is nothing to prevent us from cheating a little. Obviously, the "Enterprise" couldn't simply use brute force to push past the speed of light. Is there any other way to achieve the same ends, then?

Well, there may be. Einstein's limits depend only on normal space. Some scientists realized that Einstein was talking about masses approaching the speed of light, and that the closer they got to the speed of light, the harder it was to get them to go just a little faster. Trying the same equations from the other side revealed that objects could indeed (theoretically) travel faster than light, and in that case, they had the same problems if they tried to slow down to the speed of light. In the case of such particles, they could only travel faster than light. They were named tachyons. Theoretically, they exist, but there's not a lot of chance of us catching one. They can travel much faster than anything we know.

Another method is that of "Star Trek." Einstein's speed of light factor only limits us if space stays normal. If space could (somehow) be warped, then perhaps the problem of speed vanishes. This is how the "Enterprise" does it. It somehow twists the fabric of space, so that instead of being "straight," it is warped. If you take a piece of paper six inches long, then the ends are six inches apart. If you fold it over, however, then the ends are touching — at the same spot, virtually. The "Enterprise" somehow makes the space it travels through smaller than the same space in the real Universe. It can thus apparently travel at terrific speeds, far faster than light.

Interestingly, in the latest films, the "Excelsior" is referred to as having trans-warp drive. Whatever that may be, it clearly is the next stage of evolution in starship engines. Presumably it bears the same sort of difference in speed factors to a warp drive ship as the Concorde does to a Model T Ford. However, there is no indication yet as to how it may possibly work.

To achieve warp speeds evidently takes a great deal of power. The engines need to be carefully tuned, and a great deal of attending. They cannot be allowed to stop their reaction, since it used to take a good deal of time to start them when they were cold. However, Spock and Mr. Scott did calculate a risky cold- start formula to achieve the needed power almost instantly (in "The Naked Time.")

There are times, of course, when warp power is not appropriate, or not available. To orbit a planet, for example, in warp drive would be impossible. the constant course corrections required would be overwhelming. Also, in cases of emergency the ship may need (or be forced) to travel slower. It then relies on impulse power. This is similar to the rocket power known for thousands of years, and works adequately over short periods of time.

Once the "Enterprise" is in motion, using whichever means of propulsion is chosen, then there are further considerations. It isn't sufficient to simple set a starship going and crew it. It must have a life-support system aboard to provide the staples of life for the crew. The "Enterprise" uses a system that recycles everything. It would be completely impractical for the ship to constantly have to stop off for food, water and air to breath. Instead, these items are all prepared via the sophisticated ship's systems. The Recreation decks on the ship help convert carbon dioxide breathed out by the crew back to oxygen, since the decks are filled with plants and trees. Any imbalance is chemically treated. Water is simply recycled and purified.

The food is much more interesting, for there are two ways to prepare it. The ship has a chef ("Charlie X"), but very little real food. The ship's synthesizers make all of the food required from its basic molecules, stored in the ship. The rec rooms and various other rooms contain food machines, with a larger, changing menu. All a person has to do is to "dial" the food they wish, and it is processed by the computers and delivered to the desired spot. Almost anything may be created in this way. Wastes and spillages can then be broken back down and used to create fresh food for other meals.

A more curious problem is that of gravity. In space, there is no real gravity, and everything operates in free fall. This is fine for short hops into space (such as that made by the NASA space shuttle), but over long periods of time is impractical, and possibly dangerous. To counter this, the "Enterprise" uses a system of artificial gravity. Quite how this works is difficult to say. We know nothing nowadays that can achieve this — or its reverse, null gravity. A few hundred years from now, perhaps gravity may be manipulated as simply as we manipulate heat.

What the gravity generators on the "Enterprise" do is to create an artificial appearance of the ship being on a planet. All floors are "below" to the people inside, so it seems as though they are walking normally on a planetary surface. This way, the crew can act naturally, and when they go to various worlds, don't suffer from any problems going back to a ground with normal gravity. In trying to make the gravity compensation seem as natural as possible, certain instabilities have been left in. If the ship, for example, shakes, then the gravity field "shakes" also with it. If the ship must make a sudden turn, then the crew feels the momentum from this.

An interesting sidelight on this is that it then becomes possible to negate this artificial gravity in certain places. The area negated then returns to the zero gravity of the area of space they are in. Using clamp-on units, this makes carrying even the heaviest of articles very simple (as in "The Changeling"). They weight nothing, and all that a person must do is to watch out for building up momentum carrying things. Transportation of anything about the ship then becomes much simpler. Naturally, such anti-gravity devices work only in space and not on planetary surfaces. They don't negate real gravity, simply the artificial fields produced in the ships.

The "Enterprise" is primarily a ship for research, exploration and mapping. Accordingly, it has both a sophisticated computer system and also extremely sensitive scanners. The computer can be either voice-activated, programmed with a keyboard, or fed data from microcassettes. The scanning system, known as the sensors, is tied into the computers for analysis. The "Enterprise" can send out electromagnetic pulses, which are then reflected back to the ship and analyzed. Whatever they contact changes their response subtly, and the computer scans such responses to determine what the ship is to shortly be encountering. Naturally, the computer can only identify objects that are within its memory banks. Various forms of energy can also be detected by these scans.

No matter how peaceful the mission of the "Enterprise" is, it would have been the height of foolishness not to equip it with some form of armaments. Not everyone that Captain Kirk and his crew would encounter could hope to prove peaceful and friendly. Accordingly, the ship is well armed, and so are the crew members when they take part in exploration or defense of the ship.

The primary means of defense for the "Enterprise" is the ship's phasers. These are located below the central disc section. (When they were originally named, they were lasers, but then the decision to call them something more futuristic sounding was taken, hence the final choice of name.) They are energy weapons of varying capabilities. Even from planetary orbit, they can be directed to small areas on the planetary surface with incredible accuracy. They can destroy single structures (like Apollo's temple in "Who Mourns For Adonais?") to simply knocking out individual thugs (as in "A Piece Of The Action"). They are also the prime defense in space fights.

Power for the phasers is drawn from the engines, through yet more dilithium crystals. Boosted and concentrated into tight beams, it is then fired at the desired setting and at the desired target. The "Enterprise" has two main phaser banks, both capable of independent action.

For away team work, the landing parties (and ship security) carry portable phasers. These come in three varieties. First is the smallest, which slips into the palm of the hand. It has settings from "stun" to "disintegrate," and is normally carried on the stun setting. Starfleet personnel never take life unless it is considered unavoidable. The only problem with these smaller phasers is that they have limited battery power, and must be recharged constantly. Also, since they are held in the palm, they are not overly accurate over any distance.

This is when the second phasers come in. The small phasers can be clipped into a larger unit. This has a grip for the hand, and extended power cells. It will last several times as long as the first form of phaser, and can be aimed extremely accurately. The third form of phaser is the rarest — the phaser rifle. (It was seen only once, in "Where No Man Has Gone Before," in fact.) This has a massive difference in power available, and can virtually slice the top off a mountain. It is extremely accurate, but also very bulky and heavy. For the most part, it is overkill — the main two forms of phaser being perfectly acceptable for normal operations.

"The Cage" saw another specialized form of the phaser, this time as a cannon. The heavy, bulky unit was one of the phaser cannons for the ship's defense system (presumably). This was before the decision was taken that the ship could use such cannons from orbit. The phaser cannon was used to try and blast through a mountain to recover the lost Captain Pike. It was extremely effective at this, though its effects were covered up mentally for a while.

Phasers are obviously some advanced weaponry developed from the principle of the laser beam. Energy is expended in a tight, focused beam. Depending on the setting, it can either stun (presumably by overloading the sensory inputs of whatever life- form it hits), to kill (an extreme form of the first setting), to completely destroy (by pouring in so much energy that the person or thing is literally vaporized).

The "Enterprise" itself has another method of defense that is far more potent than the phasers — the photon torpedo. These are housed with the phaser banks, but have an independent means of firing, rather like old-time torpedos from submarines. Each photon torpedo is about six feet long and cylindrical. They are frequently adapted as coffins for burials in space. The torpedos, after firing, are detonated either on a timing device, or by remote control. They explode with tremendous power, converting matter and anti-matter directly into light energy.

To augment these armaments, the "Enterprise" has a series of shield generators. These establish overlapping force shields about the ship, which can absorb and reradiate the energy of an attack. Like all forms of defense, however, the shields can only take so much punishment. They will eventually weaken and fail if the attack is pressed home long enough. The "Enterprise" has automatic deflector shields for the most part, capable only of repelling small particles of matter and meteoric matter in interstellar space. Full shields have to be established manually, as they drain a great deal of energy whilst in operation.

The concept of a defensive force-shield has a long history in science fiction, and is something that would be most useful to have around. At the kind of speeds at which the "Enterprise" travels, if it were to hit even the smallest of particles, considerable damage could be done. Clearly, to be able to function at all, the ship has to have automatic fields that deflect oncoming particles away from its path. This could be done magnetically, perhaps, or — far simpler — by using the same technology that produces the artificial gravity in the ship. The same use of focused gravitational fields is clearly needed for the tractor beam.

The "Enterprise" uses this to "lock" an object into the same path that it is taking, to tow it, or to draw something to itself. Gravitational manipulation is the obvious method to use. The same device, if reversed, could be used as a pressor beam, to send objects out of its path — much as the deflector shield must do for micro particles.

On the other hand, this sort of defense would not work as a shield against fire-power from another ship. The main defensive shields, then, clearly must operate in a different manner. They are some form of energy barrier that absorbs localized increases in energy and spreads them out throughout the shield. This would make the incoming energy bursts controllable. Obviously, though, absorbing the energy fired at it would tend eventually to overload a shield's capacity, and it would then blow out — as tends to happen from time to time in the show.

The other major device on the "Enterprise" is the transporter. There are presumably more than one, though on the series only the one was ever seen. This device was invented mostly from a need on the part of the production staff to get the crew of the ship down to a planet as quickly and cheaply as possible. Despite this, it was definitely one of the most effective concepts in the show.

Quite how a transporter would work is another matter. Arthur C. Clarke has made mention of the difficulties involved in such a device, and he is inclined to disbelieve in the possibility of one ("Profiles Of The Future"). It's hard not to agree with his reasoned objections. First, you have to scan a human being (or whatever else you may be transporting) completely. This means literally every molecule and sub-atomic particle in the body. The problem with this is that according to Heisenberg's Uncertainty Principle, such an act of scanning would alter the very information that you were trying to record. Not only that, but it would have to be a scan done at an instantaneous moment. Sub- atomic particles are constantly moving, and if the scan took any time at all, the particles would have changed their positions, making the information incorrect.

Let's suppose for a moment, though, that this could be done. Perhaps some form of stasis could be developed, so that every single particle in the body were literally frozen into place whilst the scanning was done. This information would then have to be recorded. We are talking here about billions and billions of particles — which means that there are billions and billions of bits of information to store, and they have to be stored correctly. Given that, which is not a simple task, then we have another problem. The transporter then has to break down the body into component energy — effectively, it has to kill whoever is in the beam. This energy must then be transmitted with absolute precision from the ship to the target point. It must also, obviously, be done without any loss of signal. You wouldn't want to materialize ten pounds slimmer, if part of that ten pounds consisted of various parts of your body, rather than simply fat.

Then, once the exact same amount of energy was somehow held in position on the planet, it would have to be restructured back into the original form. Again, this would have to be done with utter precision, and it must be done instantaneously. If it weren't, you'd have bits of the body appearing at different times — both messy and dangerous.

There is, as can be seen, an awful lot of room for error. Almost anything could go wrong with the system — and often does on the show. I'm with Dr. McCoy, considering his reservations about using it as a method of transport. It sounds too potentially lethal! Not only that, it's hard to believe that so many problems with such a system could ever be resolved. (Presumably, the disintegration booths used on Eminiar VII in "A Taste Of Armageddon" were simply variations on the transporter idea — only instead of turning matter into energy and then back, it stopped half-way.) On the other hand, it sure beats all that tedious mucking about in shuttle craft.

The "Enterprise" has a number of shuttles. In the original show, it was supposed to have about eight at a time, all named after famous astronomers. (The "Galileo" is the most famous, due to it having been featured in a story on its own.) For the animated series (which didn't have the same budget restrictions as the original series, several variants on the shuttle were found, including ones adapted to water travel ("The Ambergris Element") and to armored needs ("Mudd's Passion"). This is a logical extension of the concept of the shuttle, and a clever move for the animated show.

The shuttles are simply short-range craft, whose engines are charged before flight. In a number of cases, they fell short of fuel — "The Menagerie," "The Galileo Seven" and "Metamorphosis" for example. (In "The Galileo Seven," Scotty refuels the shuttle by draining power from the phasers. As has been noted, all the Federation equipment seems to work from common power supplies.) They are intended mostly for space-to-planet hops from a starship, or perhaps starbase-to-orbiting-ship hops. They are useful for when the transporter is inoperable or inadvisable, and for making planetary explorations simpler.

Interestingly, neither the movies nor "The Next Generation" has used the shuttles at all. The more reliable transporters seem to have caused the shuttles to fade away entirely. The movies do use transportation pods as a means of travel from space dock to ships in the dock, but that's about it. Otherwise you walk, or hop a transporter beam.

Communications becomes a problem in the show that is neatly side-stepped. One of the biggest problems that any Empire or organization can face is extended lines of communications. Many problems have been caused by the inability to check back with base. With the "Enterprise" zipping about in unexplored space, communications back to Starfleet Command become essential. This is done through sub-space communication.

Just what that might be is never answered. Communications devices that we know of are limited to the speed of light, and line-of-sight. Such devices would be completely useless to the "Enterprise." What would be the point of transmitting a message to Starfleet that would take a hundred years to reach them, when you could be home in your ship in a week?

Instead, the "Enterprise" can somehow punch holes through space that are shorter and faster. They are never really instantaneous, and often take several hours or days to penetrate back to the nearest starbase. Still, this is better than hundreds of years. Quite what sub-space is, or how the ship can use it, are never explained.

The communicators that the crew members take with them when away from the ship work (probably) on a similar principle, since there never seems to be a time delay between sending a message from the planet to receiving it on the ship, no matter how far out the "Enterprise" is. We do know that the communicators contain the basic components that hold the mysteries of all Federation technology ("A Piece Of the Action"). This presumably includes those ubiquitous dilithium crystals.

The dilithium explains another property of the communicators. Two can be phased in together, and then explode. This is presumably done through overloading the dilithium crystal ("Friday's Child.) The transporter also can lock in on the signals of the communicator to get a fix for beaming back to the ship.

An interesting variation on the communicator is the transponder of "Bread And Circuses." Injected under the sky, such devices provide monitoring capabilities from the ship, and have the advantage that they cannot be lost or taken from the crew if they are captured. The only reason that they were never used again in the show is that they limited plot possibilities. On the other hand, if the stories were meant to be as real-life as possible, each crew-member would have a transponder surgically implanted. It would make excellent sense, not merely for landing parties but also from a medical point of view. They could monitor the life signs of the person, and then flash emergency signals back to sickbay in case of any problem.

For the first film, the communicators became small wristwatch- like devices. They were not too useful, and reverted with the second film to roughly the same thing as in the show. With "The Next Generation," they have been miniaturized so much that they can be fitted within the small Federation badge that each member of an away team can wear. These are activated by touch.

Allied to the communicator is the universal translator. This works by analyzing the speech patterns of an alien race, and then translates directly what is spoken. Though it translates words, it does not translate inflections, nor does it chose the sex of the speaker. Sex is, apparently, a universal constant that the translater can recognize ("Metamorphosis"). The "Enterprise" has a translater built directly into the communications board, but away parties are forced to take along a special translator for any meetings with races that do not speak standard.

Another device used by landing parties is the tricorder. Though there are many specialized forms of tricorder, including medical and psychological ("Wolf In The Fold"), the main type used is a science tricorder. It is standard for a landing party to take two or three tricorders along. The devices are useful for scanning and analysis, as well as recording and storage. Like the main sensors on the ship, tricorders can scan for energy and elements, or analyze any object that they are focused on. A small reading screen tabulates the results of such a scan. This screen can also act as a video recorder ("The City On The Edge Of Forever"), and the machine functions as a taping device also.

Medical equipment is often used for landing parties, since danger is often present. Dr. McCoy and the rest of the medical teams carry along small pouches that contain basic medications, including a sedative, a surgical laser and various forms of bindings. For more substantial problems, the ship-board sickbay is of paramount importance.

The main obvious feature of the sickbay are the diagnostic beds. These units have built into the pallet of the bed an array of scanning devices. The results from these are monitored by the medical practitioner from a screen above the head of the bed. These scanners are calibrated so that floating pointers stay central if they are within tolerable limits, enabling them to be read at a glance. Heartbeat is monitored as a pulsing sound, adding that element to the display. Changes can thus be simply seen and corrected.

The diagnostic bed concept is so staggeringly obviously useful that they have actually been developed as an off-spring of the show. Remote monitoring is nothing new to medical science — it has been used in the space program, for example, from almost the beginning, to enable ground-based doctors to monitor the health of orbiting astronauts. The diagnostic bed is then simply an extension of this concept.

McCoy and his staff have a number of other instruments at their disposal. These include lasers to conduct operations with, such as knitting bones and sealing off wounds. These are quite legitimate ideas, prognosticated from the use of lasers in surgery at our time. Another useful ally McCoy has is artificial skin to seal in the healing process. Various forms of this have been developed, though not with complete success as yet.

One of the more interesting concepts of the show was the spray-hypodermic that McCoy used to inject drugs into the bodies of patients. This would work using some form of air-pressure to force the drug into the body, rather than by current methods of using crude mechanical force to stick a needle into a vein — never the easiest or most pleasant of tasks either for the doctor or the patient. Again, this idea is an extension of methods being currently investigated. It, too, seems quite promising.

What is perhaps the most interesting thing about all of the devices used regularly on the show is that they were all introduced in the initial series. Nothing substantially different has been introduced in either the films or "The Next Generation." This is not a reflection of the imaginations of the writers and production staff of either; it simply shows that the original series covered everything that would be required logically for use in the world of "Star Trek." All that the films and shows that followed could do was to update the inventions originally introduced for the show back in 1966.

The one real exception to this is in "The Next Generation," which uses a substantial device for recreation — the holodeck. This area (introduced properly in the animated series) had been one thing that Gene Roddenberry had desired to include in the original show, but had never been able to afford. So, though it is new, it is an offspring of the original plans for the first series. It is also rather badly misunderstood and used.

The concept of the holodeck is that it projects very realistic illusions about the person in the room, which look and feel real. Presumably, this is an updating of the idea of a hologram, formed by laser light beams. The idea of a room so sophisticated that it can from a memory bank extract and recreate scenes of other times and places is a little hard to accept. For one thing, you'd expect people to then cast "shadows" onto the images. Still, if this was all that was involved, you could take it. What causes the real problems with the idea is that in "The Next Generation," these holograms are REAL. In "The Big Goodbye," guns become lethal weapons. In the following tale, a hologram girl can deliver a real kiss to Ryker.

This is simply too much to believe in. (The stories work well enough, but it's the science that's unreal.) There is little doubt that by this point in the future, computers would be sophisticated enough to "create" characters that can be moved by the computer in response to a programme selected by the person who wants to use the holodeck. That these "people" could interact by talking with the real humans is quite possible. That they could then kiss them is impossible. They are, when all is said and done, creatures of light — they are not solid. How could they deliver a real kiss? How could they fire a real gun?

Part of the problem may simply be the poor use of terminology in the show. In the pilot, "Encounter At Farpoint," we are specifically told that some of the material present is real. The computer stores it in its memory (as it does with transporter information) and then recreates it on demand. The big problem with accepting this is the old one of energy. To create even a matchstick from energy would require more than the output of a nuclear reactor — how much more so then a tree? A forest? Where the heck do they get all this energy from? Still, if the computer does somehow create parts of the "hologram," it would help resolve a few of the problems with the holodeck. It would explain how Wes could hit the Captain with a snowball ("Angel One"). It would not, however, answer everything. In the same episode, an epidemic on the ship begins from an infection picked up from the holodeck!

What happened? Did the computer create a new bug? Did it somehow make the people infected merely think that they were sick? Aren't we taking things just a tiny bit too far in these cases? It stretches the power to suspend belief just a bit too much to accept such a silly idea as being able to catch diseases from an illusion. It would be like going to see "War And Peace" and getting shot by a cannon from onscreen.

The holodeck concept is a nice idea, but it is clearly one that has gotten out of control of the show. It should be placed way out of the scripts for a good long time, and then brought back only once the concepts behind its mechanisms has been worked out better.

One device never seen in the show but mentioned significantly is the ion pod of "Court Martial." What exactly it was is not explained at all, but seems to have been some sort of external add-on to the ship transparent to ion storms, and used to measure them from. The pods can be jettisoned, so perhaps they are external work units?

Devices

The first part of this File took a look at the devices that were seen from week to week on "Star Trek." Naturally, though, a number of other devices have appeared during the run of the series either only the once or else just a few times. Some of these were simply tool that were used, say, in Engineering, and need no further discussion. Others were used by the villains to create problems for the ship. Still others were simply there for Kirk and the rest to investigate.

Other "devices" were used for recreation. In the original series, the tri-dimensional chess set was seen a few times, first in "Charlie X." This was an attempt to invent a game of the future, and there have already been attempts to market similar games for the public in our time. None have really taken, though. In the same episode, we were shown playing cards of the future, which were rather impractically circular. Spock also uses a Vulcan "harp," which is obviously something like a stringed instrument crossed with an electronics package.

In "Where No Man Has Gone Before," we are shown an automated lithium cracking plant. This makes the fuel (before it was called dilithium) for starships. It's such a boring job, the whole system is automated.

"What Are Little Girls Made Of?" was the first episodes with androids in it. Though androids are in some definition "devices," these have been covered elsewhere ("The Star Trek Villains File: Computers, Robots And Androids"). The machine that created the androids, however, was a pure example of a "visiting device." It was used only for this story, and consisted basically of a circular table divided into two halves. The person to be duplicated was strapped to one side of the table, and a blank form on the other. The table was then spun, and equipment scanned the live person, accurately reproducing characters and features on the blank form. When the table stopped, the process was complete. The spinning was simply a neat trick that looked good on screen, allowing use of a split screen to use the same actor as both the man and android. (It's not a very efficient method of duplication, and it's surprising that Kirk wasn't giddier when he came out of it!)

"Dagger Of The Mind" had the neural neutralizer in it. This was simply a chair fitted with restraints to prevent a patient from escaping. Above this was what looked like a light that pulsed and sent out ultra-sonic noises. The neutralizer simply blanked out people's thought processes, leaving the mind open to whatever suggestions the operator wished to implant. Naturally, this device was used for evil, to recondition minds to think as Tristram Adams wanted them to, and at the end of the tale (after it killed Adams), it was destroyed to prevent further abuses. The idea of mental control by machines would crop up again in the show, as in "The Return Of The Archons," for example. Brainwashing had become a catch-phrase back in the Sixties, and the possibility of using machines to change a person's mind rather worrying.

"The Menagerie" re-introduced Captain Christopher Pike, who had had a terrible accident, leaving his body a ravaged shell. His still-brilliant mind was trapped within this useless body. He used an advanced form of wheelchair for both life support and movement. Though his mind was active, it could not be used to control the chair, beyond making a light blink on or off. This seems somewhat crude, but may be simply that there was a shell of kinds about his mind that could not be broached even with the medical techniques of that future time.

"Balance Of Terror" introduced a device that has recurred down the years: the Romulan cloaking device. The idea behind this is simple, and a concept introduced (inevitably) by H.G. Wells: invisibility. The cloaking device simply bends all light and other radiation about the ship it is housed in. This includes detection by sensing devices, so that a ship with the device is invisible to detection. Whether such a concept is possible is uncertain, but it seems safe to assume that if artificial gravity is possible, then so is a cloaking device. Light rays are affected by gravitational fields (as predicted by Einstein, naturally), so by making a special field about a ship, it should be theoretically feasible to bend all forms of radiation to make it seem as though nothing was there. The device returned in a modified form in "The Enterprise Incident," when Kirk had to steal it for analysis. It then switched over to the Klingons for "The Search For

Spock." The Romulans and Klingons obviously trade.

We are told that there is a major problem with the device: it take too much energy to operate, so cannot be maintained for long. This is perfectly understandable. Also, it must be turned off before the Romulans can use their weapons. Again, this is logical, since the artificial gravity shield would work to keep the Romulans from detecting anything outside their screens, or from firing through them. If light rays are deflected about the ship, then there is nothing incoming for them to get information from. This problem is ignored in the story, and the Romulans can somehow use their sensors through their own shield.

"Shore Leave," on the other hand, introduced an idea that was probably impossible — but who cared? The idea of a monster computer that could scan the minds of people vacationing on the surface of the planet, and then construct what the people were thinking about and transport it to them is a trifle far-fetched. There's a lot of stages to go through, and it's probably (but no more than probably) unlikely that any such device could be constructed. It's even less likely that it could work so fast that it could create a white rabbit right out of "Alice's Adventures In Wonderland" and program it to behave properly in almost nothing flat. On the other hand, the story is so darned delightful that it's hard to voice these objections at all strongly. If the Shore Leave planet is impossible, then we're all the poorer for it. (The world returned in the animated episode "Once Upon A Planet," but was used so badly in that story.)

Weapons are constantly a source of new devices. The Gorns in "Arena" use disruptors, devices that Kirk and his men are familiar with. They appear to act like cannons, but presumably operate by disrupting the forces holding materials together, causing them to explode. Kirk and Spock use updated forms of a mortar to counter-attack.

A different kind of disruptor is used by the Klingons in "Errand Of Mercy." (The actual guns were simply the Eminian weapons of "A Taste Of Armageddon" slightly reworked.) The Klingon weapons, rather than killing neatly like Federation weapons, work on a nastier level. They disrupt the nervous system, which eventually proves fatal. Generally, on low power settings, it simply causes a great deal of agony and torture first. On higher settings, it can kill instantly, however. The Klingons don't consider this as much fun, though.

"The Return Of The Archons" has Landru's Lawgivers using staffs as gun-like devices. Interestingly, the staffs are hollow, and do not have a power source as such. They utilize broadcast power, and focus it. Broadcast power is what its name suggests — energy that is continually emitted, and which can be picked up by special receivers and then used to do work. The idea is to eliminate batteries and wiring. The drawbacks to the concept, however, are so enormous that it is unlikely to prove to be ever used. First of all, if the power is being broadcast continually, there is going to be a terrific amount of wastage, since not all of it could possibly be used. How many power sources could continue with constant wastage? Secondly, to be available in enough concentration to do any good as a power supply, it seems logical that the power level broadcast would probably have to be high enough to affect living things as well... The idea of using broadcast power that also cooks you while you use it is not an attractive one.

On the other hand, it might be possible if tight beams could be used — but then we have the second problem only worsened. The beam would burn anyone it touched to death. Let's stick with batteries and wires, folks. It's safer.

When we were shown the world of Vulcan for the first time in "Amok Time," there were interesting weapons used. These were clearly traditional weapons, from the deep past of the race, used only for ritual purposes. Most fascinating was the combination of blade and club that Kirk and Spock were forced to fight with. Similar weapons recurred later that season for the battles of "The Gamesters Of Triskelion."

"Mirror, Mirror" had a lot of novelty going for it. Among other things (such as parallel universes and one of those inevitable transporter malfunctions), the Kirk of this place had a secret weapon that enabled him to remain on top of the rat heap — the Tantalus Field. This was a monitoring device that could tune into anyone anywhere on the ship. A second control then disintegrated them — presumably by transfer of energy from the Tantalus Field to the spot where the victim stood. Another rather nasty device used in that alternate universe was a neural agonizer (similar to the Klingon one of the normal universe). Its sole purpose was to produce terrible pain in the victim as a punishment for carelessness or rebellion.

To destroy the vampiric cloud of "Obsession," Kirk utilities a specially-constructed anti-matter bomb. This is triggered by a timing device, and Kirk escapes in time via the transporter beam. In "The Immunity Syndrome," similar bombs are used to destroy the giant amoebic creature that threatens to Galaxy.

A very different kind of weapon is that used by the Kelvans in "By Any Other Name." Their device somehow analyzed the human body, and then converted it into an "essence," a small geometric shape that contained all the basics of that person, as well as somehow storing their minds and personalities. The process was reversible, with no ill effects — provided that the "essence" was not damaged in any way. Such a weapon seems totally impossible, at least by any method that could be imagined by science known to us. To the Kelvans, this was not a problem. After all, they had managed to change their own bodies to look and act human. The shifting of shape seemed a simple thing to them.

"The Wrath Of Khan" introduced the Genesis Device. This was not intended as a weapon at all, but did strike both Khan and the Klingons with its potential for being used as such. Since it could restructure an entire world along pre-programmed lines, it could be used to destroy any world and to create whatever the user wished.

"Space Seed" introduced the medical decompression chamber, which would later return in "The Lights Of Zetar." Such a device would certainly be useful on the ship. Working in various levels of pressure from normal to the vacuum of space could cause hazards in the crew. Greater pressures might even occur, in which case the problem would become similar to that of deep-sea divers with the bends (nitrogen narcosis). The chamber could be used to help in such cases.

"Devil In The Dark" showed us a Pergium mining center. Though this was partially automated, it was mostly a manned affair. The place was powered from a central Reactor, of an obsolete form. The Horta, out for revenge on the humans, stole the main circulating pump, causing considerable problems for a while. Most of the plant in the story was never seen, save as shots through the manager's windows.

In "Who Mourns For Adonais?" we are introduced to Apollo. He is one of the group of beings taken for gods by the Greeks, thanks to their amazing abilities. These are in fact the result of their being able to absorb and utilize a special form of energy through a bodily organ. Apollo's power source (like that of Trelane in "The Squire Of Gothos") was external. The "Enterprise" destroyed his generator, thus depriving him of the power he needed to function as a "god." A similar solution was used in "Catspaw" to destroy the Transmuters, who used a similar external energy source to create apparent miracles. They even used their transmuter to change their own appearances and to pass for human.

"The Changeling" itself was a device — once a simple NASA probe, and then transformed through an accident into Nomad, a mechanical intelligence. Alien science allowed it to think, move and even resurrect the dead Scott. Just how it could do any of this was never explained; it was simply the wonders of alien technology. A similar case occurred with V'Ger in the first film.

For "The Apple" we were given another malevolent computer. Interestingly, though, this one could communicate with the Feeders Of Vaal, because the natives all had implanted antennae in their heads. Vaal didn't talk much, but when he did, his people had no option but to listen to what he had to say. Malevolent or dangerous computers were staple ingredients of the series, and have been dealt with in the relevant File.

The Providers of "The Gamesters Of Triskelion" were brains kept alive by computers and nutrients. Their life support systems are an extension of much modern-day thinking. The idea of keeping alive simply the brain — the seat of the mind — after the death of the body is both appealing and revolting. Survival of what would otherwise be death is an obvious urge in most of the human race. Yet, survival at what cost? These Providers turned out to be bored and frequently callous in their disregard for other life-forms. Survival alone is hardly worthwhile if the quality of life is not high.

Also in this story were the obedience collars that forced the Thralls to obey the instructions of the Providers or be punished. Similar devices were used in "Spock's Brain" to quell trouble-makers, and are similar to the implanted devices of "For The World Is Hollow And I Have Touched The Sky." The concept is a pretty obvious extension of current technology. Some convicted criminals are placed under house arrest, and forced to wear monitoring devices that confirm their compliance with the sentence even now. (Just how effective this is is being debated still.) Obviously, taken from this, the devices could be turned into pain-inducers by tapping into the nervous system. They can then be triggered by remote control to deliver calculated doses of pain as a punishment for transgression.

Different types of life-support systems occur in the show. "Return To Tomorrow" has three survivors of a dead world contained as pure intellects within computer spheres. This is an interesting idea, and one that will be more topical if ever the human race can work out some way to scan the human mind and transfer the information from there to a computer. The human brain appears to work on electrical impulses in a way similar to a computer. Could a mind then be created (or recreated) in a computer? At the moment, the answer is clearly no, but this may be simply due to the "small" size of computer memories compared to the human brain. On the other hand, perhaps such storage of a person in a computer will never be possible. The only way to know for certain is to try it and see.

"Spock's Brain" also had a life-support system to keep his displaced brain alive. It was also used to run the city of the people who had stolen him. The idea of a brain functioning in the place of a computer is fascinating. Spock himself was enthralled with the idea. The people of this society were based in the study of the mind, though ironically their own had atrophied through underuse. They relied on a teaching machine to give them the kind of information that they needed for any task at hand.

To keep Spock's body alive without a brain, Doctor McCoy used a headband that enabled the amazing Vulcan body to move and survive until the brain could be restored to it. This device somehow tapped into the basic bodily functions, and enabled McCoy to direct the body like a robot. Frankly, the concept is completely silly, and the whole story is rather on the ludicrous side.

"The Paradise Syndrome" gave us an alien artifact used as a tractor/pressor beam to save an Indian culture from extinction. The tremendous technology evidenced by the Collectors was never explained, but it might have tapped into geothermal energy to power the device. Then again, it might have used a self-enclosed source of power unknown to the human race.

"Wink Of An Eye" uses a device that will put the "Enterprise" crew into a deep freeze. The Scalosians of this story need live humans to continue their race, and they see the arrival of the ship as a great source of the human material that they need. They aim to put the spare humans into cold storage, to be thawed out as needed. Kirk and Spock manage to defeat this plot, and the device is never completed or utilized.

"The Way To Eden" has the space hippies and Doctor Severin use a sonic device to attack , stun and (its ultimate purpose) kill. this is quite a reasonable weapon. Sound is something that affects people strongly — witness the complaints from neighbors when a stereo is turned up too loud! Ultrasonic sounds can be used as a cutting tool, and clearly a focused beam of sound has great potential as a weapon of war. Many attempts have been made to develop such a device.

"The Cloud Minders" has a city in the clouds that is beautiful and highly appealing. The idea of living in the clouds, far from the surface of the planet, is intriguing, provided you aren't bothered by heights. Given the anti-gravity technology of the Federation, such a city is not intrinsically impossible. The problems with it are mostly psychological, in fact. Looking down on the world literally may cause (as in this tale) a feeling of genuine superiority. The heights are definitely corrupting to mankind.

"Turnabout Intruder" had another alien device, this one used to transfer minds between bodies. Quite why anyone would ever develop such a device is hard to understand. At least, in a democratic society, that is. Why should people wish to exchange bodies with other people? The only mutual possibility is for the purpose of entertainment — a dubious reason at best. Of course, in a society where everyone is not equal there are other reasons for such a device. Rulers in tired bodies, or sick ones, could then appropriate the forms of "lesser" beings, and thus lengthen or improve their own lives. It wouldn't be as nice for the recipients of the old bodies, of course.

This transference device seems rather improbable at the least. It would involve somehow recording the mental patterns of two people, and then somehow transferring them to the opposing bodies. The question is whether a personality is nothing more than the sum of their mental patterns. Could a personality be transferred if the mental patterns were? Or would it create a different personality in the process? Could the original mentality in that brain be somehow blanked out, or would the two minds somehow overlap? Could two distinct mentalities perhaps inhabit a single mind and body?

Other Starships

One of the most obvious uses of devices in the show was in the form of other starships. The "Enterprise" and the shuttle craft have already been dealt with, but there were a number of other ships also seen in the series. On the other hand, for a number of stories, the ships were never actually seen — they were either just out of scanner range, shown as pinpoints of light and one — ridiculously! — even invisible ("Let That Be Your Last Battlefield)!

There was the Class J cargo ship used by Harry Mudd in "I, Mudd." This, along with the "Antares" of "Charlie X," were simply introduced and then destroyed without any attempt to talk about them at all. The first ship shown at any length was the beautiful "Fesarius," piloted by Balok of the First Federation. This immense ship was a beautiful sphere, made up of smaller units, at least one of which could be detached from the main vessel. The "Fesarius" also used a warning buoy, a spinning cube, to try and warn off the "Enterprise." The "Fesarius" seemed to have almost unlimited power, but was kept at bay through Kirk's invention of "The Corbomite Maneuver." It was only with the successful resolution of the tale that Kirk was invited aboard to meet Balok. The interior of the ship was sumptuously laid out, and virtually automatic. Balok himself seemed to do little if any of the work of controlling the monster ship.

"Balance Of Terror" introduced the superb Romulan "Bird Of Prey" ship that captured the hearts of the fans. An excellent design, though never credited in the series. (Allan Asherman corrects this by crediting Wah Chang for his excellent work in "The Star Trek Compendium.") The model was either destroyed or lost after this story — the tales of its fate vary a lot — so it could never be re-used. When the Romulans returned in "The Deadly Years," it was thanks to stock footage from this tale. Their next appearance in "The Enterprise Incident" showed them using Klingon ships. This is a great loss, and it is to be hoped that when the Romulans return — either for the films, or for "The Next Generation" — they will revert to their Birds of Prey. (Confusingly, the Klingon warships were also called Birds of Prey, though they did not have anything like the same appearance as the Romulan vessels; they do, however, look like birds in flight, which perhaps accounts for the mixing of titles.)

This same story also used the idea of the Outposts watching the Neutral Zone. Though not shown on screen, they were described convincingly as hollowed-out asteroids, fitted within with small bases. The concept is extremely sound, and will undoubtedly be used in the relatively near future to construct bases in space. Using asteroids has three great factors going for it. First, they are already in space, and cut down on transportation costs. Second, many of them are ferrous-mixtures, which means that they can be mined and the ore used in the construction of the base itself. As the tunnels are hollowed, the rocks would be processed for use. Third, the rocky outer layer would serve as excellent protection for the crew against the dangers of radiation and cosmic rays. Many suggestions for both starships and space colonies have evolved from the idea of using asteroids as starting materials.

"Space Seed" gave us another famous ship, the DY100 class "SS Botany Bay." This was another idea seriously under consideration, that of the sleeper ship. Given only conventional power supplies — and even some unconventional ones — it would take years or centuries to reach a desired star in a spaceship. Accordingly, there are two possible solutions to making the journey. "Space Seed" used the first of these, that of suspended animation. The idea is that it might be possible to somehow suspend life in a human being somehow, then allow that person to sleep through the journey, and to awaken them at the destination.

The most popular method suggested to do this is through cold storage, or cryogenics. If the body could be cooled down somehow, it might simply suspend life. The problem is not that of freezing, but that of unfreezing. Freezing tends to kill people, and attempting to defrost a frozen person has never met with success at all. Freezing the body causes the water in the cells to expand and rupture the cells. It seems like a (pardon me) dead end quest to work on survival through freezing. (Those "body banks" storing frozen heads for re-attachment to convenient bodies later are thus in trouble to begin with.) Perhaps suspended animation might be possible through drugs or something, but then deterioration of the body structure becomes a major problem. Bed sores develop after a few weeks in bed — what shape would a person be in after a couple of centuries?

The other possible method is far more likely to be used — that of the generation starship. "For The World Is Hollow And I Have Touched The Sky" was "Star Trek's" entry into this idea. The original crew cannot possibly make a journey to the stars in their life-times. What they must then do is to have a carefully controlled number of children, and train them to operate the ship when the original crew is either too old or dead. Theoretically, this would work, but there are ethic and scientific problems with this also. First, what the original crew is doing is condemning perhaps many generations to live and die in space, and forcing them to become nothing but starship crews. Is that any life for those people? Does the crew have the right to make that choice for their descendents? Or will their children simply become the technological equivalent of slaves for the original crew?

The scientific aspects of the problem are that it isn't possible with small numbers of human beings to accurately predict breeding patterns. Statistically the chances are small, but what if every child born on the ship were male? That would cause problems in finding a third generation... Also, would long-term living in space cause mutation or perhaps even sterility? It's not possible to give anything like a definite answer to any such questions — but anyone who seriously plans a generation starship would have to consider them fully first.

The ship model used in "Space Seed" was reused later in "The Ultimate Computer" as a drone ship.

An extremely different form of ship is owned by Lazarus in "The Alternative Factor." It is some form of time machine, but it is also capable of crossing barriers between parallel universes. Time machines have been popular in fiction since H.G. Wells' notable literary invention. Travel across parallel dimensions is also an old hope in literature. Mind you, neither of them have a shred of possibility according to what we know of the laws of physics. Parallel universes may or may not exist. If they don't, there is no way to travel there. If they do, how the barriers could be breached is impossible to say.

Time, on the other hand, clearly exists. What it is may be hard to say, but there was a yesterday, and there will presumably (hopefully!) be a tomorrow. Can they then somehow be reached? The problem is that time seems to flow in one direction only — forwards. Moving against the flow would seem to be more than difficult, and perhaps impossible. (Having made which proclamation, it's worth noting that if psychic powers do exist — another doubtful supposition — then they offer a method of practical time travel via the mind.)

Moving forwards in time is extremely easy, since we do it constantly ourselves. Moving forward in time faster than the normal rate is also relatively (excuse me) easy. According to the theory of relativity, as something speeds up, time slows down for it. If a ship could somehow reach the speed of light, time would cease to have any practical meaning for it. (This is theoretically impossible, of course.) At slightly slower speeds, the passage of time slows significantly. Everyone has heard of the possibility of setting out at near-light speeds for another star, taking a few years there and back, only to return and discover centuries have passed for those unfortunates left on Earth at fairly normal speeds. That kind of time travel is extremely possible. It's also extremely one-way, since once you are in that future, you are stuck there. (Unless you want to continue the trip again by another hop to the future...)

Time travel devices were a theme of the show. The earliest and the best was the Guardian of Forever (in "The City On The Edge Of Forever"). Apparently little but a stone circle, the Guardian was an advanced mechanism — semi-sentient at the very least — from some long-dead civilization. It offered, through an undefined method, time travel into the past of whatever species was viewing the images it flashed up. No attempt is made to explain how the Guardian can lock into the past of its visitors. Can it, perhaps, encompass the history of the entire Galaxy somehow? Still, no matter — the story is fascinating, and the Guardian very archetypal. It would be used again in the animated episode "Yesteryear."

A different sort of device was the time travel portal of "All Our Yesterdays." Trapped on their world under the looming threat of their sun going nova, the people of Sarpedon retreated into their own past. One of the interesting side-lights of this tale is that travelers into the past had to be conditioned to be able to survive there. Despite our often idyllic images of what life in the past would have been like, it was often filthy, unsanitary and grindingly dull. I suspect that some of the conditioning that the Sarpedon people must have undertaken was to enable them to cope with such changes as the lack of proper medical care, poor diets and ignorance. The past is a nice place to visit, but you wouldn't want to live there.

The portal was a nice idea. Images recorded through it could be observed, so that the escapee could select the time and place that they preferred to live. Once conditioned, they simply stepped through into the time and place they had chosen, and there was no return for them.

Whether "The Doomsday Machine" was a weapon or a space ship is something of a moot point. It was probably simply a mobile weapon whose function was destroying entire planets. To accomplish this, it needed starflight capabilities. The energies of the planets it destroyed were used to fuel it to move on to the next target. Designed as a weapon of war, the Machine was well armored and virtually indestructible.

In "The Trouble With Tribbles," we are shown Deep Space Station K7. As a result of the Organian Peace Treaty, the Klingons and Federation have to prove their ability to best use Sherman's Planet. K7 was thus used as a supply base and rendezvous point for the world. A neat design (actually merchandised as a model kit, it was so popular), the Station served as a place for R&R also. Such a station is obviously of use in areas where no suitable local planet can be used for one of the inevitable Star Bases that the Federation prefers to construct. The Stations are clearly temporary answers to the need for a presence in an area. They can be towed into position by starships, and when replaced by a permanent base they can then be moved on to wherever they can then best serve.

Space stations are such obvious and useful devices that it is in one way surprising that they were not used more extensively in the show. They weren't used any more after this single story simply because the model work would have been too costly for the series' budget. The films, with their larger money-spending abilities, have used the theme over and over. The vast orbital space docks of Earth in the first two films are fine examples of this. Constructing a starship in orbit is sound economic sense, especially when the ship — like the "Enterprise" — is not meant to take off from or land on a planet. The third and fourth film have shown us Starfleet's orbiting Spacedock. This was used for ships to enter and dock, to be refitted or overhauled, and to allow the crew to rest and refresh themselves.

More specialized was Regulus One, of "The Wrath Of Khan." This orbital station served as a scientific base for the Genesis project. Again, this makes perfect sense — isolating potentially disastrous inventions in an orbital station is a perfect answer to the problems of containment. Another specialized station was the Epsilon 9 monitoring station close to the Klingon Empire. This was the equivalent of a US spy satellite, serving to keep watch on the Klingons. It was destroyed by the approach of V'Ger.

Memory Alpha of "The Lights Of Zetar" was another specialized station. It was a huge library, one of several in the Galaxy, that functioned as a repository of knowledge. Again, it was some form of hollowed-out asteroid.

The Klingon cruisers used in the show and then in the films are perhaps the most well-known ships after the "Enterprise" itself. They are very effective in their appearance, and have continued into the movies almost without a change. It wasn't until the first film, though, that we actually saw inside one. They tend to be cramped (since the Klingons feel that comforts are decadent), and ill-lit, since the Klingon eye is slightly different to a human one. According to Scotty, they stink of Klingons also! For the third and fourth film, Kirk and his abbreviated crew took over a Klingon ship, renamed it the "Bounty," and used it for their own craft. It was destroyed at the end of "The Voyage Home," after helping save the Earth.

In "The Tholian Web," we are shown the peculiar but fascinating Tholian ships. Wedge-shaped, they have the ability to extrude what seem to be solid bars of light, which they use to attempt to imprison the "Enterprise" for trespassing. This is presumably some kind of sophisticated force field of an unknown kind. It is a nice example of alien thinking, and not something that a human would develop or utilize.

"The Voyage Home" had the Intruder. This ship was never explained. It may have been somehow a living entity, or else perhaps just a ship containing other beings. Since the nature of the Intruder was never considered, speculation is really rather useless in this case.

Throughout the show and the films, various other Federation starships had been featured. The ones from the show were simply redressed models of the "Enterprise." For the films, with their larger budgets, fresh and different ships have been created. In "The Wrath Of Khan" we were shown the "USS Reliant." This was small and less effective as a battleship than the "Enterprise," and intended mostly as a science exploration craft.

"The Search For Spock" introduced the "USS Excelsior." This was the next generation of starships after the "Enterprise" type. It is fitted with the transwarp drive (whatever that is), and can run circles around any other ships. Obviously, though, there are hidden problems with this sort of drive — beyond the fact that Scotty can sabotage it so simply — since by the time of "The Next Generation," starships still don't travel that much faster than they used to.

The new "Enterprise" of that show is the fifth in the line begun with the original craft. Updated in the first film, the original "Enterprise" met its end in "the Search For Spock." "The Voyage Home" introduced the second "Enterprise." Obviously over the years there have been others — either destroyed, or simply replaced by fresher models. Still, both the name and the legend have continued.

5715 N. Balsam Rd. Las Vegas, NV 89130

Pioneer Books wants to be your entertainment book company and make you happy by producing the best books we can about your favorite subjects. Your voice is important in choosing which books we publish. Please complete this questionairre and either photocopy it or tear it out and send it back to us. Your help is greatly appreciated!

Is your first Pioneer book? yes___ no___ What Pioneer book(s) do you have?___________________________

How did you hear about our books?___________________________

Rate the book(s) on a scale of 1-5 (5 being the highest)____

How could we make the book(s) better?___________________________

Other than bookstores and mail order, where else would you like to be able to purchase our books (i.e. gift shops, Walmart, Target, K-MART)?___________________________

Why did you purchase the book(s) (ie gift, personal, job related)?___________________

What publications do you subscribe to or read on a regular basis?___________________________

What are your favorite T.V. shows?___________________________

What other books would you like to see us publish?___________________________

Couch Potato carries a full line of Pioneer Books. Would you like to be added to the list to receive notice of upcoming new releases and a free catalog of all titles? yes___ no___

Name ___________________________ Age: 18-25___ 26-35___ 36-45___ 45+___

Address: ___________________________

Occupation ___________________ Education: High School____ College_____ Adv. Degree_____

Yearly Earnings: under $25,000___ $25,000-$50,000___ $50,000+__ Sex: male___ female___

Please add any other comments you may have:

THANK YOU VERY MUCH!

David Marin

T.E.

THE MAN WHO CREATED STAR TREK: GENE RODDENBERRY

James Van Hise

The complete life story of the man who created STAR TREK, reveals the man and his work.

$14.95 in stores ONLY $12.95 to Couch Potato Catalog Customers
160 Pages
ISBN # 1-55698-318-2

TWENTY-FIFTH ANNIVERSARY TREK TRIBUTE

James Van Hise

Taking a close up look at the amazing Star Trek stroy, this book traces the history of the show that has become an enduring legend. James Van Hise chronicles the series from 1966 to its cancellation in 1969, through the years when only the fans kept it alive, and on to its unprecedented revival. He offers a look at its latter-day blossoming into an animated series, a sequence of five movies (with a sixth in preparation) that has grossed over $700 million, and the offshoot "The Next Generation" TV series.

The author gives readers a tour of the memorials at the Smithsonian and the Movieland Wax Museums, lets them witness Leonard Nimoy get his star on the Hollywood Walk Of Fame in 1985, and takes them behind the scenes of the motion-picture series and TV's "The Next Generation." The concluding section examines the future of Star Trek beyond its 25th Anniversary.

$14.95.....196 Pages
ISBN # 1-55698-290-9

THE HISTORY OF TREK

James Van Hise

The complete story of Star Trek from Original conception to its effects on millions of Lives across the world. This book celebrates the 25th anniversary of the first "Star Trek" television episode and traces the history of the show that has become an enduring legend—even the non-Trekkies can quote specific lines and characters from the original television series. The History of Trek chronicles "Star Trek" from its start in 1966 to its cancellation in 1969; discusses the lean years when "Star Trek" wasn't shown on television but legions of die hard fans kept interest in it still alive; covers the sequence of five successful movies (and includes the upcoming sixth one); and reviews "The Next Generation" television series, now entering its sixth season. Complete with Photographs, The History of Trek reveals the origins of the first series in interviews with the original cast and creative staff. It also takes readers behind the scenes of all six Star Trek movies, offers a wealth of Star Trek Trivia, and speculates on what the future may hold.

$14.95.....160 Pages
ISBN # 1-55698-309-3

THE MAN BETWEEN THE EARS: STAR TREKS LEONARD NIMOY

James Van Hise

Based on his numerous interviews with Leonard Nimoy, Van Hise tells the story of the man as well as the entertainer.

This book chronicles the many talents of Leonard Nimoy from the beginning of his career in Boston to his latest starring work in the movie, Never Forget. His 25-year association with Star Trek is the centerpiece, but his work outside the Starship Enterprise is also covered, from such early efforts as Zombies of the Stratosphere to his latest directorial and acting work, and his stage debut in Vermont.

$14.95.....160 Pages
ISBN # 1-55698-304-2

TREK: THE UNAUTHORIZED BEHIND-THE-SCENES STORY OF THE NEXT GENERATION

James VanHise

This book chronicles the Trek mythos as it continues on T.V. in “Star Trek: The Next Generation,” telling the often fascinating conflict filled story of the behind-the-scenes struggles between Roddenberry and the creative staff. It includes a special section on “Star Trek: Deep Space Nine,” a spin-off of “The Next Generation,” which will begin syndication in early 1993.

$14.95.....160 Pages
ISBN 1-55698-321-2

THE NEW TREK ENCYCLOPEDIA

John Peel with Scott Nance

Everything anyone might want to know about the Star Trek series of television shows and movies is conveniently compiled into one volume in *The New Trek Encyclopedia.*

This detailed volume covers the original T.V. series, all six feature films, “Star Trek: The Next Generation,” and the animated show. It provides descriptions, explanations, and important details of every alien race, monster, planet, spaceship, weapon, and technical device to appear in all the shows—all listed in alphabetical order for easy reference. It also includes every person who worked on the shows or movies!

$19.95.....300 Pages
ISBN 1-55698-350-6

TREK: THE MAKING OF THE MOVIES

James Van Hise

TREK: THE MAKING OF THE MOVIES tells the complete story both on-screen and behind the scenes of the biggest STAR TREK adventures of all. Plus the story of the STAR TREK II that never happened and the aborted STAR TREK VI: STARFLEET ACADEMY.

$14.95.....160 Pages
ISBN # 1-55698-313-1

TREK: THE LOST YEARS

Edward Gross

The tumultouos, behind-the-scenes saga of this modern day myth between the cancellation of the original series in 1969 and the announcement of the first movie ten years later. In addition, the text explores the scripts and treatments written throughout the 1970's, including every proposed theatrical feature and an episode guide for STAR TREK II, with comments from the writers whose efforts would ultimately never reach the screen.

This volume came together after years of research, wherein the author interviewed a wide variety of people involved with every aborted attempt at revival, from story editors to production designers to David Gautreaux, the actor signed to replace Leonard Nimoy; and had access to exclusive resource material, including memos and correspondences, as well as teleplays and script outlines.

$12.95.....132 Pages
ISBN # 1-55698-220-8

THE TREK FAN'S HANDBOOK

Written by James Van Hise

STAR TREK inspired its millions of loyal fans to put pen to paper, in order to discuss the various themes and issues being raised by the show's scripts, explore the characters in minute detail and ponder where both STAR TREK and humanity are headed in the future. THE TREK FAN'S HANDBOOK offers a guide on who to write to, what products are available, information on the various STAR TREK fanclubs, addresses, membership information nad details on the fanzines they publish.

THE TREK FAN'S HANDBOOK allows the reader to tap into the basic backbone of what has allowed STAR TREK to thrive over the past quarter century.

$9.95.....109 Pages
ISBN # 1-55698-271-2

TREK: THE NEXT GENERATION

James Van Hise

They said it would not last, and after its cancellation in 1969, it looked as if it wouldn't. But the fans refused to let it die and now *Star Trek* is thriving as never before. The *Next Generation* television series continues the adventure. This book reveals the complete story behind the new series, the development of each major character, presents a complete episode guide, and gives plans for the future.

$14.95.....164 Pages
ISBN # 1-55698-305-0

THE TREK CREW BOOK

James Van Hise

The crewmembers of the starship Enterprise as presented in the original STAR TREK television series and feature film spin-offs. These fascinating characters, beloved by millions of fans, are the primary reason for the phenomenal on going success of this Gene Roddenberry created concept. Never before has a book so completely revealed this ensamble of fine actors, focusing on their careers, examining their unique portrayals of their most famous on-screen alter egos, profiling the characters themselves and presenting in-depth interviews with William Shatner, Leonard Nimoy, DeForest Kelly, James Doohan, George Takei, Walter Koenig and Nichelle Nichols.

$9.95.....108 Pages
ISBN # 1-55698-257-7

THE BEST OF ENTERPRISE INCIDENTS: THE MAGAZINE FOR STAR TREK FANS

Edited by James Van Hise

Unlike most televison series, STAR TREK inspired its millions of fans to put pen to paper in order to discuss the various themes and issues raised by the show's scripts, or to explore the nuances of the various characters, and ponder where both STAR TREK and humanity are headed in the future.

THE BEST OF THE ENTERPRISE INCIDENTS: THE MAGAZINE FOR STAR TREK FANS, is devoted entirely to such discussions, providing a collection of informative articles that have appeared over the years in ENTERPRISE INCIDENTS, the most successful STAR TREK fanzine ever published. This unique volume is written by fans for fans, and edited by the author of the TREK CREW BOOK, as well as ENTERPRISE INCIDENTS for over a decade.

$9.95.....108 Pages
ISBN # 1-55698-231-3

THE COMPLETE LOST IN SPACE

John Peel

DANGER. . . DANGER. . . DANGER!

Don't miss this book!

The complete guide to every single episode of LOST IN SPACE including profiles of every cast member and character

The most exhaustive book ever written about LOST IN SPACE.

$19.95.....220 Pages
ISBN # 1-55698-145-7

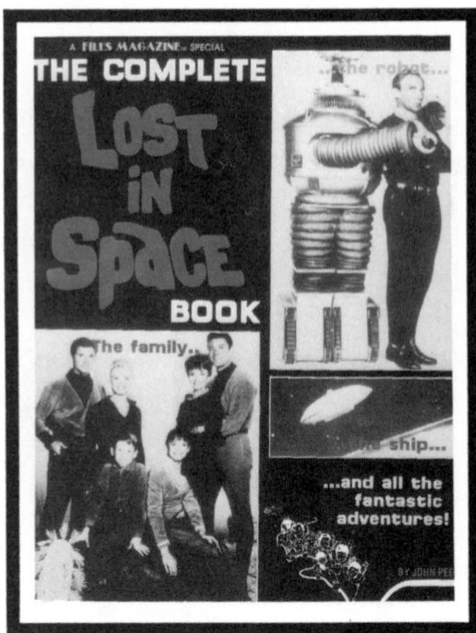

THE DOCTOR WHO ENCYCLOPEDIA: THE BAKERS YEARS

John Peel

This volume contains references for *all* the characters who appeared during the Baker years, and then examines all if the monsters that have come up against the good doctor in a special section. Want to know who the Trakenites are? Or where the Synge hails from? The answers are all here. THE DOCTOR WHO ENCYCLOPEDIA: THE BAKER YEARS is the perfect companion piece to John Peel's THE TREK ENCYCLOPEDIA

$19.95.....171 Pages
ISBN # 1-55698-160-0

THE LOST IN SPACE TRIBUTE BOOK
James Van Hise

LOST IN SPACE remains television's second most popular science fiction series, only falling behind the legendary STAR TREK. The show began in 1965 and ran for five seasons, but has continued to live on in syndication ever since, with legions of fans clamoring for a reunion film. Now for the first time ever, Pioneer presents THE LOST IN SPACE TRIBUTE BOOK, the ultimate guide to this unique television series.

Author James Van Hise presents a guide to every episode aired during the series' run, plus exclusive interviews with the late Guy Williams, June Lockhart, Marta Kristen, Mark Goddard, Angela Cartwright, Bill Mumy, the Robot and, of course, Jonathan Harris, as well as various behind-the-scenes personnel. As a special bonus, the book features blueprint reproductions and a guide to the Jupiter 2 spacecraft.

$14.95.....164 pages
ISBN# 1-55698-226-7

LOST IN SPACE WITH IRWIN ALLEN
James VanHise

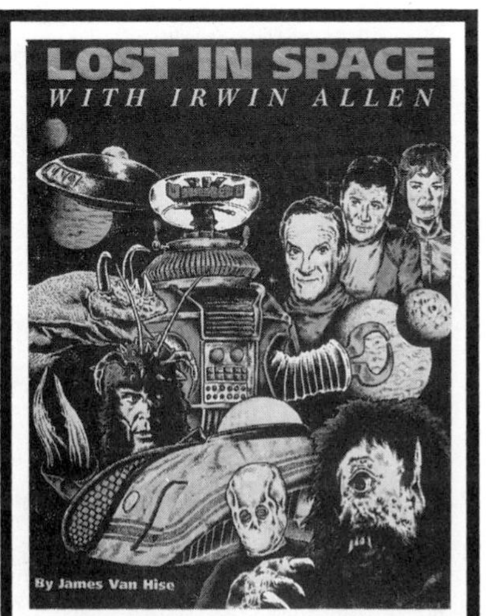

This much awaited book documents Irwin Allen's career in movies and T.V., especially "Lost in Space," his most popular concept. You will get an in depth history of *The Poseidon Adventure*, *Towering Inferno*, *The Lost World*, and *Voyage to the Bottom of the Sea.*

This book also covers the history of his four popular T.V. series including "Time Tunnel", and "Land of the Giants." What's more, you will learn about his unsold T.V. ideas, such as "Man from the 25th Century," and his success in the disaster-film genre in the 1970's.

$14.95.....160 Pages
ISBN # 1-55698-323-9

THE DARK SHADOWS TRIBUTE BOOK

Edward Gross and James Van Hise

THE DARK SHADOWS TRIBUTE BOOK is the ultimate guide to the series, providing interviews with the cast and crew (including Jonathan Frid) who detail the inner workings of the show: a look at the phenomenon the series inspired, a DARK SHADOWS history and a guide to the first 600 episodes following Barnabas' initial appearance and complete names and addresses of fan clubs and magazines. This volume is unlike any that has been published on the show before.

$14.95.....164 Pages
ISBN # 1-55698-234-8

MONSTERLAND FEAR BOOK

Edited by James Van Hise and Forrest J. Ackerman

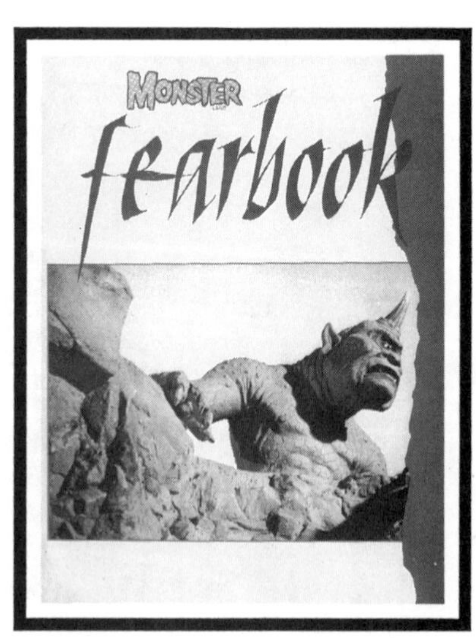

Devoted to horrors past and present, the MONSTERLAND FEARBOOK presents profiles of classic films of terror, and interviews with those people who have brought them to screen. The macabre ingredients of this volume indepth examinations of *20 Million Mile to Earth, The Beast From 20,000 Fathoms, Freaks, The Seventh Voyage of Sinbad, Halloween, and Curse of the Demon.* In addition, it features an interview with Stephen King and a guide to creating your own monster masks. The perfect gift for for your favorite monster!

$14.95.....85 Pages

BORING, BUT NECESSARY ORDERING INFORMATION

Payment:

Use our new 800 # and pay with your credit card or send check or money order directly to our address. All payments must be made in U.S. funds and please do not send cash.

Shipping:

We offer several methods of shipment. Sometimes a book can be delayed if we are temporarily out of stock. You should note whether you prefer us to ship the book as soon as available, send you a merchandise credit good for other goodies, or send your money back immediately.

Normal Post Office: $3.75 for the first book and $1.50 for each additional book. These orders are filled as quickly as possible. Shipments normally take 5 to 10 days, but allow up to 12 weeks for delivery.

Special UPS 2 Day Blue Label Service or Priority Mail: Special service is available for desperate Couch Potatoes. These books are shipped within 24 hours of when we receive the order and normally take 2 to 3 three days to get to you. The cost is $10.00 for the first book and $4.00 each additional book .

Overnight Rush Service: $20.00 for the first book and $10.00 each additional book.

U.s. Priority Mail: $6.00 for the first book and $3.00.each additional book.

Canada And Mexico: $5.00 for the first book and $3.00 each additional book.

Foreign: $6.00 for the first book and $3.00 each additional book.

Please list alternatives when available and please state if you would like a refund or for us to backorder an item if it is not in stock.

COUCH POTATO INC. 5715 N. Balsam Rd Las Vegas, NV 89130 (702)658-2090

Use Your Credit Card 24 HRS — Order toll Free From: (800)444-2524 Ext 67

ORDER FORM

_____ Trek Crew Book $9.95
_____ Best Of Enterprise Incidents $9.95
_____ Trek Fans Handbook $9.95
_____ Trek: The Next Generation $14.95
_____ The Man Who Created Star Trek: $12.95
_____ 25th Anniversary Trek Tribute $14.95
_____ History Of Trek $14.95
_____ The Man Between The Ears $14.95
_____ Trek: The Making Of The Movies $14.95
_____ Trek: The Lost Years $12.95
_____ Trek: The Unauthorized Next Generation $14.95
_____ New Trek Encyclopedia $19.95
_____ Making A Quantum Leap $14.95
_____ The Unofficial Tale Of Beauty And The Beast $14.95
_____ Complete Lost In Space $19.95
_____..doctor Who Encyclopedia: Baker $19.95
_____ Lost In Space Tribute Book $14.95
_____ Lost In Space With Irwin Allen $14.95
_____ Doctor Who: Baker Years $19.95
_____ Doctor Who: Pertwee Years $19.95
_____ Batmania Ii $14.95
_____ The Green Hornet $14.95 ____ Special Edition $16.95
_____ Number Six: The Prisoner Book $14.95
_____ Gerry Anderson: Supermarionation $17.95
_____ Addams Family Revealed $14.95
_____ Bloodsucker: Vampires At The Movies $14.95
_____ Dark Shadows Tribute $14.95
_____ Monsterland Fear Book $14.95
_____ The Films Of Elvis $14.95
_____ The Woody Allen Encyclopedia $14.95
_____ Paul Mccartney: 20 Years On His Own $9.95
_____ Yesterday: My Life With The Beatles $14.95
_____ Fab Films Of The Beatles $14.95
_____ 40 Years At Night: The Tonight Show $14.95
_____ Exposing Northern Exposure $14.95
_____ The La Lawbook $14.95
_____ Cheers: Where Everybody Knows Your Name $14.95
_____ SNL! The World Of Saturday Night Live $14.95
_____ The Rockford Phile $14.95
_____ Encyclopedia Of Cartoon Superstars $14.95
_____ How To Create Animation $14.95
_____ How To Draw Art For Comic Books $14.95
_____ King And Barker:an Illustrated Guide $14.95
_____ King And Barker: An Illustrated Guide II $14.95

100% Satisfaction Guaranteed.

We value your support. You will receive a full refund as long as the copy of the book you are not happy with is received back by us in reasonable condition. No questions asked, except we would like to know how we failed you. Refunds and credits are given as soon as we receive back the item you do not want.

NAME:_______________________

STREET:_______________________

CITY:_______________________

STATE:_______________________

ZIP:_______________________

TOTAL:________ SHIPPING________

SEND TO: Couch Potato, Inc. 5715 N. Balsam Rd., Las Vegas, NV 89130